PETERSON & DAVIE

What We Talk About When We Talk About Systems

Essays on the Systems Approach

SYSTEMS APPROACH LLC

PUBLISHED BY SYSTEMS APPROACH LLC

ISBN: 978-1-7364721-8-7

The cover photo of the Golden Gate Bridge (San Francisco) is by Bruce Davie.

First printing, April 2025

Contents

6

Foreword

The selection of essays that Bruce and Larry bring together is an outstanding read on how and why we got "here." Rarely do we get the opportunity to read the lineage of thinking of two prominent leaders in the network and systems field, and follow the intellectual leaps they take to the next lily-pad. Following their thinking, how they view a problem or architecture, how they intellectually deconstruct and analyze a topic by looking through different facets of problem definition (often their perception that the problem was incorrectly defined), requirements, use-cases, solution design, solution design patterns, and choices is like peering into their minds and how they work. That alone is the worth the price of admission.

   Now the book isn't meant for the coffee-table, it's meant to catalyze debate! If you've ever had the opportunity to correspond or talk w/ Larry and Bruce, neither believe they hold "the only answer" and that's why they are so enjoyable as humans. I've known BSD [Bruce] for over 25 years and worked alongside him on many of the journeys he and Larry have presented in this book. I must admit, that while reading many of the essays, I found myself arguing with the book and needing to call Bruce immediately to speak with him on how my views differ or how some minutia is vital to the argument. I am certain he is smiling, because over our friendship and careers, that was our relationship. I so value my time and interaction with great minds, it's made me a better engineer, thinker and listener.

   Interestingly, one strong thought came to mind while reading, it is that the book may be incorrectly titled. The set of essays that demonstrate their analysis (taking apart) of various problems, are a synthesis (coming together). I don't mean to attribute that the authors are reductionists or that synthesis holds some intellectual superiority but, that every analysis requires a synthesis to verify, correct and build upon its results; and this is the subject of so many of the essays. That, and the book is a collection of essay and thus, a synthesis—but I digress.

What you read in this book is in fact a demonstration of the duality between analysis and synthesis and constant progression of thought. What's different is that the topic, as Larry and Bruce always give us, is at the level of understanding the architecture and construction (and deconstruction and rebuilding!) of the Internet architecture. How they thought through a problem, grabbing from far-reaching ideas from other disciplines, experiences with other design patterns, and then built products, protocols, state machines, data interactions and systems. What is inherent in their writing, and never fully discussed is that both authors realized that, to lead new designs, architectures and new ways to build on the Internet, it wasn't solely a challenge to others to "keep up" with them but, in fact their desire to bring the community "with them." As once was said to me, "you don't launch a community, you build one."

What makes this book fascinating for the reader is that it tackles the early days and adolescence of Software Defined Networking and many "fixes" to the limitations of early protocols on the Internet. It allows us all to understand how hard, and why it was so hard to move forward with new ideas; the options for solutions, and the pitfalls of the choices. Protocols have limitations and thus new systems, and design patterns, must be created to solve them. Reading how the authors thought through the very walls they created for themselves, rebuilding and solving the limitations of the very protocols, systems and products they invented and made ubiquitous; it's reading how two great minds reinvent themselves.

With this absolute fascinating book, Bruce and Larry deliver the goods. They bring all of us with them on the journey of their minds and careers. As the Internet architecture continues to evolve rapidly with new problems to solve, new use-cases, services, requirements and solutions; I read this book as a reminder to something Bruce said to me in 2000, "architectural purity is not a reason to think something is a better idea, than any other solution to the problem."

David Ward

Capitola, California

Introduction

The Systems Approach author team has been working together since the early 1990s and published our first jointly authored text book in 1996. Having worked on six editions of that book (so far), there came a time when we started to think about doing a broader series of books together, and whether that might be a suitably fulfilling activity to be our "main jobs" when we reached a certain stage of our careers. 2020 turned out to be the year in which we decided to put that idea into practice. We founded "Systems Approach, LLC" and started working on the first book that we would write without the support of a big, traditional publisher. *"Software-Defined Networks: A Systems Approach"* was the first book to come out of this partnership (with the help of several co-authors). We also decided to supplement our book-writing efforts with a regular newsletter, as a way to write about our experiences and developing thoughts on the world of networking and related systems topics.

The books and articles we have written over the last 40 years could be viewed as "reporting from the front-lines," as we told the story of the maturation of the Internet: from a research experiment that escaped from the lab, to today's ubiquitous and essential global infrastructure. We were fortunate to have excellent vantage points to report from, ranging from established vendors (Cisco, VMware) to disruptive startups (Nicira, Verivue) to open source initiatives (PlanetLab Consortium, Open Networking Foundation, Linux Foundation). Throughout those efforts we were active in the forums tackling the next technical challenge, including the IETF and the IRTF's End-to-End Research Group, and ACM's Special Interest Groups on networking (SIGCOMM) and operating systems (SIGOPS).

Our newsletter, and now this book, draws on these experiences and tries to distill the essential lessons from them. Ever since we started writing books in the 1990s we have tried to get at the timeless essence of computer networks rather than just describe the most recent technology or some long-lost piece of networking history. Some of our essays have held up better than others over time—we've picked the ones that seem to have the most longevity for this collection.

One might wonder what is the value of compiling a set of essays into a book. Each essay explores a particular question in system design with the help of a real-world example. What we have tried to do with this book is identify themes that arise repeatedly across these examples, and make them as clear as we can. Our hope is that this broader perspective will help people who work in computer science, whether as practitioners or researchers, gain a deeper understanding of the principles that are applied when building and deploying systems.

Homage to The Mythical Man-Month

As we started organizing our essays, it became clear that we needed to pay homage to another book of essays about the challenges of building large systems: Fred Brooks' classic "The Mythical Man-Month". Brooks focuses more on the software engineering side of building large systems, whereas our essays are more focused on the design side, but the interplay between implementation and architecture is an obvious (and important) bit of overlap. Brooks is also the person that coined the term "Second System Syndrome", a condition with which we are quite familiar!

It's also the case that the Mythical Man-Month is grounded in Brooks' experience as project manager for the IBM System 360 and later for OS/360, whereas we draw on our experiences with the Internet. Both are complex systems, but the differences between engineering projects within a single company and the competitive-cooperation among a wide-range of stakeholders in the Internet makes for an interesting dynamics. Navigating those dynamics to a successful outcome is at the heart of what this book is about.

Just as there is no perfect way to decompose a network into a set of protocol layers, there is no perfect way to group our essays. However, there are a number of themes that we want to emphasize and we have organized the book around these themes. Sometimes we've written a whole book on a topic where the systems approach can be applied (e.g. SDN, TCP Congestion Control, 5G). Some themes just keep appearing, as we've studied the evolution of the Internet over the decades, such as the tension between centralization and decentralization.

One of our favorite reviewer quotes from our first book, which appears on the first edition jacket, is this:

"This book is incredibly rich in perspective!" — Chris Edmondson-Yurkanan

That quote captures a lot of what we think the systems approach entails. You can't just look at a piece of technology in isolation—you need to step back to gain perspective, looking at how it fits into a bigger, system-level view.

What every essay does in this book is to examine a topic where the systems approach helps us understand certain problems and offers approaches to solving them. So before we jump into the main body of the book, here is our early newsletter entry on the meaning of "A Systems Approach".

Defining A Systems Approach

We recently noticed that our book, *Computer Networks: A Systems Approach*, was discussed in a thread on Hacker News. It was nice to see mostly positive commentary, but we also noticed a fairly involved debate about the meaning of "Systems Approach". Some readers had a pretty good idea of what we meant, others mistakenly took it for a reference to "Systems and Cybernetics", which we definitely never intended. Others interpreted it as an empty, throw-away term. "Don't these people read prefaces?" we thought, before remembering that we dropped the definition from the latest edition, thinking it was old news. Clearly, we had been making some assumptions that left many of our readers in the dark. Rather than just rescuing the old preface from the recycling bin, we thought it would be timely to revisit the meaning of "Systems Approach" as we're now building a whole series of books around that theme.

The term "systems" is used commonly by computer science researchers and practitioners who study the issues that arise when building complex computing systems such as operating systems, networks, distributed applications, and so on. At MIT, for example, there is a famous class 6.033: Computer System Design (with an excellent accompanying book) that is a typical introduction to the systems field. The required reading list is a tour through some of the most influential systems papers. The key to the systems approach is a "big picture" view—you need to look at how the components of a system interact with each other to achieve an overall result, rather than fixating on a single component (either unnecessarily optimizing it or trying to solve too many problems in that one component). This is one of the important takeaways of the End-to-End Argument, a landmark paper for system design.

A systems approach also has a strong focus on real-world implementation, with the Internet being the obvious example of a widely-deployed, complex networking system. This seems incredible now, but when we wrote our first edition in 1995, it was not yet obvious that the Internet would be the most successful networking technology of all time, and organizing our book around the principles that underlie the design and implementation of the Internet was a novel idea.

The systems approach is a methodology for designing, implementing, and describing computer systems. It involves a specific set of steps:

- Defining the problem (or the need for a new system) which is typically a combination of (a) identifying a new use case/application, and (b) incorporating a new technology or technological capability.

- Specifying requirements, taking into account multiple stakeholders (e.g., those who use the system, those who administer the system, those who pay for the system, and so on).

- Considering design alternatives and articulating the rationale for selecting one implementation choice over another.

- Empirically evaluating the effectiveness—with respect to the requirements—of a realization of the design.

- Extracting the lessons learned (i.e., contributing best practices and general design principles back to the field).

Over time, this leads to the iterative evolution of computing systems, for example, from time-sharing mainframes, to client/server LAN-based distributed systems, to wide-area scalable services, to today's cloud services.

In following this methodology, there are requirements that come up again and again. Scalability is an obvious example, and appears as a key design principle throughout networking, e.g., in the partitioning of networks into subnets, areas, and autonomous systems to scale the routing system. A good example of cross-disciplinary systems thinking is the importing of techniques developed to scale distributed systems such as Hadoop to solve scaling challenges in software-defined networking.

Generality is another common requirement: the way that the Internet was designed to be completely agnostic to the applications running over it and the class of devices connected to it distinguishes it from networks like the phone network and the cable TV network, whose functionality has now been largely subsumed by the Internet.

And there are a set of system-agnostic design principles that are used extensively to guide systems designers. They are not mathematically rigorous (compared to, say, Maxwell's Equations or the Shannon-Hartley theorem) but are considered best practices:

- Separation of policy and mechanism

- The end-to-end argument

- Scalability through hierarchical aggregation (Information Hiding)

- Optimization through caching

- Separation of control and data planes

- The use of abstraction to limit complexity

Most of these and more can be found in the iconic paper by Turing award winner Butler Lampson: *Hints for Computer System Design*.

In applying the systems approach to networking, and to our books, you'll notice that we start every chapter in *Computer Networks* with our problem statement. In chapter 1 we go on to develop requirements for a global network that meets the needs of various stakeholders, satisfies scaling objectives, manages resources cost-effectively, and so on. Even though the Internet is already built, we're walking the reader through the system design process that led to it being a certain way, so that they are learning systems principles and best practices like those mentioned above. We call many of these out explicitly in "Bottom Line" comments throughout the book.

One of the most challenging aspects of teaching people about networking is deciding how to handle layering. On the one hand, layering is a form of abstraction—a fine system design principle. On the other hand, layering can sometimes prevent us from thinking about how best to implement the system as a whole. For example, in recent years it's become clear that HTTP, an application layer protocol, and TCP, a transport layer protocol, don't work terribly well together from a performance perspective. Optimizing each independently could only take us so far. Ultimately by looking at them as parts of a system that needs to deliver reliability, security, and performance to applications, both HTTP and the transport layer evolved, with QUIC being the new entrant to the transport layer. What we have tried to do is give readers the tools to see where such system-level thinking can be applied, rather than just teach them that the 7-layer model was handed down from on high and can't be touched.

Hopefully this helps give some clarity around what we mean by "A Systems Approach". It's certainly a way of thinking that becomes natural over time, and we hope that as you read our books and these newsletters it will become part of your thinking as well.

Bruce Davie, March 2021

Closing Remarks

In this book we are trying to help our readers gain a better appreciation of what a systems approach is and how to apply it to their jobs, whether as researchers, teachers, or implementors. So at the end of every chapter, we look back on the material covered and try to extract a few key messages that will be of practical value in other settings. Our goal is to enable our readers to apply the lessons of the chapter to any system-building situation they are likely to encounter. This is in keeping with an important tenet of the systems approach, which places value on being a generalist.

While the Closing Remarks sections summarize the highlights, much of the book's value is in the details and color the essays provide. Readers are likely to recognize aspects of the systems they know or work with in our stories. Seeing the connections between different systems is part of the fun.

One final note about the collection of essays that follow. While we often refer to them as essays, they were also newsletter posts published over four years. This book does *not* present the posts in chronological order, so we have edited any reference one post makes to another to match its place in the book (rather than when it occurred in time). Apart from fixing these and similar "cross references" (plus cleaning up a few poorly constructed sentences), the posts/essays are as they originally appeared.

Explore Further

Fredrick Brooks Jr. *The Mythical Man-Month: Essays in Software Engineering* (Anniversary Edition). Addison-Wesley Publishing, 1995.

Jerome Saltzer and Frans Kaashoek. Principles of Computer System Design: An Introduction. Morgan Kaufmann, 2009.

MIT OpenCourseWare. 6.033 Computer System Engineering. MIT, 2018.

Butler Lampson. Hints for Computer System Design. ACM SIGOPS Operating Systems Review, October 1983.

Jerome Saltzer, David Reed, and David Clark. End-to-End Arguments in System Design. ACM Transactions on Computer Systems, November 1984.

System and Network Architecture

Because the systems approach takes a holistic, end-to-end perspective on system design, it makes sense to start our discussion at the architectural level. And with the Internet serving as our primary example system, there is no better case study for exploring what factors go into making an architecture effective (or not).

The rest of the book looks at specific technologies and asks more focused design questions, but we begin with general observations, starting with the most basic question: exactly what constitutes an architecture? This is a question we asked—and attempted to answer—in the first essay. But instead of putting the issue to bed, it triggered the series of reactions and subsequent responses that follow. That's the nature of the topic: architectures are defined using some helpful design principles and quite a bit of judgement, much of which comes through experience. This book reports our experiences and the conclusions we draw, and hopefully, in the process, sheds a little light on the topic.

What is Network Architecture, Really?

Pamela Zave and Jennifer Rexford's new book *The Real Internet Architecture* strikes a chord on two topics that I always find interesting: (1) how we teach networked systems, and (2) how networked systems evolve over time. These two topics are strongly connected for me, and at the heart of any book that puts a discussion of architecture front and center.

The book focuses on the compositional primitives that can and have been used to evolve the Internet. These primitives include familiar mechanisms like bridging (concatenating two networks) and layering (running one network on top of another network), but framed to help the reader appreciate that the Internet is just a large modular program running on a widely distributed collection of boxes. We can evolve the Internet by evolving (adding to, changing out, and removing) its modules, just as we would extend or modify any long-running program. Using the compositional primitives of networking ensures that we preserve the connectivity (or isolation) we want the network to deliver.

I'm oversimplifying—and you should read the book for yourself—but I find this general approach appealing in that it helps to distinguish the conceptual foundations of networking from the artifacts that we too often focus on. (As for artifacts, I'm including both products and standards.) Those conceptual foundations define the invariants of networking that have always been true, whether we fully articulate them or not. And the proof of the pudding is in the eating: the Internet has evolved continually since the first RFC was published and the first router came online.

About Ossification

Clearly, everyone who succeeded in finding a way to extend the Internet over the years understood these invariants at some intuitive level, which raises the question of why the networking research community went through so much hand-wringing about ossification. Chapter 1 of Zave and Rexford draws attention to this hand-wringing, but mostly to highlight the limits of the "textbook definition" of the Internet architecture, not to explain the ossification complaint. Having been in the middle of those discussions (and benefiting from 20/20 hindsight) I think it was more about the loss of control than anything else.

In the earliest days of the Internet, we didn't have to ask anyone's permission to "fix" the Internet. It was our experiment and we had the ability to make radical changes. At some point that was no longer the case, and commercialization had shifted the center of power to the vendors and operators. Anyone involved in a large software project will recognize the transition from "pre-release freedom" engineers enjoy to "post-release constraints" imposed by product managers. (This is an interesting topic in its own right, but I'll leave it as an unsubstantiated claim at this point.)

I wrote previously about a specific "aha" moment for me—leading to PlanetLab, and evolution through layering—but it's also the case that the research community had a point: Vendors controlled the ability to make fine-grained changes "inside" the existing code base, forcing innovation to the "edges". Function placement can be important in a large distributed system, but Internet history is full of examples of how we were able to find ways to make new ideas work, helped by the fact that the cloud is effectively distributing the programmable edge more widely. Multicast and mobility are prime examples, but even real-time communication found a way to work over-the-top, despite the argument that timeliness had to be addressed inside the network because the end-points couldn't make a late packet arrive earlier.

About Teaching

As to how we teach networking, I think the perspective of Zave and Rexford is a valuable one, although we might debate whether their "Real" architecture is the right starting point for an introductory course, or whether it is better to guide students gradually to that end point. The simple hourglass model of the Internet architecture is certainly just a snapshot in time, but I think it's an appropriate place to start, with the expectation that the evolutionary power will be revealed (and appreciated) incrementally throughout the course. Bruce and I tried to capture these "architectural invariants" as Key Takeaways in our book, with Chapter 1 introducing two that are most relevant to this discussion:

> **Key Takeaway 1:** The main idea to take away from this discussion is that we can define a network recursively as consisting of two or more nodes connected by a physical link, or as two or more networks connected by a node. In other words, a network can be constructed from a nesting of networks, where at the bottom level, the network is implemented by some physical medium.

> **Key Takeaway 2:** Of these three attributes of the Internet architecture, the hourglass design philosophy is important enough to bear repeating. The hourglass's narrow waist represents a minimal and carefully chosen set of global capabilities that allows both higher-level applications and lower-level communication technologies to coexist, share capabilities, and evolve rapidly. The narrow-waisted model is critical to the Internet's ability to adapt to new user demands and changing technologies.

Inspired by Zave and Rexford, I think I would work harder (if we do another edition) to revisit these themes throughout the book, rather than leave it to students to connect dots. In the end, the goal should be to help students appreciate—at a deep level—the power they have to effect change.

Architecture in Other Domains

Thinking about architecture in networked systems naturally leads us to look for connections to architecture in other domains. The design and construction of houses is an obvious place to start, and in fact, we talk about Tracy Kidder's book "House" in a later chapter. Many years ago, fellow textbook author Jim Kurose recommended another book—Michael Pollan's "A Place of My Own"—in which the author deals with an architect and a builder as he tries to construct a one-room structure for writing. It's in part a story about the tension between design and implementation.

Kidder and Pollan's books are two great sources of war stories many networking people will recognize. A favorite example is Pollan quoting Frank Lloyd Wright saying "Of course it leaks, that's how you know it's a roof." which reminds us of the oft-heard refrain: "It's a feature, not a bug." But maybe there's a deeper lesson in FLW's attitude about leaky roofs, as architect Dave Clayton explains in a blog post about perfection, entitled "What Frank Lloyd Wright Taught Me about Roof Leaks".

About Architecture

I think it's fair to say that an important property of any network architecture is its ability to adapt to new technology and new use cases. Real Architecture is a careful study of how this works for the Internet, with the compositional primitives the book puts forward being an important part of its success.

The case for modularity being a requirement for evolution is compelling, but it's not the whole story. I would argue that an architecture also needs to have a fixed point that is not easy to change. The genius of the Internet is how this fixed point was kept minimal, allowing everything else to evolve around it. This gets to how one defines "architecture" in the first place, which is a question I kept asking myself while reading Real Architecture. I have always liked a definition I once heard from David Clark: *"An architecture tells you what you cannot do.*" You have to disallow some things, otherwise it's not an architecture. (Even a program written in a type-safe modular language can grow unwieldy and be impossible to reason about.)

The important contribution of this book is to describe, in a rigorous way, the design patterns that govern how evolution happens to the pliable parts that revolve around such a fixed point. Taking a step back, the Internet is the perfect case study for understanding what constitutes an architecture, and how to evaluate its value.

Larry Peterson, August 2024

How the Hourglass Won

Competition on the Information Superhighway

After Larry paraphrased David Clark saying *"Architecture tells you what you cannot do"*, I started looking at what else David Clark had to say about architecture. I have just read the opening chapters of his 2018 book, *"Designing an Internet"*, which is a great resource: it not only describes the current Internet architecture, it imagines what other architectural choices we might make. I was hoping for a short definition of "architecture" in the networking context, but it takes a whole chapter of the book to explain. One important takeaway is that network architecture includes the things we have to agree on—such as the meaning of IP addresses—while leaving a lot of flexibility for variations in the design and implementation of specific networks.

David is known as "the architect of the Internet" and has written the foreword for each edition of our textbook. Less well-known is that David is the person who introduced me to Larry. Sometime in the early 1990s I was working with David on Aurora, a gigabit networking project involving MIT, UPenn, IBM, and Bellcore, where I worked. I was building a high-speed (for its time) network interface, which I have come to describe as "the accidental SmartNIC". David made an intro to Larry (then at the University of Arizona) and we would go on to collaborate, with his student Peter Druschel writing software to make my NIC useful. This also gave me an excuse to visit Arizona during the New Jersey winter for several years in a row. This collaboration went well enough that Larry later invited me to be his co-author on the first edition of *Computer Networks: A Systems Approach*.

At the time that we were working on Aurora, David was also involved in an effort, supported by the National Research Council (of the U.S.) to shape the agenda for "National Information Infrastructure (NII)". This work took place in 1993 and 1994, at a time when the term "Information Superhighway" was very much in vogue but there were at least three main competing views on what such a "superhighway" might entail. The result was a book-length report *Realizing the Information Future*. This book had a huge influence on my thinking, and one reason is that it introduced me to the idea of the Internet's architecture being pictured as an hourglass. The hourglass was popularized later in the 1990s by Steve Deering, who gave a talk entitled *"Watching the Waist of the Protocol Hourglass"*. If you go searching for pictures of the Internet hourglass, you are likely to end up with a slide from Steve's talk such as the one shown below.

We discussed the hourglass in our textbook in 1995 as an important aspect of the Internet architecture, but didn't go to the effort to draw it as tidily as above. I reached out to David Clark last week to see if he could recall when the hourglass first appeared. He admitted it was shrouded in the mists of time, but thought it likely that the first publication of the hourglass image was the 1994 RTIF report, even though the idea predated the book. Importantly, the breadth of the hourglass at the top and bottom captures the notion that there is room for flexibility in the Internet architecture.

Competing Visions For Networking

It's important to consider the context in which this picture of the Internet emerged. Older readers will remember the "net-heads vs bell-heads" debates, essentially a struggle between a telco-centric view of networking and an Internet-centric one. When I joined Bellcore in 1988, fresh from my PhD studies, I had almost no background in networking. While the team I joined was one of the least "bell-headed" within Bellcore, the system we were building was based on ATM and the telephone-company-led plan to build "Broadband ISDN (B-ISDN)". So my first real exposure to network architecture was through the eyes of the telcos. Working with David and Larry,

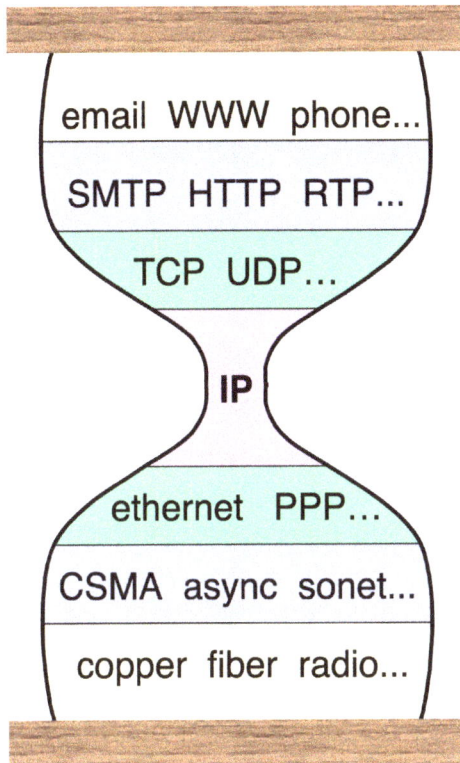

The Internet Hourglass as Drawn by Steve Deering

and reading Realizing the Information Future, were important correctives to this.

It is hard to believe now, but there was a third competing vision for the future of information infrastructure at this time, based on an expansion of the cable TV network. Cable TV was ubiquitous in the US and digital video was starting to emerge. One view of the "information superhighway" was often summarized (depressingly) as "500 channels of video". The view was that digitization and other technological advances would allow the cable network to deliver hundreds of channels, with limited upstream data enabling including some interactive and on-demand services. To a degree, this is what the cable system turned into, but it didn't become the centerpiece of national information infrastructure that its proponents were arguing for in

1994. Importantly, the cable industry was quick to realize that their infrastructure could also be used to offer broadband Internet access, so that cable modem-based access emerged as an early high-speed alternative to dial-up for home Internet users.

What Realizing the Information Future did brilliantly was to highlight the key differences between these competing visions of the future of networking. While the Internet could be modeled as an hourglass, ATM looked more like a funnel: the entire bottom part of the stack was pinned down to a small set of technology choices, with ATM requiring SONET and a specific set of link technologies. And the cable-TV version, with the view that the only application that mattered was video, was the inverse of this, narrowing to a single application class at the top.

RTIF didn't claim that the Internet architecture was the one true choice for the future, but it did point out the drawbacks of narrowing either the top or the bottom part of the hourglass to a small set of choices. If you narrow the bottom, you rule out a whole lot of current and future technology choices for the link layer, such as Ethernet and WiFi. By contrast, IP just keeps working over every new link layer technology that gets invented, embracing all sorts of link layer innovations such as various generations of cellular data and a proliferation of broadband access technologies. It also provided a clear deployment path leveraging existing networks that ATM lacked. And if you narrow the top, you rule out the diversity of applications that have flourished since the Internet was invented.

Recall that the World Wide Web was in its infancy in 1994, and voice and video applications barely worked due to low link speeds. One of the claims of the ATM camp was that it had inherently superior performance to IP due to the small cell size (and hence would better serve video and voice). This was arguably true in 1994 but turned out to be irrelevant as faster links became available and a combination of new router designs and Moore's law enabled high-speed routing to flourish. So in the end it was breadth at both the top and bottom of the hourglass that really enabled the Internet to emerge as the dominant architecture. Its support for innovation in both applications and underlying technologies has been critical to its success.

By the time Larry and I started working on our first edition in 1995, I was pretty convinced that the Internet was going to be the winner in this war of competing visions. (In a related move, I left Bellcore for Cisco the same year.) Hence we structured our book around the Internet architecture—a novel choice at the time—although we made a point of including alternative approaches as well. One of our guiding principles was: don't assume that today's technology is the one true approach. Explain the foundational principles that have gone into making the Internet work the way it does, and explore alternatives, so that students will learn how they might design the networks of the future. Clark's Designing an Internet takes this approach as well—hence the indefinite article in the title.

This goes back to a tension we highlighted in a prior post: teaching students about an idealized architecture doesn't necessarily reflect the reality of the Internet today. But if you focus too much on how the Internet looks today, you can miss the core principles among all the artifacts that have been built over the decades. This is not just an issue of teaching theory versus practice, but also a matter of trying to help students understand what is really fundamental to network architecture. Our sense of what is fundamental may change over time—tunneling, for example, feels like a basic building block of today's networks in a way that it did not in 1995. (For a strong version of that view, see the blog from Tailscale.) To reiterate a point from Larry's post, if we can teach students that they have the power to change the Internet, and give them the tools to do so, that is more valuable than just telling them how it works today.

Bruce Davie, August 2024

This is Not a Pipe

But is it an Architecture?

Our last two posts on network architecture have generated a fair amount of interest, including some comments that got me thinking about what more can be said on the topic. (I also sense a rat hole, so I'll proceed with caution.)

One reaction is to ask exactly what constitutes an architecture, and correspondingly, how would one judge if an architecture is good. My starting point is to think of an architecture as essentially a working model of a system: it is both descriptive of the current system and prescriptive of how the system is expected to evolve over time. Looking back in time, if an architecture is not reasonably descriptive, it provides little value for understanding what's been built so far (and it needs to be updated). Looking forward in time, even with a disciplined engineering team, it's challenging to enforce an architecture's prescriptive power, so it had better do a good job of capturing the invariants that are expected to hold across a wide range of possible futures.

Another helpful way to think about an architecture is that it is a process that bridges a set of requirements and constraints to a realization of a system (i.e., an implementation). If you talk in terms of actors—and substitute a house for a computing system—an architect produces a design that simultaneously satisfies the home owners and can be realized by carpenters using readily available construction materials (building blocks). Elegance is a factor, for reasons that are appreciated by other architects, but seldom understood by either owners or carpenters.

So is the hourglass an architecture? No, not any more than Magritte's famous painting is actually a pipe. If you're not familiar with the story of Magritte's pipe, he supposedly said of his painting:

The famous pipe. How people reproached me for it! And yet, could you stuff my pipe? No, it's just a representation, is it not? So if I had written on my picture "This is a pipe". I'd have been lying!

Magritte's picture is easy to find on the Internet, but since we do not have permission to reprint it here, we offer a photo Bruce took of the Pipe Bridge at the Fairfield Park Boathouse in Melbourne as a stand-in.

Back to the hourglass, it is a helpful visualization of an important design principle that the early Internet architects understood at an intuitive level, even if they weren't able to draw the diagram until later. I would go so far as to say that the Hourglass Design is one of the most important intellectual contributions of the Internet, because of its general applicability to any system that aspires to widespread adoption. It's OK to call it an architecture, but it's probably better to say it's an architectural principle that can be applied in many settings.

The key is judgement in how one applies the principle, where the genius of the Internet hourglass is the narrowness of the narrow waist. When designing a system, it's natural to try to address as many of the known tech-

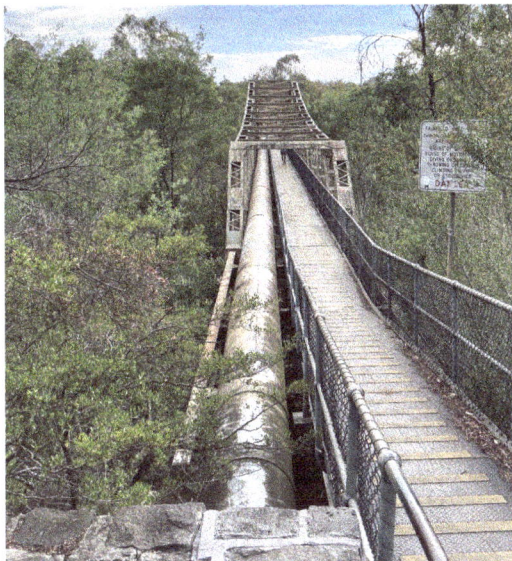

This Is Not the Pipe Bridge

nical requirements as possible, and in doing so, over-engineer the system. That important judgment call was to solve exactly one of the many problems it might have tried to address—defining a global addressing/routing scheme that could exploit any communication channel—and to punt on everything else, including reliable delivery, security, mobility, quality-of-service and so on. This left ample room for others to innovate, and claim a stake in the Internet's future.

For example, the original design did not address security, but had it tried to, it most likely would have not anticipated all the real-world threats, yet would have made wide-spread adoption more difficult. There have been many attempts through the years to establish "universal" networking technologies (ATM is an example Bruce talked about in his last post), but the lesson is that if you have to achieve universal buy-in, agreeing to the minimal and least controversial thing is necessary to get started. The design principle is inspired by the idea of late binding: Create a minimal-but-general framework today and postpone filling in use-case specific details for others to tackle tomorrow, when everyone better understands their requirements. This is an advantage system software has over home construction.

(It's also a disadvantage, because violating the architecture is a simple matter of programming.)

This approach effectively plans for evolution. We often take this for granted, but not all communication architectures are defined this way, with the mobile cellular network serving as a great counterexample. Each generation of the mobile network introduced new technologies, but unnecessarily (in our view) coupled the architecture with the technology. This ensured that every time the technology changed, the architecture had to change as well.

In the case of the Internet, TCP obviously extended IP with support for reliable byte-streams, and including it as part of the reference implementation (but not the narrow waist) was essential. And with the Socket API bootstrapping the TCP/IP platform, over time the platform then grew to address security (notably with TLS—Transport Layer Security), mobility (with DHCP, HTTP redirects, for example), and universal object identity (Uniform Resource Identifiers), with HTTP's RESTful interface capping off today's ubiquitous platform. This platform has not only fueled a generation of cloud apps, but it has also made it possible to realize many of the features originally targeted at the Internet core (multicast is a great example) as cloud-hosted services.

What About Commercial Reality?

This story is familiar to anyone "raised" on the Internet, making it easy to overlook the fact that this entire discussion of what constitutes a good architecture is technical—one could even say academic—with no particular attention given to commercial concerns (other than the broad goal of "cost effectiveness"). Some of the comments we received on our earlier posts raised business-related issues, and one could certainly argue that a system architecture ought to be judged on the commercial value it generates.

Of course there's no denying the economic value generated by the Internet, which I largely attribute to an architecture that enabled innovation. This created new business opportunities. But there are many cases where architectures have been defined to protect existing revenue streams, effectively controlling (if not stifling) innovation. In such cases, the architecture organizes the design space and draws module boundaries according to existing markets and products; technical considerations are secondary. Take the OSI Reference Model as an example. Without re-fighting the Protocol Wars of the past, I've always been of the opinion that the best explanation of "Why seven layers?" is simply that it was the result of a negotiated way to organize a set of committees populated primarily by telcos. This is an inevitable consequence of defining an architecture in a standards body, but the standardization process is not unique—see my post on Venn Diagram Engineering in the next chapter for discussion of this exact same phenomenon in the open source world.

The common thread in these examples is the influence of commercial concerns in the definition of an architecture. One possible conclusion is that the "goodness" of an architecture depends on its purpose: Is it technically driven with the goal of enabling unrestricted innovation, or is it economically driven with a goal of protecting current business models and revenue streams. Or said another way, an architecture is shaped by its inputs—if you start by putting business-motivated constraints on the available building blocks (or assumptions about how technology will or will not be commoditized), then you will end up with a different outcome, serving a different purpose. Catalyzing disruptive innovation is not everyone's goal, but there are always opportunities and people willing to pursue them.

Larry Peterson, September 2024

The Importance of Thinking Across Layer Boundaries

There was a moment early in my career when I realized that strict layering was not always the best way to think about protocols. And that realization hit me again with force when I started to look into QUIC to add it to our textbook a few years ago. One way to think about QUIC is that, after 30 years of running HTTP over TCP, we're finally getting a chance to revisit the layering decisions that we've lived with since the creation of the Web. And the development of QUIC tells us a lot about layering, as well as the challenges of introducing new protocols to the Internet in its current form.

The design of HTTP/1.0 is a pretty good case study in how layering can go wrong. HTTP, being an application layer protocol, makes the reasonable assumption that the transport layer below it reliably delivers the bytes fed into it. Unfortunately, HTTP/1.0 opened a fresh TCP connection for every object on a web page, which generated a huge amount of extra work and latency to open and close all those connections, including a flurry of three-way handshakes, while ensuring that many connections would be too short to ever get out of the slow-start phase of congestion control. HTTP/1.1 addressed many of these shortcomings, but over time more problems have arisen with the layering of HTTP over TCP. In particular, the addition of another layer (TLS) to secure HTTP compounded the issues to the point where it made sense to consider an alternative transport to TCP. This alternative transport has now been developed as QUIC.

As I've read through a few hundred pages of QUIC RFCs, one thing that keeps jumping out is the difficulty of getting layering "right". Take the layering of transport security for example. Before QUIC, the layering is roughly as follows:

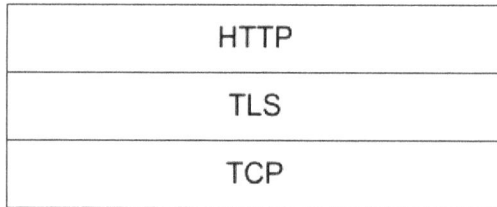

HTTP
TLS
TCP

HTTP Over TLS Over TCP

This looks nice and clean, like something straight out of a networking textbook. In RFC 9001, which defines how TLS works with QUIC, however, the picture is less tidy, as follows:

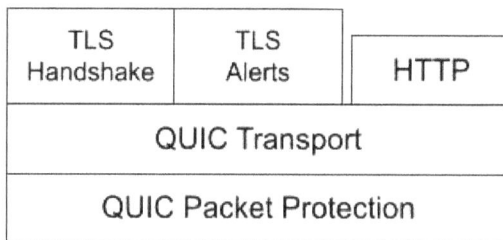

TLS Handshake	TLS Alerts	HTTP
QUIC Transport		
QUIC Packet Protection		

Protocol Layers for QUIC

As the RFC says:

> *Rather than a strict layering, these two protocols cooperate: QUIC uses the TLS handshake; TLS uses the reliability, ordered delivery, and record layer provided by QUIC.*

Why the departure from strict layering? Because the old way of doing things inserted multiple round trip times (RTTs) of delay at every layer. First a three-way handshake to set up TCP, then a TLS handshake to set up the required security (authentication, encryption), then finally the HTTP layer gets to start asking for something like a web page. In fact, these problems of layering are called out in the original QUIC design document. A similar line of reasoning led to the decision not to use SCTP over DTLS (a Datagram variant of TLS), even though at first glance that combination would have met many of the goals of QUIC. The strictly layered approach would again have introduced multiple RTTs of setup delay before HTTP got a chance to send its first application-layer request.

My high-level takeaway from this discussion is that while layering makes it easier to think about protocols, it's not always the best guide to design or implementation (a point also made by David Clark in the foreword to our first edition). When the designers of HTTP/1.0 thought about TCP, they apparently had a model of "this layer makes sure our commands get to the other side"—which is correct, but massively oversimplifies the situation once you start to think about security and performance. The designers of QUIC, with the benefit of decades of experience of running HTTP over TCP, came to the conclusion that the abstractions offered by TCP and TLS were not quite right for HTTP, and used the requirements of the application layer to revisit the design for the transport and security layers.

The other really interesting thing about QUIC is the realization that middleboxes are a fact of life in the modern Internet. This realization was already dawning at the time HTTP/1.1 was designed (the mid 1990s), as that protocol recognizes the existence of caches and proxies sitting between the true ends of an HTTP connection. But the prevalence of middleboxes such as Network Address Translation (NAT) and firewalls has ballooned since then, and led to the conclusion that the only option for a new transport protocol to succeed in today's Internet was for it to sit over UDP. (SCTP stands as an example of a new transport that failed to take off for this reason.) In other words, QUIC, a transport protocol, needs to run over UDP, a transport protocol, because the Internet no longer really allows any transport protocol other than UDP or TCP. (See the comments above about ossification.) The only way to get a new transport protocol deployed is to run it over one that already exists (and QUIC over TCP is off the table for reasons that are hopefully obvious).

This isn't really what was expected when the Internet was designed, and it is the sort of thing that has often been lamented by members of the Internet community who remember a simpler time before middleboxes. But QUIC deals with the world as it is rather than wishing for a different one, and it's hard to fault that approach.

There is yet one more interesting aspect of QUIC, which is its approach to congestion control. Having just written a thousand words on that topic for our upcoming book, I won't try to cover it in depth here. But strengths of the congestion control approach in QUIC include (a) collecting all the decades of experience of TCP congestion control into a new transport protocol design, and (b) recognizing that congestion control continues to evolve and thus allowing new algorithms to be added to QUIC over time. If you read RFC 9002 and the work it references, you would actually end up with a pretty good understanding of the advances that have been made in congestion control since 1988. It would, however, be more efficient to read our book on TCP Congestion Control.

Now that I've invested the effort in understanding the design and rationale of QUIC, I find that I'm quite impressed with the results. I say that as someone who worked on many IETF standards over the years: it's not an easy environment in which to reach consensus and make progress on a protocol design. The design team seized the chance to accommodate a large amount of collective experience in congestion control, and transport protocols more broadly, into a single design. And the end result shows an awareness of cross-layer interactions that is all too rare.

Bruce Davie, September 2021

Closing Remarks

One reasonable conclusion to take away from this chapter is that architecture is frustratingly hard to define. We have given a few examples here, drawing on insights from the respected "architect of the Internet" David Clark:

• An architecture tells you what you cannot do.

• An architecture comprises the things we have to agree on (like IP address semantics) while leaving many other things open to alternative solutions (such as the infinite choices available for the links below the IP layer).

That an architecture both restricts options and makes room for alternatives sounds contradictory, but that's exactly what makes architectural decisions so important to the enduring success of a system (or as we'll see in later chapters, the key to preserving the status quo and thwarting competition). In all cases, judgement is required.

The point about enabling alternative solutions is also important to remember whenever discussions of layering come up. We have been party to many discussions where someone tried to shut down an idea because it was a "layer violation", which would imply that there is only one correct way to use layers in the Internet. But in fact layering is a useful tool to *understand* the Internet, not a rigid constraint that prevents us from doing things. The example we highlighted above was the way layering had to be rethought in the context of reliable transport, security, and Web applications. By changing the arrangement of layers that had built up in the early days of the Web, the designers of QUIC have provided us with a more efficient way to deliver security, reliability, and congestion control for the Web, while also working within the constraints of the Internet architecture and its modern implementation.

Layering in a network protocol stack generalizes to the problem of how one factors any complex system into a collection of modules. The systems approach is always open to refactoring—rethinking the modularity of a system—as the right way to achieve a desired outcome. Just tinkering with the existing modules is often too limiting.

Explore Further

Pamela Zave and Jennifer Rexford. The Real Internet Architecture: Past, Present, and Future Evolution. Princeton University Press, 2024.

Michael Pollan. A Place of My Own: The Architecture of Daydreams. Penguin Putnam, 2009.

Tracy Kidder. House. Houghton Mifflin Company, 1985.

Dave Clayton. What Frank Lloyd Wright Taught Me about Roof Leaks. August 2019.

David Clark. Designing an Internet. MIT Press, 2018.

National Research Council. Realizing the Information Future: The Internet and Beyond. National Academies Press, 1994.

Avery Pennarun. The New Internet. Tailscale blog, 2024.

Larry Peterson, Lawrence Brakmo and Bruce Davie. TCP Congestion Control: A Systems Approach. Systems Approach, 2022.

Open Source Software

All of our books are informed by open source software, keeping with the value we place on systems-building (and being able to talk about and learn from those systems). It's often the case that others have been responsible for those open systems, but in some cases, the software we include in our books is the product of open source communities that we've been active in. That participation gives us insights into both how software ecosystems work, and the role open source plays in the industry.

We start this chapter with an ending: a retrospective about Larry's time at the Open Networking Foundation (ONF) at the point it closed up shop. That background sets the stage for a deeper dive into our experiences with the process of both creating and leveraging (finding value in) open source software. It also gives us perspective on how open source, by itself, isn't always sufficient; the barrier-to-entry can still be too high for mere mortals.

All Things Must Pass

Seems like not that long ago I posted my reflections on PlanetLab as we shut it down, and now I find myself doing the same for ONF. All things must pass (h/t George Harrison). The easy part is to catalog the software ONF has released, since that's what we've been doing the last few years as part of our Systems Approach Series; see our Software-Defined Networking, Private 5G, and Edge Cloud Operations books. But I think it's fair to say that the journey to produce the systems described in those books is at least as interesting as the software itself.

ONF, and its sister organization, ON.Lab, were created by Nick McKeown and Scott Shenker to catalyze SDN, in the early days of the initiative.

(Read John Markoff's NYT story for insight into what made ONF unique.) Both were non-profits: ONF wrote standards (e.g., OpenFlow) and ON.Lab wrote open source platforms (e.g., ONOS, the Open Network Operating System), with the two merging in 2017 under the ONF banner. I became aware of the ON.Lab/ONF mission when Bruce called me in 2012 to ask my thoughts on an offer he had to join ON.Lab as CTO. He was also weighing an offer from Nicira (the SDN startup Nick and Scott founded with Martin Casado). I don't remember the specifics of the conversation, but Bruce ended up at Nicira and is now retired and living the good life in Melbourne. (Bruce's "retirement" of course includes co-running Systems Approach.) But that call got me thinking, and the next time I saw Scott and Nick—at the O'Hare Hilton, where we were pitching an SDN-meets-PlanetLab edge cloud story to an National Science Foundation working group—I asked if I might join them.

Why would anyone in his right mind leave a tenured position at Princeton to join a six-person non-profit you might ask? Lots of factors go into a decision like that, but it was simultaneously a natural next step after PlanetLab and an exciting new opportunity to change the world. It felt like joining a startup, except, of course, there was absolutely no equity upside. Most importantly, after having spent 25+ years in academia, with occasional side trips to industry, I saw a sweet spot that appealed to me.

That sweet spot is one that walks a fine line between academia and industry. It was an opportunity to build systems that were new and disruptive, but to do so in collaboration with networking companies trying to address real-world problems. The systems had to be real, but we had the freedom (or rather, the mandate) to stick to our guns when it came to architectural integrity. We wanted our software to be adopted and deployed—and there were often spurts of "get it ready to ship"—but the "product" we were selling was actually more the potential of a new way to build networks than any single feature that could be immediately monetized. Questions of return on investment were always being asked, but that mostly happened inside our industry partners, leaving our merry band of disruptors to build systems the way we thought they ought to be built. (I'm idealizing a little here, but more on that in a moment.)

Not surprisingly, the partner companies that championed our mission played a critical role. Over the years they included both network operators (AT&T, Google, Comcast, Verizon, NTT, DT, SKT, China Unicom, Turk Telecom) and network vendors (Intel, NEC, Ciena, Radisys, Netsia, Cisco, Ericsson, Nokia, Huawei, Juniper, Edgecore, Adtran). Some were there to keep tabs on how we might impact their current business models, some were there to stay on the good side of their operator customers, and some were there to get better pricing from their equipment providers. But all cynicism aside, there was a good-faith belief that change was important and necessary among all the individuals involved (if not their employers).

Most of these companies made important contributions, but I think it's fair to say that AT&T (promoting Domain 2.0) and Google (advocating cloud technology) provided the lion's share of the thought leadership from the industry side, with Urs Hölzle (Google) and Andre Fuetsch (AT&T) serving as the two Chairs of the ONF Board. (Those of us from the academic side had been telling this story for years, so we were more than eager to continue evangelizing for programmable networks.) And towards the end, when the corporate excitement started to wane, DARPA made a significant investment, giving us the opportunity to build Aether, the capstone project of the ONF experiment. Aether now continues as a funded project of the Linux Foundation (LF).

I talk about how ONF's unique position in the networking industry colored my view of open source software in the next post—where my cynicism is on full display—but that doesn't change the fact that ONF gave me the opportunity to work with an outstanding collection of engineers to design and build systems that we wanted to build, in the way we wanted to build them—the sweet spot I mentioned earlier. And I think the 30+ engineers at ONF—ranging from fresh PhDs who had worked on SDN-related research projects to seasoned developers who had spent years in the corporate world—would say the same thing. The ONF executive team, particularly Guru Parulkar (Executive Director) and Bill Snow (VP Engineering) deserve the credit for creating such an environment, absorbing the brunt of the impedance mismatch between the industry and academic halves of our mission.

Going forward, the three projects moving to LF's stewardship represent ONF's tangible legacy. One is the P4 programming language, which already has an active community focused on creating deeply programmable networks. The second is LF Broadband, which brings SDN to fiber access networks and is already deployed in production throughout the world. The third is Aether, which leapfrogs Telco-centric solutions, and shows the way to democratizing 5G. I will continue to be involved with Aether, and am looking forward to working with new industry partners to realize real-world deployments.

Larry Peterson, January 2024

Venn Diagram Engineering

And Other Tactics in Weaponizing Open Source

Open source software has been the subject of many essays, of which Eric Raymond's insights in *The Cathedral and The Bazaar* still serves as a thought-provoking example. For those who haven't read that piece, Raymond examines the conflict between what had been his experience with open source software:

> *I believed that the most important software... needed to be built like cathedrals, carefully crafted by individual wizards or small bands of mages working in splendid isolation, with no beta to be released before its time.*

and a different approach he witnessed the Linux community using with great success:

> *The Linux community seemed to resemble a great babbling bazaar of differing agendas and approaches ... out of which a coherent and stable system could seemingly emerge only by a succession of miracles.*

His observations came to mind as I reflected on our experiences at the Open Networking Foundation (ONF) over the last decade, leading me to write down a few of my own observations on one particular corner of the open source ecosystem.

ONF's mission has been to disrupt the networking industry, with open source software serving as its primary tool for catalyzing that change. That disruption is widely known as Software-Defined Networking (SDN), but focusing on that term misses the point, which is that the overriding goal is to transform the networking industry from a vertical market to a horizontal market, and in doing so, both spur innovation and improve the opportunity for network owners to control their destiny. That mission has its roots in a 2001 National Academy report on the ossification of the Internet, but my take is that the goal is simply to lower the barrier for those who wish to program and control networks. The ONF journey has involved a long list of open source platforms and components (some of which are described in our SDN book), but rather than retrace the history of the specific projects, I'd like to focus on a few lessons we learned along the way.

Beyond its mission to be disruptive, ONF has two other distinctive attributes. First, it has its own engineering team, and that team has no allegiance to any commercial product. (Mozilla is the only other similar example that comes to mind.) The objective is to push the principles of SDN—open source software, disaggregation, commodity hardware, cloud practices—into any space that provides an opportunity. There is no legacy business model to protect. Second, although the individual software components each have stand-alone value, with their own constituents driving requirements and their own development teams doing the work, they have been designed with an eye towards working in concert across the entire portfolio. This proved important because it provided in-house use cases that drove iterative improvements, which ultimately led to the creation of new platforms with their own set of requirements and use cases. This approach is arguably a hybrid Cathedral/Bazaar model, but more on that point below.

So what did we learn? The top-level lesson is that we knew we were making progress on the disruption mission because there was constant resistance. It's impossible to know how much change to directly attribute to ONF given everything else going on in the industry, and making such a claim would be silly. But when you are trying to disrupt an entrenched industry, resistance is a sure sign that you are doing your job. Interestingly, this resistance came from stakeholders up-and-down the stack. It started with the incumbent network vendors who the network operators wanted to disrupt, but it ended up including the network operators themselves, whose approach to operationalizing the network is now being challenged by cloud native approaches. For fun, we report a few "ah ha" moments along the way. Some technical. Some, not so much.

- I learned a new term early in the journey: *weaponizing open source*. Make of that what you will.

- It became clear after we started to deliver successful platforms that we were a pawn on a larger chess board. We were effectively serving as a stalking horse for operators to negotiate better pricing from their vendors. Of course that was the case. The surprise was hearing it said out loud.

- Standing up vendor-backed open source projects is the go-to approach for doling out incremental change, a strategy known in some circles as "throwing sand in the gears." This happened with Open Daylight (ODL) in the SDN Controller space, and the O-RAN Software Community (OSC) in the RAN Intelligent Controller space. (See our post on SD-RAN for an example of the point of contention in the 5G space.) When vendors bring all the engineering resources to a "community" effort, they retain control over the agenda. ONF's vendor-neutral/engineer-led approach offered a counter-weight in both cases, which led to tangible features that would otherwise be missing.

- A tried-and-true approach to discrediting a new (disruptive) technology is to brand it as a "research project". This was a constant refrain, and of course any new approach isn't going to be as mature as the incumbent solution. That should be expected. But time is a great equalizer, and in the case of ONF, much of its software now runs in production networks. But that isn't necessarily the point; it's just a more measurable outcome than indirectly impacting the openness and programmability of commercial alternatives.

- The best traction for a disruptive technology is in deployments facing generational upgrades, as was the case in the access network (e.g., DSL to PON/GPON and 4G to 5G). This is obvious in retrospect, but then again, SDN likely needed small wins in established settings to be a credible alternative in new environments.

- Uncountable hours can be spent doing *"Venn Diagram Engineering"*, a term I coined to describe the process of mapping the constraints on any potential solution (before it's implemented or fully understood) to respect existing business models and stakeholder boundaries. That's certainly not how the Bazaar works. Creating new platforms requires freedom to refactor as you gain experience, and that refactoring may very well disrupt current business models.

- Building complete solutions (and not just components) is a necessary first step in gap analysis, helping to identify the breadth of issues that need to be addressed to make a technology viable. The second step is to use and operate your solution, and not just throw it over the wall to someone else. Operational experience (aka "eating your own dog food") is the best way to turn a proof-of-concept into a commercially viable solution. ONF is now doing this with Aether, a capstone project that combines its SD-Fabric, SD-Core, and SD-RAN components with a comprehensive operational platform to provide a managed edge cloud service.

These last two points are the main (technical) takeaway. The ONF approach to open source software includes elements of both the Cathedral and the Bazaar, but is also different in its open-ended approach to mapping out a new space. There is a shared set of architectural principles and a concerted effort to ensure that the components work together to build operational end-to-end solutions (the cathedral). But at the same time, each component is allowed to reinvent itself and fork new components, as necessary, to follow emergent opportunities (the bazaar). There is no prescribed framework that fixes interface boundaries a priori. This isn't a revolutionary new approach: it's just the natural consequence of making a system open and programmable.

Larry Peterson, February 2022.

Open Source: Another Value Proposition

Open source software has become an integral part of today's technology marketplace. We've written above about weaponizing open source software in the context of our experiences using SDN to disrupt the networking industry. It's also common to hear people talk about business models for monetizing open source software, for example, by selling support (think RedHat) or cloud services (think Databricks operationalizing Apache Spark). Discussions of this kind typically reduce to an exercise in defining a value proposition for open source software; if you're going through that exercise in a business setting, that value has to be direct and quantifiable.

But there's another way to think about value, which struck me recently as we went to press with our Private 5G book. Without consciously adopting it as a strategy, I realized that all four of the Systems Approach books we've written recently are strongly influenced by—and in most cases, organized around—open source software. The Private 5G book describes Aether as a combination of SD-RAN, SD-Core, and SD-Fabric (all open source); the SDN book describes a software stack that starts with a P4-programmable forwarding plane, and builds through a Switch OS, a Network OS, and a set of control applications (all open source); and the Edge Cloud Operations book describes how to build a cloud management platform from a combination of over 20 open source projects ranging from Kubernetes to Keycloak to Elastic Stack. Even the TCP Congestion Control book leans heavily on the implementation in the Linux kernel (which, as I've argued in another post, is effectively the specification of the algorithm). And as Bruce recently reminded me, one of the reasons I decided to write the original Computer Networks book was that I was able to leverage open source protocol stacks that I had been working with. I should have seen this pattern long before now; I thought I was just being opportunistic.

I'm not sure what name to put on that value, or even the right way to characterize it. Part of it is my own internal drive to understand how complex systems work, and part is wanting to share that understanding with anyone struggling with the same questions—but it definitely feels like value to me. I guess the easy label would be educational value, but with understanding comes empowerment to make the ideas your own, adapt them to your purposes, and ultimately, to innovate. None of these are easily quantifiable, and I have no idea how to go about computing the return on investment, but that doesn't make the value any less real.

Looking Under The Hood

But I'm getting ahead of myself. I think there's more than meets the eye to the conclusion that open source software leads to understanding and know-how. For example, it's obvious that open source makes it possible to see the engineering details of a given software tool. That's important, but what I have found to be equally true is that having access to a breadth of implementation detail is essential to having a deep conceptual framework for complex systems such as the Internet or the cloud. Or said another way, seeing the "Powerpoint rendition" of a system often leads to a superficial understanding unless you also have an opportunity to look "under the hood", and ideally, play with the code. Here are three other observations that I came to appreciate about the topics we've been reporting on in our book series.

Starting with SDN, it is well known that the objective was to catalyze a horizontal market around the historically vertical networking industry, and to this end, our book describes all the components that go into building an end-to-end Software-Defined Network. There comes a point about three-quarters of the way through the book where we acknowledge that everything discussed up to that point merely *"reproduce(s) functionality that already exists"*, at which point we are finally ready to start talking about SDN's supposed value proposition: the ability to rapidly evolve and customize the network. But if you stop and think about it, that first 75% is a complete blueprint for how to build a modern high-speed L2/L3 switch, which until fairly recently has been the proprietary know-how of a handful of device and chip vendors. (And this understanding is now finding its way into undergraduate networking courses; see for example CS 422 at Purdue.) It's impossible to predict how a widespread understanding of the internals of packet forwarding will impact the future of networking (even at a time when the commercial viability of programmable hardware is being questioned), but I have no doubt that it will.

There is a similar story about 5G, arguably with the potential for even greater impact. An in-depth understanding of the mobile cellular network has been known only to a handful of incumbents for 40 years. The availability of an open, software-defined RAN and Mobile Core changes that dynamic. And even though the Mobile Network Operators are starting to pull back from Open-RAN, presumably because the incumbent vendors have given them good business reasons to do so, I think it's fair to say that there's no turning back. It's now the case that even I am able to bring up a 5G network; surely others will figure out ways to leverage that know-how in innovative ways. Making it easier for anyone to do that is the motivation behind the book's hands-on appendix, which is starting to find its way into courses like CS 596 at UMass.

The final example is from how to operate an edge cloud. The know-how needed to operationalize an inert pile of code (whether it's open source or proprietary) is substantial enough that we're willing to pay other people to do it for us. Ease-of-use is often worth paying for, but doing so should not be due to a belief that wizardry is required. This is especially true since all the tools you need to operationalize cloud services are readily available as open source (complete with excellent tutorials). At the very least, you should know what you're paying for when you outsource the problem. It's also the case that the steepness of the learning curve is partially related to the newness of the technology, with lots of overlapping tools competing for mind-share. Once enough people understand the space in a principled way, we should expect to see a distillation that simplifies the toolset, hopefully lowering the barrier to entry.

At this point it's fair to observe that someone has to pay for it, and it's difficult to fund open source software for its educational value alone. Fortunately, the educational angle is usually not the whole story. Sometimes the technical people get out in front of the business people and make their code available without an obvious business model. That happened many years ago at Bell Labs, and still happens with researchers who value impact over monetary reward. Sometimes governments pay for it as a matter of public policy (or national security). That is what's happening today in the 5G space. Sometimes companies take a long-term perspective as a way of growing a market rather than focusing on their share of an existing market. You could argue Google has done that by releasing tools like Kubernetes, or Nicira with Open vSwitch. But I suspect that most of the time, it's software for which someone originally put together a business plan that ends up delivering this indirect and unquantifiable value (whether or not the business plan ever panned out).

These observations may be obvious in hindsight, but I think they are easy to overlook in a field so often focused on entrepreneurship and business value. There's the marketplace of products, but also the marketplace of ideas, and how those ideas are manipulated impacts all of us. Learning from open source software—as a means of internalizing the know-how that went into building it—is one way to consume it. Our books aim to be an aid in finding and extracting that value. As we noted previously, we are primarily motivated by our potential impact, and open source software is one of the best ways we've found to deliver it.

Larry Peterson, June 2023

Repeatability: As Difficult as it is Important

We all understand that reproducibility of experimental results is a cornerstone of the scientific method. It should be possible to consistently replicate a finding, and this should be just as true for experimental systems research as for any scientific field. One could also argue that the bar ought to be higher for systems research, since it should be possible for others not only to reuse software artifacts developed for our experiments to replicate the results, but also to perform follow-on experiments.

Reproducibility—or rather, repeatability, if you want to replicate a result starting with the authors' software artifact rather than just based on your reading of a technical paper—has not historically been a strong suit of the experimental systems research community. This is my takeaway from Collberg and Proebsting's 2016 article *"Repeatability in Computer Systems Research"*, which is well worth reading if you're not familiar with it. In addition to documenting the embarrassing state of affairs in 2016, the paper talks about several challenges, which includes both having the right incentives and addressing the technical barriers. In response to the incentives issue, conferences like SOSP and SIGCOMM now put an emphasis on the availability of research artifacts per ACM badging policies. But the technical challenges of getting someone else's software to work for us does not get any easier.

(Note that Collberg & Proebsting use the terms "reproducibility" and "repeatability" differently than the ACM badging policy statement. Our usage is consistent with Collberg & Proebsting, which we prefer because it focuses on artifacts rather than teams.)

For reasons that will become clear, I find myself thinking about this highbrow principle in the context of open source, where the goal is to lower the barrier for others to replicate and use your software—to repeat the process of deploying a system, but for their own purposes rather than just to verify your results. In this case, the incentives are clear (there are measurable outcomes instead of badges), but the technical challenges are equally daunting, if not more so.

Tooling For Repeatability

In simple cases, widely used tools are sufficient. Specify the Ubuntu release and provide a Makefile (along with the source code) and you're done. But this is limited to self-contained programs. Once there are dependencies (beyond the OS), you need to specify those as well. This forces the "consumer" to know their way around package management tools like APT or pip, and for you to carefully document all those dependencies. Be sure to start with a clean Ubuntu install, because there's no way to remember all the assumptions you're making about what runs on your test environment. Or you can assume Docker containers, which works until you need to install multiple containers, or better yet, do so on some other system, such as a cloud platform so you can scale performance. Now we've crossed the line into release management. Search for "release management tools" and you'll quickly appreciate how this problem quickly unravels. (You might also search for "Kubernetes distributions" if you've never encountered all the choices available to you in bringing up a "simple" Kubernetes cluster.)

The problem is that, as we have created ever more powerful frameworks for building complex systems by integrating existing components, we have made it increasingly difficult for others to replicate what we've done. To complicate matters, the tools themselves are often complex systems constructed from the integration of multiple components, so it's no simple matter to bootstrap the process. And finally, just to add an additional level of difficulty to the challenge, replicating a research prototype so you can reproduce a particular experimental result corresponds to a single "use case". In general, the open source variant of this "repeatability" problem needs to support multiple use cases and/or deployment options.

Managing (or Punting) Complexity

My experience is that a common way to manage complexity is to punt it to someone else. Here's one example, but it is by no means unique. The Linux Foundation has defined blueprints for assembling multiple components to deploy a 5G network: an edge cloud stack from Project X, a set of 5G Network Functions from Project Y, a 5G management plane from Project Z, and so on. Each blueprint is backed by a Proof of Concept (typically a demo showing the particular combination of components working, along with supportive slideware), with links to the documentation provided by the individual projects to help the user who wants to replicate the blueprint. Clearly, the burden falls to the consumer to do the heavy lifting, although in fairness, these blueprints typically target companies with sufficient engineering resources to take on such a burden.

But that's more than a little depressing. We often think of open source as leveling the playing field, but the complexity of actually deploying state-of-the-art cloud-based systems keeps the barrier to entry quite high. My own recent focus on 5G, where the stock talk I give is entitled "Democratizing 5G", focuses attention on how 5G/NextG networks are no longer strictly the purview of global carriers, but can now be deployed by anyone (aka Private 5G). But I've come to add the subtitle "Open Source and Much More" as I come to appreciate that the availability of open source doesn't mean anything if you don't have the wherewithal to take advantage of that open source.

Based on my experience trying to lower the barrier for replicating Aether, this translates into three additional requirements. The first is that blueprints—the recipe for replicating a system—be executable rather than just a collection of documents. For Aether, that "executable" is an Ansible playbook (used in a stylized way), with its vars file serving as the root of the blueprint specification. Yes, this is a tool the consumer still has to deal with, but it's a necessary starting point, and leads me to the next two requirements.

The second requirement is that the tooling needed to execute the blueprint make as few assumptions as possible, and in general, be minimal, open, and widely used. Said another way, the tool(s) must be transparent and explicit, and not hide any of the steps behind an opaque "single click install" button. Full automation may be called for in an operational system, but the overhead of full automation can be a hindrance to adoption. Simplicity is often a judgment call, and my sense is the tooling must be sufficient to bootstrap the process of replicating the system, but no more. Ansible checks all the boxes, which not only enables resource-limited users, but also has the benefit of not getting in the way of sophisticated users who want to substitute their own (arbitrarily wonderful) management tools.

And finally, because there is still some amount of documentation required to use the replication tooling—and hence the risk of hidden assumptions or misunderstandings—the third requirement is that an example execution be provided. For Aether, this takes the form of an open source Jenkins pipeline that doubles as a nightly verification test that the blueprint still works. Users trying to replicate my work can see the exact sequence of calls I invoke, and proof that it works.

I doubt anyone would argue with the aspirational goal of making it easy for others to run any code you've written and put on GitHub. But it takes more than good intentions, especially as we build ever more complex systems by integrating existing components. It takes care in selecting the tools others will be forced to use to build and install the software, and it takes thorough documentation to walk them through the process of applying those tools. Obvious things to do, but hard to prioritize and surprisingly hard to deliver.

Larry Peterson, October 2024

Closing Remarks

You may have heard someone say "open software is not the same as free software." The point they are usually trying to make is that software has to be maintained, so even though you might not be charged on day one, you will accrue costs over time to keep it running. But ongoing maintenance is just one hidden cost of open source. Getting software to run in diverse environments—reproducibility—is another. We should be aware of these costs whenever we decide to leverage some open source project.

Another important thing to remember is that open source software is written (and hence effectively funded) by someone whose incentives may not be entirely altruistic. There is typically a business rationale (or in some national interest) for making source code widely available. It's important to understand what those incentives might be.

This is not to say open source software is inherently suspect. In many cases, it defines a common platform that makes it possible for anyone to compete to build applications that run on that platform. This can spur innovation. Another important benefit is that open source software is a good way to share know-how. This gives it both pedagogical and research value. The challenges with open source are numerous, but so are the benefits. As with so much of systems design, it is important to weigh the tradeoff between costs and benefits before trying to make use of "free" software.

Explore Further

John Markoff. Open Networking Foundation Pursues New Standards. New York Times, March 2011.

AT&T Domain 2.0 Vision White Paper. November 2013.

Jimmy Clidaras, Urs Hölzle, and Luiz André Barroso. Datacenter as a Computer: An Introduction to the Design of Warehouse-Scale Machines (2nd Edition). Morgan and Claypool, 2013.

Eric Raymond. The Cathedral and the Bazaar. February 2010.

Looking Over the Fence at Networks: A Neighbor's View of Networking Research. The National Academies Press, 2001.

Christian Collberg and Todd Proebsting. Repeatability in Computer Systems Research. *Communications of the ACM*, February 2016.

ACM. Artifact Review and Badging. August 2020.

Larry Peterson. SD-RAN: A Familiar Tussle Unfolding. Systems Approach blog, September 2021.

Judgement in System Design

Despite our insistence that every technical question has a right and a wrong answer, system design is not an exact science. Technical arguments can usually be made to justify this or that architectural decision (as we saw in the Architecture chapter), but those arguments are always rooted in some judgement about what is and is not important. Viewed in this way, defining a system architecture is a balancing act—weighing the requirements of different stakeholders—and at the end of the day, it depends on the judgement of the architect.

This chapter explores the idea of judgement in system design, drawing on parallels with the design process in other, very different, domains: writing about systems and building houses. In looking at the creative side of system design, one soon encounters *elegance* and *simplicity* as important consideration. How do you know if a system is elegant? It takes good judgement, of course.

If all of this seems too far afield from computing, we're not actually plowing new ground. Scott Shenker's seminal talk on Software-Defined Networking (SDN), for example, takes inspiration from Don Norman's thesis on the importance of extracting simplicity. Not coincidentally, Don Norman is best known for his iconic book: *The Design of Everyday Things*.

Trial By Fire

Our insight that weighing competing requirements is an essential aspect of system design is hard-earned. During the mid-2000s, Larry was the technical lead for the GENI project, an attempt to build a "large scientific instrument" for the networking research community, akin to Physics' Large

> *Hadron Collider and Astronomy's Hubble Telescope. (See the John Markoff article cited below for a general introduction to GENI.) GENI attracted requirements and constraints from nearly every corner of Computer Science, meaning we were dealing with a seriously over-constrained design space. We produced a feasible architecture that rested on a report that made our underlying value statement explicit.*
>
> *That report defined eleven requirements (none are surprising), seven tensions (points of conflict between various of those requirements), and six engineering principles (pragmatic steps to realize GENI in finite time). The tensions are the most interesting part of the report, and to give one example, there was a sticky question about how to balance slicability (the ability to share GENI resources) with fidelity (the ability to run experiments that are representative of the real networks). The report didn't resolve the conflict, per se, but it did define a "virtual knob" for managing virtualization (the crux of the issue in this case). It also punted the question of how to set that knob down the road to a future governing board; the evolution of both open and closed systems ultimately must defer to a board of directors of some kind.*

Stakeholders and #2 Pine

I would guess most people who read our books and posts are familiar with Tracy Kidder's Pulitzer Prize-winning *The Soul of a New Machine*. It's essential reading for any Computer Scientist or IT professional. But the book by Kidder that has always resonated with me is *House*—a story about the seemingly ordinary process of building a house on a pasture just outside of Amherst, Massachusetts.

That I'm drawn to a story like this is not surprising, when you consider the first line of our Computer Networks book that I put to paper: *"Suppose you want to build a computer network…"* Whether it's about a computer, a network, or a house, Kidder had me at "building". And House delivers with a wealth of detail about that process, from the art of putting together a bid for the job to trying to shave costs by picking through a stack of #2 pine boards for a handful without too many knots, and everything in between. It's a meaty and satisfying end-to-end story.

But that's not what has stuck with me over the years since I first read the book. For me, the compelling feature of the story is the tension between the three principal stakeholders: the architect, the lead carpenter, and the owners who pay to have the house built. The parallels to my professional experience building computing systems are unmistakable, with the system architect, the engineering team, and the customer (or the product line manager serving as a proxy for the end customer) reading from an eerily similar script. It's easy to believe that our high-tech challenges are unique, but they are not. Whether you are building a house, a new computer, or a network, you are part of a human endeavor, and in the case of House, Kidder makes the story about the people.

The book describes the conflicts that are bound to arise in such a collaboration, many of which will sound familiar—the architect having to translate a vague wish-list into a feasible blueprint, or the builder having to put a price tag on it—but one of my favorite exchanges happens midway through the process, with distinct overtones of feature creep:

> *Jonathan [the owner] stands in the driveway, looking up at the house. "Enough is enough. It has a taste of a Greek temple. Fine. But it's not a Greek temple, and we're not Greeks." He and Judith have resolved to put red shingles on their roof. "That gives it a little color, a little fun, in what could be a pretentious house," says Jonathan. But New Englanders, Jim [the builder] learns to his slight surprise, have not taken to red shingles. No one has them in stock.*

But it's the tussle between the architect and the builder that keeps bubbling to the top, or maybe it seems that way because it's the one that is most familiar to me (as someone who has both architected computer systems and worked on construction sites with power tools and a tool belt). There is plenty of finger pointing, but also mutual admiration and respect. An example of conversation that Kidder excels at capturing involves Jim [the builder] complaining to a friend that *"I haven't ever built a house that I really like."* The friend responds by telling Jim that he should be an architect, to which Jim replies: *"I can't do it. I can't conceive the grace of line, starting from nothing."*

The architect may be the one able to "conceive the grace of line" but it's the person wielding the hammer who more often than not has the last word, as I once learned when discussing a feature we were trying to support in a software product for which I was the lead architect.

Engineer: I'm going to support that feature by doing x, y, and z.

Me: You can't do that. It violates every tenet of the architecture.

Engineer: Sure I can. I just have to code it.

That's one lesson that seems to hold across domains, although houses suffer a different kind of technical debt than computer systems. Another is that projects are successful when there is a well-functioning team, with engineers who value the architect's judgement, and an architect who appreciates the practical issues that the engineers face. (Spoiler Alert: The house does get built and you can find it on Zillow with only a little bit of effort.)

There are many other "big picture" takeaways that make House well worth the investment of your time, plus Kidder does a great job weaving historical tidbits throughout the story. One in particular jumped out at me because of the connection it makes to the book-writing endeavor Bruce and I have undertaken:

Jim [the lead carpenter] explained a number of technical details to Bill [the architect], such as the usual height of cabinets on kitchen walls. A few hundred years before, in England, this same species of information would have fallen into the category of "secrets and mysteries of the trade." Some historians think that the publishing of books that revealed those secrets partly accounted for the decline of apprenticeship and guild systems in carpentry and opened the way for the rise of professional architects.

I'm not a big fan of "secrets and mysteries of the trade", and that has a lot to do with why I've made a career of teaching and writing about whatever it is that I happen to discover (or figure out how to build). In fact, much of what we try to do at Systems Approach is to re-capture the excitement we felt when we first understood a new technology and to pass that excitement onto our readers.

Larry Peterson, December 2022

Omission by Design

Writing about systems has a lot in common with building them, and one of the secrets of writing that I've come to appreciate over the years is knowing what to leave out. This starts with deciding what topics are in-scope versus out-of-scope, and then for the selected scope, knowing what's important to say and what can go unstated. The best (and most entertaining) discussion of this topic I've come across is John McPhee's *Draft No. 4: On the Writing Process*, a book that helped me appreciate how much of my job as a CS Professor was spent practicing (as a researcher) and teaching (as an advisor) Creative Nonfiction. McPhee makes many insightful observations about the writing process, but one that particularly resonates with me (especially with my systems hat on) is his chapter on Omission.

Deciding what is in-scope versus out-of-scope is something all authors face. Our TCP Congestion Control book forced us to make many decisions to leave stuff out, for the simple reason that we had to select a small subset of the hundreds of available algorithms to report on, to illustrate the fundamental principles at work in Congestion Control. From the first edition of *Computer Networks: A Systems Approach* we have tried to provide perspective on what is fundamental, not to produce an encyclopedia. As another example, we made a decision to treat QoS as out of bounds, but we did so by first mapping the larger design space for resource allocation, and then declaring what parts of that space are not covered in the rest of the book. To my eye, there is a direct connection between this aspect of writing about a system and the process of distinguishing between requirements and non-requirements when building a system.

Deciding where to draw the line between important concepts and details that can be safely omitted has obvious parallels with the art of defining abstractions, which anyone trained in Computer Science will have an appreciation for. The high-level concepts are codified as modules, the implementation details go unstated, and the relationships and dependencies among modules are made explicit. I'm a strong proponent of clearly describing a system you're building (beyond simply documenting its API) as an integral part of the design process. Writing helps with clarity of thought, which is important to the simplicity, consistency, and completeness of a system's design. My experience is that if you can't clearly describe a system (or component) you've built, you're probably not done designing it yet.

Known Unknowns

Our experience writing the Edge Cloud Operations book highlights a less obvious (but equally important) aspect of omission: Knowing what you don't know. The book—which describes a system we also built—focuses on three stakeholders: cloud operators who manage one or more edge clouds, enterprise users who take advantage of services running on an edge cloud, and service developers who build those edge services. The relationships among these three stakeholders are well understood by the hyperscalers when applied to the central clouds they've built, which support two models: (1) the hyperscalers offer their own services (e.g., AWS DynamoDB), so users see no distinction between the cloud operator and the service developer; or (2) the hyperscalers provide infrastructure (and building block services) to 3rd-party service developers who in turn interact with users, hiding the cloud operator as an implementation detail.

The complication is that these relationships are more nuanced when the edge cloud is deployed in enterprises. In our approach to building (and describing) edge cloud operations, we decided to support the possibility of all three stakeholders being distinct: Operator A manages an edge cloud running on-prem at Enterprise B, delivering services built by Service Developers X, Y, and Z. And while it is a viable option for an enterprise to select one of the existing hyperscalers to also operate its edge cloud (and they are more than happy to do that, with Google's Anthos, Microsoft's Azure Arc, and Amazon's ECS-Anywhere being prime examples), a major point of the book is to show that the bar for an enterprise being its own cloud operator is not insurmountable. This commonly means that edge services are deployed on Kubernetes clusters and optionally paired with centrally hosted services. So how would that work with respect to the stakeholders?

One option is for the edge cloud operator to mimic the hyperscaler model: start with an IaaS foundation and give each Developer the freedom to acquire vanilla infrastructure and then build whatever operational support they want on top of that infrastructure; for example, they get to provision their own Kubernetes clusters and define their own Lifecycle Management toolchain. In our view, having to install and operate an IaaS layer before you can begin to deploy Kubernetes-based services is a non-starter for edge deployments because it dramatically increases the complexity, so we look for other possibilities.

A second option is for the edge cloud operator to prescribe a particular operational platform (e.g., the book describes a Lifecycle Management toolchain constructed from a combination of RKE, Jenkins, Rancher, Terraform, and Fleet), which forces the service developer to either adapt to those practices, or make their service available as standard artifacts (e.g., Docker images and Helm charts) that can be fed into different CI/CD pipelines. This option shifts responsibility (and pain) from the operator to the developer, which could prove equally problematic.

A third option is to accept that a multi-cloud will emerge within enterprises. Today, most people equate multi-cloud with services running across multiple hyperscalers, but with edge clouds becoming more common, it is possible (if not likely) that enterprises will invite multiple edge clouds onto their local premises, some hyperscaler-operated and some not, each hosting a different subset of edge services. This approach again shifts the burden, this time onto the enterprise.

None of these options is ideal, with each shifting the burden/pain to one of the other stakeholders. So how did we resolve this in the book? We didn't. In fact, it was while trying to write the architectural overview chapter that we came to appreciate that we were butting up against a hard problem that we could not immediately solve. The book outlines the design space, but we did not let the lack of resolution on this question delay or limit the value provided by the rest of the book (or the system the book describes). This is consistent with one of my favorite system design principles: *Solve no problem before its time.* McPhee's essay on omission makes a similar point with an anecdote about the author, then a 19-year-old college sophomore, meeting General Eisenhower five years after the end of World War II. I can't possibly do the story justice, so I urge you to read it for yourself. But the takeaway is this: systems, books, and even paintings of bowls of fruit are often improved by what we decide to leave out.

Larry Peterson, July 2022

————————————————————

Elegance: The Undervalued System Requirement

I've downsized my CS library multiple times over the last several years, whittling it down to only the few dozen books that have some meaning to me. It still includes the *Pascal User Manual and Report (2nd Edition)*, so of course I took note of the In Memoriam column for Niklaus Wirth in the March issue of CACM. I have a strong affinity for his perspective on the systems we build:

> *Wirth's overriding philosophy was that systems should be simple, efficient, and "elegant". He forcefully (some colleagues have said "ruthlessly") advocated for the reduction of both features and overhead in systems, often frustrating his colleagues and students when this removed functionality they wanted.*

Wirth was a major force in laying the foundation for modern programming languages during the 1960s and 70s, with a hand in the design of ALGOL, Euler, Modula and Modula-2. But for a generation of students like myself, he is best known for Pascal, a language designed to teach students block-structured programming. Pascal was, in part, a response by Wirth to his experiences with "commercial languages" that were so large and complex that "nobody can understand them in their entirety." Wirth insisted Pascal be simple enough to learn how to program and to efficiently implement. Not surprisingly, I also appreciate the connection he made between simplicity and teaching, which I argue has a corollary even in the commercial world: *Until you can clearly describe and explain your system to others, it's not as simple or elegant as it should be.*

Simplicity is not a radical idea, at least in theory. Most practicing software developers have heard of the KISS Principle (Keep It Simple, Stupid), and the Second System Syndrome is a well-known adage about simple, elegant systems being followed by over-engineered and bloated successor systems. In practice though, it seems that we just can't help ourselves. We like the challenge of complexity, and as a one-time collaborator of mine was fond of saying once we started to make progress on a system design: *"This problem has become too easy; let's make it harder."*

One thing we can do is draw attention to cautionary tales. Programming languages provide plenty of examples, not the least of which is PL/I, a contemporary of Pascal designed by IBM. (Yes, I also wrote programs in PL/I.) The goal of PL/I was to "bring together the power of three different programming languages: FORTRAN, ALGOL, and COBOL." It's difficult to imagine a better example of second system syndrome... unless it's Ada, another Pascal contemporary, built to meet the requirements of the US Department of Defense to "supersede over 450 programming languages used by the DoD at that time."

Calling out blatant examples of questionable design is fun, but of limited value. It would be more helpful if we could extract a few lessons and some deeper insights from less obvious examples. To this end, one of my favorite case studies is a subsection of our networking textbook that I've insisted on keeping in every edition, despite the fact that it's drawn from the ARPANET, a network that hasn't been operational for decades. It's about how to assign link costs (metrics) that get used by the routing algorithm to select the shortest path to a destination.

The original ARPANET routing metric measured the number of packets that were queued waiting to be transmitted on each link, meaning that a link with 10 packets queued awaiting transmission was assigned a larger cost weight than a link with 5 packets queued. It turned out that using queue length as a routing metric did not work well—it moves packets toward the shortest queue rather than toward the destination, a situation all too familiar to anyone who has hopped from line to line at the grocery store.

A second version of the ARPANET routing algorithm took both link bandwidth and latency into consideration and used delay (rather than queue length) as a measure of load. Although an improvement over the original mechanism under light load, at heavy load a congested link would start to advertise a very high cost. This caused all the traffic to move off that link, leaving it idle, so then it would advertise a low cost, thereby attracting back all the traffic, and so on. The effect of this instability was that many links would spend considerable time being idle, which is the last thing you want under heavy load. (The approach had other problems, including a dynamic range for metrics that was too large.)

A third approach addressed these problems, but that algorithm also turned out to be too complicated for real-world network deployments, and in the end, conventional wisdom arrived at the conclusion that dynamic metrics are too unstable. Today, static metrics are the norm.

This example reinforces the argument that simpler is better, but it also illustrates that sometimes you need to gain experience to understand how much simplicity is appropriate. To paraphrase Einstein: A system should be as simple as possible, but no simpler. Routing was a new problem in the ARPANET's day, and while it may seem obvious in retrospect that static metrics were both the simplest solution and the best solution, the assumption that dynamic metrics were required needed to first be debunked. Credit is due to those who learned from the ARPANET experience, rather than stubbornly continuing down the path of trying to further optimize dynamic metrics.

Sources of Complexity

Networking has lots of examples of creeping complexity—adding support for multicast was once the easiest way to make an otherwise solvable problem suitably hard—but they are probably best saved for another time. The interesting question is why so much complexity is introduced in the first place, and what we can do to avoid it. Academic researchers who are often rewarded for cleverness are surely one source. And our attraction to opportunities to optimize—producing an easy-to-quantify result, without considering the difficult-to-quantify costs—is certainly a contributing factor. Ambitious government/international initiatives that include too many requirements, thereby over constraining the problem, are yet another source. And last but not least, a product development team following the path-of-least-resistance to adding a new feature to an existing product so as to secure a sale (no matter how elegant the product's original design) is a practice we all recognize. I can only conclude, as John Mashey, another vocal critic of complexity once did by paraphrasing Pogo: *"We have met the enemy and they are us."*

While I value simplicity, and view elegance as a legitimate requirement in system design, I'm not so naive as to believe complexity can magically be wished away. The question is how to manage complexity, which, after all, is what the systems approach is all about. I'm convinced that the conservation of complexity is a law of system design—you can break complex systems into smaller components, moving bits of complexity around in the process, but doing so doesn't eliminate any complexity; it just makes it more manageable. Still, much as it is our job to manage complexity, I also believe as a discipline we are overly attracted to it, often embracing unnecessary complexity. On this point I believe Wirth had it right: Sometimes it's necessary to forcefully—even ruthlessly—say no.

Larry Peterson, March 2024

More Thoughts on Elegance and Simplicity

Judgment about What's Important (Today)

In retrospect, I realize that my last post on Elegance focused mostly on poor decision making (and the causes), and not so much on what makes for an elegant design. I can think of lots of examples, many of which adhere to Edsger Dijkstra's "simplicity and clarity" school of programming. Dijkstra is oft-quoted on the topic of simplicity (see the references at the end of the chapter), but the following example sums it up for me:

> Simplicity is a great virtue but it requires hard work to achieve it and education to appreciate it. And to make matters worse: complexity sells better.

And as someone who also thinks about the craft of writing, I can't help but see the parallel to Blaise Pascal's oft-copied apology for something he wrote: *"I have made this longer than usual because I have not had time to make it shorter."* (Pascal, a 17th century mathematician, is also the person after whom Niklaus Wirth named his elegant programming language.)

What Dijkstra, Wirth, Pascal, and many other champions of simplicity are saying is that elegance requires both hard work and good judgment. That translates equally well to large systems (such as, for example, the Internet) as to individual programs, mathematical proofs, and essays. Which brings me to the example of elegant system design that I want to highlight: the Internet Hourglass, with IP serving as the narrow waist. Recognizing the power of the Hourglass design is an important first-class take away from the Internet because of its general applicability to any system that aspires to wide-spread adoption. But from the perspective of appreciating why simplicity has so much value, there's a deeper lesson in this example.

That lesson follows from the narrowness of the narrow waist. When designing a system, it's natural to try to address as many of the known technical requirements as possible, and in doing so, over-engineer the system. (Tackling additional requirements is the cause of second-system syndrome, but taking on too many requirements happens with "first" systems too.) The beauty of IP's design is that it solved exactly one of the many problems it might have tried to address—defining a global addressing/routing scheme—and it punted on everything else, including reliable delivery, security, mobility, quality-of-service, and so on. This left ample room for others to innovate, and claim a stake in the Internet's future.

People have long ruminated about not addressing security in the original design, but doing so would likely have (a) not anticipated all the real-world threats, and (b) made wide-spread adoption more difficult. There have been many attempts through the years to establish "universal" networking technologies (ATM comes to mind), but the Internet teaches us that if you want to achieve universal buy-in, you should agree to the minimal capability you need to get started (i.e., today's #1 requirement). The design principle is inspired by the idea of late binding: create a minimal-but-general framework today and postpone filling in use-case-specific details for others to tackle tomorrow, when everyone better understands the requirements.

This approach requires that you design for evolution, or said another way, that you treat evolvability as a first-class requirement. Evolution is enabled by making it easy to build new abstractions on top of the existing platform, and in the process, incrementally completing the platform. We often take this for granted, but not all communication architectures are defined this way, with the mobile cellular network serving as a great counterexample. Each generation of the mobile network introduced new technologies, but unnecessarily (in our view) coupled the architecture with the technology. This ensured that every time the technology changes, the architecture has to change as well. (5G has the potential to end that cycle by embracing a cloud-based architecture, but it also leaves the door open to continuing legacy practices.)

In the case of the Internet, TCP obviously extended IP with support for reliable byte-streams, and including it as part of the reference platform (but not the narrow waist) was essential. And over time, the platform then grew to address security (TLS), mobility (DHCP, HTTP redirects), and universal object identity (URIs), with HTTP's RESTful interface capping off today's ubiquitous platform. (More recently, QUIC refactored the upper layers, which was possible because TCP was not baked in to the narrow waist.) This platform has not only fueled a generation of cloud apps, but it has also made it possible to realize many of the features originally targeted at the Internet core (multicast, for example) as cloud-hosted services.

Engineering Decisions Matter Too

This perspective has been at the architectural level, and as every engineer who has been asked to implement a beautiful architectural diagram understands, architectures all too often appear simple and elegant because they ignore implementation realities. But that's not the definition of elegance we're talking about, which requires that abstract design and implementation details be treated as two sides of the same coin. (Re-read the Wirth quote from my previous post to see the importance he places on implementation.)

In the case of the Internet's original narrow waist, having a reference implementation of the architecture that people could build upon was key. Such an open, Minimum Viable Platform was initially defined by TCP/IP (plus UDP) wrapped with the Socket API, and it catalyzed the first generation of client/server-based Internet services. This strong connection between architecture and implementation was part of the early Internet's ethos, although the tendency to focus on over-the-wire protocol definitions has made it easy to overlook the value of a well-defined API. It's the API that spurred adoption. (One can legitimately argue that the original Socket API was far from simple and elegant in its details—mostly because it tried to be too general—but in terms of the set of operations it defined, the API is, in a word, beautiful.)

Finally, the success of the Internet arguably had as much to do with its operational practices as with its feature set, where the narrow waist again displayed its elegance by giving Autonomous Systems the autonomy to experiment with wildly different operational models. Over time, those models evolved into today's cloud practices, which have been optimized for feature velocity. This has been achieved by defining communication functionality in software running on commodity hardware (sometimes as services running on top of the cloud, sometimes as services running within the cloud substrate), resulting in a symbiotic relationship: the Internet provides the communication platform for the cloud, and the cloud provides the lifecycle management platform for the Internet (at least for those operators that have the wherewithal to take advantage of such practices).

This tour of the Internet's elegance is prone to revisionism (and only hints at some of the other contributing factors), but connecting the dots from Cerf and Kahn's 1974 TCP/IP paper to the state of today's Internet/Cloud is remarkably direct and cogent: (1) start with a minimal (i.e., simple and elegant) architectural design; (2) codify that design in a minimum viable platform with a well-defined API that others can build upon; (3) evolve the system by incrementally layering platform upon platform; and then (4) leverage that global cloud you just built to operationalize the network and increase feature velocity into the future. That also happens to be a pretty good example of applying the "systems approach".

Larry Peterson, April 2024

Closing Remarks

While this chapter makes the case for the importance of judgement in system design, it is fair to ask, how does one learn to make good judgements? And who decides which judgements are good? The examples in this chapter make clear that judgement comes from experience, and that we can learn from the experiences of those who have gone before us. One reason that certain names in our field—Wirth, Dijkstra, Clark, Cerf, Kahn—are so well known is because they demonstrated good judgement in building systems, and tried to convey their experience to others. So studying their efforts and learning from them is one way we develop good judgement. Working with an experienced mentor can be another excellent way to learn about judgement.

The other theme that jumps out in this set of essays is how much judgement and simplicity come together. Knowing what to leave out is a critical skill to develop in the pursuit of simple, elegant system designs.

Finally, it is important to remember that architectures need to be implemented. An architecture might appear elegant enough at first but prove to be unreasonably complex to implement. The best architects we have worked with had extensive implementation experience. It is through building real systems and seeing them into production that we learn to exercise good judgement in system design.

Explore Further

Scott Shenker. The Future of Networking and the Past of Protocols. Open Networking Summit, October 2011.

Don Norman. The Design of Everyday Things. The MIT Press, 2014.

Larry Peterson, et al. GENI: Global Environment for Network Innovation. August 2006.

John Markoff. Early Look at Research Project to Re-engineer the Internet. New York Times, August 2005.

Tracy Kidder. The Soul of a New Machine. Little, Brown, and Company, 1981.

Tracy Kidder. House. Houghton Mifflin Company, 1985.

John McPhee. *Draft No. 4: On the Writing Process.* Farrar, Straus and Giroux, 2017.

Kathleen Jensen and Niklaus Wirth. Pascal User Manual and Report (2nd Edition). Springer-Verlag, 1978.

In Memoriam: Niklaus Wirth. Communications of the ACM, March 2024.

Edsger Dijkstra Quotes About Elegance.

Robert Kahn and Vint Cerf. A Protocol for Packet Network Intercommunication. IEEE Trans on Communications, May 1974.

Software-Defined Networking

We have been involved in SDN now for well over a decade, with Larry having co-authored the 2008 paper that argued for a new a protocol called OpenFlow. Bruce's involvement in SDN led to his joining Nicira in 2012 as the startup was about to launch its network virtualization product. And the first book to come out of the Systems Approach stable was *"Software-Defined Networks: A Systems Approach"*. So it's not surprising that SDN topics have featured heavily in our newsletter over the years. SDN is also a topic rich with stories about systems thinking.

In the selection that follows we've traced some of the key moments in SDN history that each of us experienced. That includes the creation of OpenFlow and its subsequent adoption by both academics and industry. The rise of SDN became apparent to us because of the extent to which it was becoming a hot topic at conferences (and eventually spinning up its own conferences). And Nicira played a key role in bringing SDN to the market with a "killer app" in the form of network virtualization.

The P4 language for programmable switching has played a role that is arguably as important as OpenFlow, and we have followed it closely. The essay on P4 below tries to predict how the language and its usage might evolve as its support by hardware manufacturers has changed over time.

Finally, two essays look at service meshes. We include them here because, to our eyes, service meshes look a lot like SDN systems moved up to the application layer.

SDN and the Alignment of Planets

We've been involved in some exciting moments as we've watched the networking landscape over the last forty-or-so years. It's often only with hindsight that we can see where the important inflection points were. Sometimes we look back and think that the outcome was inevitable, but at the time, many different outcomes seemed possible. SDN strikes me as a technology that might have easily failed to launch, and certainly I wouldn't have predicted the path that it has taken. In this article we examine how SDN made the jump from science experiment to mainstream technology.

The roots of Software Defined Networking (SDN) go back a long way, but I can clearly remember the point at which I decided that it was time to start paying attention to the emerging technology. In August 2009 I was attending the SIGCOMM annual conference, and I had a lot going on because I had become chair of SIGCOMM just a couple of months earlier. Preparing your first community feedback session as SIG chair is a lot harder than you might think! But I did manage to listen to most of the talks and, more importantly from the SDN perspective, spent plenty of time at the poster and demo sessions. I remember walking out of the demo area thinking that the SDN group from Stanford, with three demos and a huge array of equipment, was on the verge of taking over the event. I resolved to take a closer look at SDN and OpenFlow when I returned to the office. For context, the term SDN had been coined in MIT Technology Review just six months earlier, while the OpenFlow "manifesto" had appeared in SIGCOMM's newsletter the previous year.

Interestingly, there was also a lot of talk about network virtualization at that conference. There was a workshop on the topic and the VL2 paper, which I often cite as an early example of network virtualization for the data center, was presented there. But at that point the connection between SDN and network virtualization was not clear to me (although, as I learned later, it was already clear to my future colleagues at Nicira).

I spent the next two years following the development of SDN. At this point I had been at Cisco for 14 years, and I wanted to figure out what the implications of SDN were for the networking industry. One mistake that I made (and I think I had plenty of company) was conflating OpenFlow and SDN. Of course SDN was much bigger than OpenFlow, which was just a piece of low-level mechanism, but it was easy for traditional networking people like me to get their heads around a protocol. And it was easy to criticize OpenFlow. The need to query a central controller whenever a new flow arrived combined two ideas that were "known" to be bad in networking: centralized control, and "reactive" installation of forwarding state. The problem of the reactive approach is that forwarding performance is sensitive to flow arrival patterns, and hence unpredictable. I'd seen enough customer complaints about earlier router implementations whose performance was traffic-dependent to know that this aspect was unlikely to fly. (We carefully avoided such an approach when creating Tag Switching and MPLS.) Centralized control—well, anyone who grew up learning Internet architecture in the 1980s and 1990s, and witnessed the success of the Internet's growth into the 2000s, knew that a fully distributed architecture was the only way to go.

To top it off, OpenFlow looked too much like other ideas we had seen before that hadn't taken off. The idea of creating an open interface between the forwarding and control planes had been tried before, e.g., by Ipsilon with GSMP and by the Forces (Forwarding and Control Element Separation) working group of the IETF. It was easy to see the theoretical advantages of creating such an interface—particularly if you want to disrupt the networking industry, as it opens up the space for innovation on both sides of the interface. But the fact that it had been tried before without much success led many of us to think there was "nothing to see here" when we looked at OpenFlow.

A New Context For Old Ideas

In fact, as I wrote in an editorial for Computer Communications Review for SIGCOMM's fiftieth anniversary, it's often worth taking a look at old ideas when they reappear, because the context might have changed enough to make them viable. I believe this is the case for both separating the control plane from the forwarding plane, and for the use of centralized control in networks. As SDN pioneers McKeown, Casado and Shenker note in their 2019 retrospective "From Ethane to SDN and beyond", factors that had changed by the time SDN emerged in the late 2000s included the rise of merchant switching silicon (Broadcom, Marvell, etc.) and the development of hyperscale data centers as a new market for networking, giving network operators the opportunity and resources to break free from traditional approaches. I would add that decades of distributed systems research and development had created the technologies to build logically centralized controllers for networks that were neither a scaling bottleneck nor a single point of failure. The viability of centralized control was something that few of us accepted in the traditional networking community, but it was essential to the rise of SDN.

Two further events in late 2011 made me start to appreciate the disruptive potential of SDN. One was the legendary talk by Scott Shenker "The Future of Networking, and the Past of Protocols" at the first Open Networking Summit. This was the talk that crystallized for me the fact that it was insufficient to simply separate forwarding from control: it was also necessary to provide logically centralized control, so that we could create better abstractions. That's a computer scientist's view of the world; you could also say we needed a way to specify intended network behavior at a higher level than individual router configurations. It was the combination of these two ideas—control plane separation, plus centralization—that provided SDN with its real power. Scott's talk helped me to see that there was something transformative going on here, way beyond OpenFlow.

The second event was triggered by a "bad day at the office" which left me feeling a bit grumpy about Cisco. That evening, I had dinner with an old friend in the industry who suggested that I should chat with the folks at Nicira. Within a few hours I had an appointment with Martin Casado, who by this point, as CTO of Nicira, was fully committed to applying SDN principles to the problem of network virtualization. Network virtualization would prove to be the "killer app" that brought SDN to a broad market. Not many enterprises had the needs or expertise of a hyperscaler, but most of them needed a better way to build and manage networks for their virtual machines, and this was the problem that Nicira tackled head-on. This wasn't just a matter of incrementally improving networks; it was solving a networking problem that had appeared insoluble with standard networking techniques. Within a couple of months I was off to work at Nicira. The rest, as they say, is history, with network virtualization turning into a billion-plus dollar business within a few years.

There is a lot more to the history of SDN than this of course. We've covered some of it in our book, and there is a good overview in the CCR article cited below. SDN continues to evolve and find new applications. I think the technology trend of programmable switching hardware with tools like P4 to customize switch behavior has a long way to run. What I find interesting about this small slice of SDN history is how the shift from research project to "known bad ideas" to successful (and industry-changing) technology took place over a few short years. A whole lot of things had to go right for that to happen: the leverage of technologies from outside of networking; successful re-examination of ideas previously discarded; new players entering the networking business; and the identification of an important problem space where SDN could be incrementally deployed without the buy-in of the traditional networking industry. I'm glad I was able to be part of the SDN movement and I look forward to seeing what comes next.

Bruce Davie, March 2022.

_____

What OpenFlow Teaches Us About Innovation

In a previous post I recounted the history of OpenFlow at ONF. That got me thinking about how to have impact, and potentially to change the course of technology. The OpenFlow experience makes for an interesting case study.

For starters, the essential idea of OpenFlow was to codify what at the time was a hidden, but critical interface in the network software stack: the interface that the network control plane uses to install entries in the FIB that implements the switch data plane. The over-the-wire details of OpenFlow don't matter in the least (although there were plenty of arguments about them at the time). The important contributions were (a) to recognize that the control/data-plane interface is pivotal, and (b) to propose a simple abstraction (match/action flow rules) for that interface.

In retrospect, one of the secrets of OpenFlow's success was its seemingly innocuous origins. The original paper, published in ACM SIGCOMM's CCR (2008), was a call to action for the network research community, proposing OpenFlow as an experimental open interface between the network's control and data planes. The goal was to enable innovation, which at the time included the radical idea that anyone—even researchers—should be able to introduce new features into the network control plane. Care was also taken to explain how such a feature could be deployed into the network without impacting production traffic, mitigating the risks such a brazen idea could inflict on the network.

It was a small opening, but a broad range of organizations jumped into it. A handful of vendors added an "OpenFlow option" to their routers; the National Science Foundation (NSF) funded experimental deployments on University campuses; and Internet2 added an optional OpenFlow-substrate to their backbone. ONF was formed to provide a home for the OpenFlow community and ON.Lab started releasing open source platforms based on OpenFlow. With these initiatives, the SDN transformation was set in motion.

Commercial adoption of SDN was certainly an accelerant, with VMware acquiring the startup Nicira and cloud providers such as Google and Microsoft talking publicly about their SDN-based infrastructures (all in 2012), but this was a transformation that got its start in the academic research community. Over time some of the commercial successes have adapted SDN principles to other purposes—e.g., VMware's NSX supports network virtualization through programmatic configuration, without touching the control/data plane interface of physical networking equipment—but the value of disaggregating the network control/data planes and logically centralizing control decisions proved long lasting, with OpenFlow and its SDN successors running in datacenter switching fabrics and Telco access networks today.

The original proposal did not anticipate where defining a new API would take the industry, but the cascading of incremental impact is impressive (and perhaps the most important takeaway from this experience). Originally, OpenFlow was conceived as a way to innovate in the control plane. Over time, that flexibility put pressure on chip vendors to also make the data plane programmable, with the P4 programming language (and a toolchain to auto-generate the control/data plane interface) now becoming the centerpiece of the SDN software stack. It also put pressure on switch and router vendors to make the configuration interface programmable, with gNMI and gNOI now replacing (or at least supplementing) the traditional router CLI.

| Control App | Control App | Control App | · · · | Control App |

Network OS

Global Network Map

Control Plane

Data Plane

Flow Rules

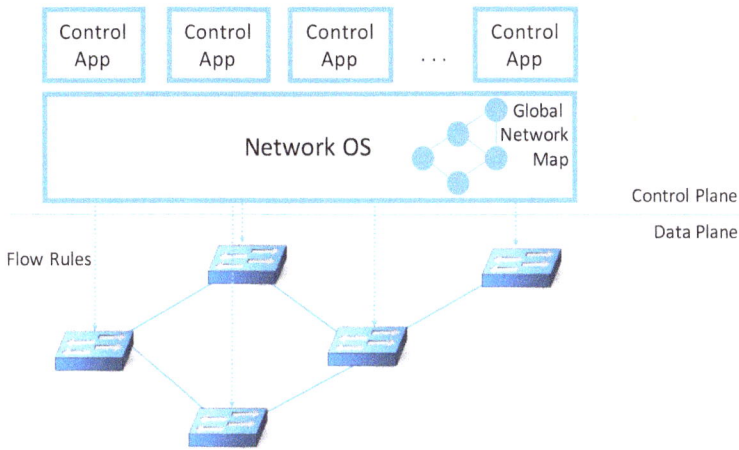

Control Plane Installing Flow Rules in the Data Plane

OpenFlow was also originally targeted at L2/L3 switches, but the idea is now being applied to the cellular network. This is putting pressure on the RAN vendors to open up and disaggregate their base stations. The 5G network will soon have a centralized SDN controller (renamed RAN Intelligent Controller), hosting a set of control applications (renamed xApps), using a 3GPP-defined interface (in lieu of OpenFlow) to control a distributed network of Radio Units. SD-RAN is happening, and has the potential to be a killer app for SDN.

One of the more interesting aspects of all of this is what happened to OpenFlow itself. The specification iterated through multiple versions, each enriching the expressiveness of the interface, but also introducing vendor-championed optimizations. This led to data plane dependencies, an inherent risk in defining what is essentially a hardware abstraction layer on top of a diverse hardware ecosystem. P4 is a partial answer to that. By coding the data plane's behavior in a P4 program (whether that program is compiled into an executable image that can be loaded into the switching chip or merely descriptive of a fixed-function chip's behavior) it is possible to auto-generate the control/data plane interface (known as P4RunTime) in software, instead of depending on a specification that evolves at the pace of standardization. (This transition to P4 as a more effective embodiment of the control/data plane interface is covered in our SDN book.)

It is now the case that the network—including the control/data plane interface—can be implemented, from top to bottom, entirely in software. OpenFlow served its purpose bootstrapping SDN, but even the Open Networking Foundation is shifting its focus from OpenFlow to P4-based SDN in its new flagship Aether project. Marc Andreessen's famous maxim that "software is eating the world" is finally coming true for the network itself!

A well-placed and smartly-defined interface is a powerful catalyst for innovation. OpenFlow has had that effect inside the network, with the potential to replicate the success of the Socket API at the edge of the network. Sockets defined the demarcation point between applications running on top of the Internet and the details of how the Internet is implemented, kickstarting a multi-billion dollar industry writing Internet (now cloud) applications. Time will tell how the market for in-network functionality evolves, but re-architecting the network as a programmable platform (rather than treating it as plumbing) is an important step towards improving feature velocity and fostering the next generation of network innovation.

Larry Peterson, March 2021.

The Future of P4, Revisited

The P4 Workshop was a couple weeks ago, and as General Chair, I went into it with a fair amount of trepidation. My concern was that Intel's announcement earlier this year that they're cancelling development of the Tofino 3 switching chip would have a chilling effect, not only on the Workshop, but also on the future of P4. That concern has been voiced in several forums, including SIGCOMM's Slack workspace, with members of the P4 Advisory Board making reassuring pronouncements in various settings. (See for example, Nick McKeown's post to the P4 Forum, and Nick along with Nate Foster and Jennifer Rexford discussing the future of Network Programmability on The Networking Channel).

I won't try to give a point-by-point replay of what Nick, Nate, and Jen and others have been saying, except to observe that at a high level it can be summarized as follows:

Programmable Networks >> P4 Language >> Tofino Switching Chip

They point out, for example, that Tofino is just one of many interesting backend targets for P4 programs (SmartNICs and IPUs being the next "big deal") and P4 is one of many tools being used to inject functionality into the end-to-end network path (DPDK and eBPF being two active projects that people are integrating with P4). Ultimately, the value of programmability comes from having visibility and control over the network, and there are many complementary approaches to making that happen. With that background, I do have three takeaways from what turned out to be an interesting and vibrant two days at the P4 Workshop (despite my initial concerns).

P4 As Specification Language

First, we're often so focused on P4 as a tool to program the forwarding pipeline that we forget the other half of its value proposition: It also provides a way to specify the behavior of a pipeline (independent of how that pipeline is implemented). We talk about this idea, and the value of being able to auto-generate the Control API, in the P4 chapter of our SDN Book. Rob Sherwood (Intel) made a similar argument at the P4 Workshop. It is now becoming a reality as companies like Google are starting to use such behavioral definitions as a Hardware Abstraction Layer, covered in Parveen Patel's workshop keynote. This makes me hopeful that we are rapidly approaching the day when a P4 program (plus the generated P4RT interface) will become the standard way network providers specify their requirements to network vendors, and proposed new features (whether proprietary or standard) will be specified by a P4 program (potentially augmenting the intuition and design rationale presented in an RFC).

As an aside, I couldn't help but notice the similarities between the architecture Parveen described and the way P4 has been used to program the forwarding plane of the 5G Mobile Core. Both include a P4-based "abstract forwarding model" that's independent of the underlying implementation details.

Second, it is common to divide forwarding pipelines into "programmable" versus "fixed function", but this glosses over what might be the more important distinction: whether the pipeline is open or closed. Even "fixed function" pipelines are increasingly flexible—it's just a question of how restrictive the vendor is in who they allow to make changes. This restriction may have the biggest impact on researchers who want to experiment with a new feature (especially ones that do not yet have a proven market), but maybe less so in the commercial world where incentives to make changes are (arguably) well-defined. Using P4 as the "spec language" (as I just outlined) has the potential to accelerate the process on the commercial side. On the research side, there is a strong argument in favor of using Tofino 2 to demonstrate the feasibility and value of new ideas (12.8 Tb/s still makes for a credible Proof-of-Concept), and repeating the refrain yet again, P4-as-spec makes for a compelling tech transfer story. If that were to happen, it would be interesting to see how vendors and chip designers adapt to reduce their spec-to-hardware implementation overhead. I would argue that programmable forwarding planes have a time-to-market advantage even for closed solutions.

Third, our focus on quantifiable metrics makes it easy to forget about the less quantifiable aspects of programmability. At its core, P4 is a programming language that does a good job of abstracting the essence of a packet forwarding pipeline. It is enormously impressive that a P4 program can be compiled onto a PISA-based switching chip that has the same performance, die area, cost, and power consumption of a fixed-function ASIC (and that equivalency was probably necessary for P4 to be taken seriously), but hitting that quantifiable mark is not sufficient. Well-designed languages are software tools that bring clarity to the intellectual challenge of programming. For me, the biggest "aha" moment of the Workshop was when Chris Sommers (long-time P4 contributor and new co-Chair of the API Working Group) started rattling off all the functions he'd been involved in writing in P4, and remarking on how natural P4 makes that process. There is certainly room to add new language features as P4 expands its domain to include SmartNICs and IPUs—as Chris and the other WG chairs are now pursuing—but having an existing target to evolve is a great position to be in.

One common thread that weaves its way through these three takeaways is that Intel's cancellation of the Tofino 3 chip is a potentially helpful forcing function: The P4 community has to demonstrate the value of the language without being buttressed by ever-improving performance numbers that have more to do with 7nm semiconductor technology than anything networking people have done. I saw a lot of evidence exactly that is happening at last month's workshop. The march to programmable networks is inevitable (in my view), and I remain optimistic P4 will play a central role.

Larry Peterson, May 2023.

Network Virtualization Revisited

When writing our Systems Approach books, we generally try to put ourselves in the shoes of a reader who doesn't yet understand the topic we are trying to explain. This might seem obvious, but it means we need to be constantly checking our assumptions about what readers can be expected to know. Back in 1995 we couldn't even assume that a reader would have spent much time on the Internet—we recently noticed a section of our big book that was quite overdue for an update since it still reflected our 1995 assumptions. In a related vein, some of our recent discussions have made us wonder how well our readers understand virtualization, especially when applied to networking, so in this article we're taking a look back at how we came to understand virtualization and its power.

I have a vague memory of hearing about server virtualization for the first time in the early 2000s when I was working at Cisco. Most of my knowledge of operating systems had been picked up early in my career, so I had a working knowledge of concepts like virtual memory, but I was pretty surprised when I learned just how popular virtual machines had become. One thing I wondered was why virtual machines had become the *de facto* means to isolate applications rather than making use of process isolation capabilities of a single operating system. I wouldn't get a satisfactory answer to that question until I joined Nicira many years later (more on that in a moment).

Even more perplexing to a networking person was to hear that the prevalence of virtual machines in data centers was driving a push towards big, flat layer-2 networks. One of the most remarkable (to me) consequences of virtualization is virtual machine migration: because a virtual machine is completely decoupled from the physical hardware on which it runs, it can be picked up and moved to another physical host without interruption. VMware's version of live migration, vMotion, was released in 2003 to considerable acclaim, as it allowed a VM to be moved across a data center without interruption to the applications running on it. But there was an unfortunate networking-related side effect to VM migration: VMs retained their IP addresses as they moved. And this is what led to the push to build big, flat L2 networks in modern datacenters: so VMs could move around without finding themselves on a subnet that didn't match their IP address.

By this time, I was convinced that scalable L2 networks were something of an oxymoron, so my first reaction was to argue that VMs should simply change their address to match the destination subnet when they moved across the DC. But that just illustrated what I didn't know about real-world applications in datacenters. The consequences of an IP address change range from a dropped TCP connection to complete breakage of an application in the case where it has a builtin assumption of L2-adjacency to some other component. From the perspective of a datacenter operator, you simply can't expect the application to respond correctly if the IP address is changing underneath it.

Fortunately there are alternatives to attempting to build datacenter-scale L2 networks. One of the seminal efforts to tackle the problem is VL2, described in 2009 by Greenberg et al. While this was not the first paper to use the term network virtualization, it did (I think) introduce the term in the way that it is most widely used today. Interestingly, Albert Greenberg (a SIGCOMM award winner) led the team that developed Azure's network virtualization system, while his co-author James Hamilton later led the networking team at AWS. VL2 gives each service the illusion that all the servers assigned to it, and only those servers, are connected by a single non-interfering Ethernet switch—a Virtual Layer 2—and maintain this illusion even as the size of each service varies from 1 server to 10,000.

Efficient, Isolated Duplicates

Too often when I read something about network virtualization, it turns out to just be some way of partitioning network resources among different users (also known as slicing). But the key word in the above quote is "illusion" because it gets to the heart of virtualization: creating an illusion of something that, strictly speaking, doesn't exist. As the seminal 1974 paper on virtualization puts it, these illusions are "efficient, isolated duplicates" of the physical thing being virtualized. Virtual memory gives processes the illusion of a massive amount of address space, generally much larger than what is physically present, completely available to that process and protected from other processes. Virtual machines create the illusion of a complete set of computing resources (CPU, memory, disk, I/O) that are so fully independent of the underlying physical machine that they can be moved across a datacenter (or further). And virtual networks create the illusion of a private switched Ethernet (in the case of VL2) that can span the datacenter, even when the datacenter is a Layer 3 network built out of routers interconnecting many subnets. So while partitioning of resources is part of the story, it's just one element in service of creating these illusions.

By the time I started working at Nicira in 2012, the team had settled on this view of network virtualization that mirrored the success of server virtualization. The idea of virtualization creating an illusion of something was core to the vision: just as a virtual machine creates the illusion of a physical machine so faithfully that an unmodified operating system and its applications can run on it—even as it migrates from one piece of hardware to another—so too, a virtual network should perfectly replicate the features of a physical network, while remaining independent of the actual underlying hardware. Just like servers, networks are complicated things with lots of moving parts, so Nicira's product needed to do a lot more than what VL2 did: not just creating a virtual layer 2 switch, but virtualizing every layer of the network. That meant (eventually) virtual layer 3 routing, virtual firewalls, virtual load balancers and so on. I used to chuckle to myself about the prospect of a 50-person engineering team managing to recreate in software all the networking capabilities that had been developed over the previous several decades by companies like F5, Checkpoint and Cisco, but that is pretty much what eventually happened (thanks to the injection of considerable engineering resources over the following years).

You can find descriptions of network virtualization as implemented at Nicira, Google, and Azure. It's a bit harder to get details on how AWS does it but a VPC is a form of virtual network. We also cover network virtualization as a key use case of SDN in our book. And it's not limited to the datacenters of the hyperscalers; VMware claims at the time of writing that their network virtualization product (following on from the work at Nicira) is used in the datacenters of 91 of the large enterprises making up the Fortune 100.

In some respects, network virtualization has followed the same path as server virtualization and for similar reasons. Nicira founder Martin Casado has talked about how virtualization changes the "laws of physics": the salient example for server virtualization is live VM migration, but there are others, such as snapshotting and cloning of VMs, made possible by recreating the illusion of a physical machine entirely in software. Not only did network virtualization bring similar capabilities to networking, but it facilitated entirely new ones such as microsegmentation, laying the groundwork for what was arguably the "killer" use case, zero-trust networking. We had a running joke at Nicira about the movie "Inception" (particularly when running virtual networks inside virtual networks). Network virtualization, with its own "laws of physics", allowed us not only to recreate the capabilities of physical networks but to create new ones.

Bruce Davie, October 2023.

―――――――――――――――――

How SDN Came to the WAN

While the early success of SDN was in local area networks (and particularly the special case of datacenter networks) it didn't take too long before it made its impact in the wide area. The WAN applications of SDN can be further subdivided: there was the application of SDN to traffic engineering of inter-datacenter networks (notably from Google and Microsoft) and then there is what came to be known as SD-WAN. This part of the story relates primarily to enterprise WANs—a huge business but not something that gets much coverage in the discussions of SDN at academic conferences. So let's look a bit more closely at enterprise WANs and why SDN turned out to be a good fit for the challenges in that environment.

My introduction to enterprise WANs came in the early days of MPLS, around 1996. My team at Cisco had published the first drafts on Tag Switching at the IETF, which would eventually lead to the creation of the MPLS working group and all the RFCs that followed. At one point we were approached by a team at AT&T whose main problem, in essence, was that their enterprise WAN business was too successful. Their core business was building WANs using Frame Relay virtual circuits to connect the offices and datacenters of enterprises. Deploying a WAN for one customer entailed provisioning a set of frame relay circuits to interconnect the sites, plus configuring a router at every site to manage the routing of traffic over the WAN. The complexity of managing these circuits and routing configurations was becoming overwhelming both because of the popularity of the service and because of the increasing desire to provide full-mesh connectivity (or something close to it) among sites.

At the time, one of the options that was being considered as an alternative to Frame Relay was to use IPSEC tunnels across the Internet to interconnect the sites. Leaving aside the fact that the Internet in 1996 was way less ubiquitous than it is today, the big downside of that approach was that it actually didn't do much to reduce the complexity of configuration. You would need to configure as many IPSEC tunnels as Frame Relay circuits, and you still need to configure the routing overlay on top of all those tunnels to forward traffic between all the sites. In rough terms, both Frame Relay and IPSEC tunnels require n^2 configuration steps, where n is the number of sites. MPLS/BGP VPNs came out ahead by reducing that configuration cost to order n, even with full mesh connectivity among sites. The full story of how that works is in RFC 2547 and in the book I wrote with Yakov Rekhter. One thing that we made sure of was that our system had no central point of control, because in 1996 we knew that central control was not an option for any networking solution aiming to scale up.

A few years later (2003) I gave the SIGCOMM talk for which I am most well known: "MPLS Considered Helpful" (in the outrageous opinion session of course). Talking to people afterwards I was struck by the lack of awareness of how widely deployed MPLS/BGP VPN service was at that point. There were over 100 service providers using it to provide their enterprise WAN services by 2003, but that was completely invisible to most of the SIGCOMM community (perhaps because universities don't rely on such services and because enterprise network admins don't show up at academic conferences).

Fast forward to 2012 and MPLS VPNs were the de facto choice for enterprise WANs. But many things had changed since 1996, and those changes were about to align to create the conditions for SD-WAN to emerge. Importantly, the idea that central control was a non-starter had been effectively challenged with the rise of SDN in other settings. Scott Shenker's influential talk "The Future of Networking, and the Past of Protocols" had made the compelling case for why central control was needed in SDN, and developments in distributed systems had enabled scalable, fault-tolerant centralized controllers such as the one we built for datacenter SDN at Nicira. The first time I heard about the ideas behind SD-WAN was when one of my Nicira colleagues told me he was leaving for another startup. The simple high-level sketch he gave of applying an SDN-style controller to the problem of enterprise WANs immediately made sense.

Whereas in 1996 we relied on a fully distributed approach using BGP to determine how sites could communicate with each other, an SDN controller allows policies for inter-site connectivity to be set centrally while still being implemented in a distributed manner at the edges. The benefits of this approach are numerous, especially in an era where high-speed Internet access is a widely-available commodity. Building a mesh of encrypted tunnels among a large number of enterprise sites no longer has n2 configuration complexity, because you can let the controller figure out which tunnels are needed and push configuration rules to the sites. Furthermore, there is no longer a dependence on getting a particular MPLS service provider to connect your site to their network: you just have to get Internet connectivity to your site. This factor alone—replacing "premium" MPLS access with "commodity" Internet—was decisive for some SD-WAN early adopters.

The other big change in the decades since RFC 2547 was the rise of cloud-based services as an important component of enterprise IT (Office 365, Salesforce, etc.). Traditionally, an MPLS VPN would provide site-to-site connectivity among branches and central sites. If access to the outside Internet was required, it would entail backhauling traffic to one of a handful of central sites with external connectivity and all the firewalls etc. needed to secure that connection. But as more business services were delivered from "the cloud", and with SD-WAN leveraging Internet access rather than dedicated MPLS circuits to every branch, it started to make sense to provide direct Internet access to branch offices. This meant a significant change to the security model for networking. Rather than a single point of connection between the enterprise and the Internet (with a central set of devices to control attendant security risks) there are now potentially as many connection points as there are branches.

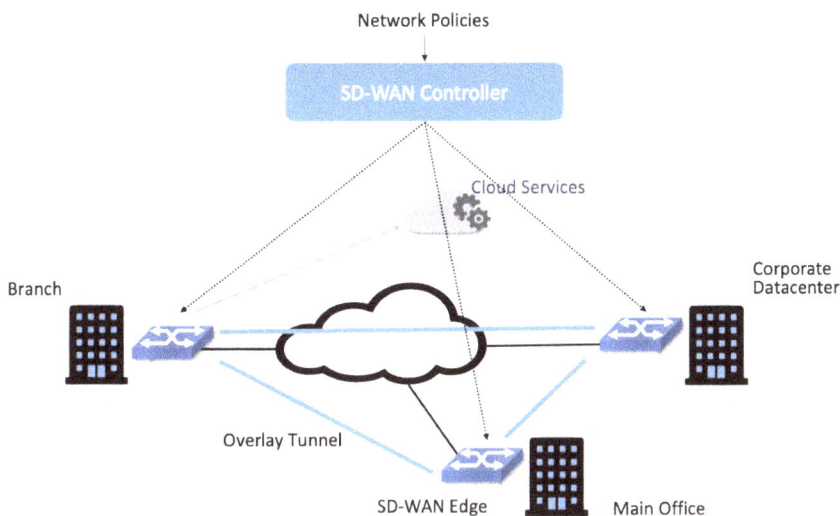

SD-WAN: Central Control Over Distributed Forwarding

So with SD-WAN and the rise of cloud services, you need a way to set and enforce security policy at all the edges of your enterprise—and now there is potentially an edge at every branch. In a sense, this aspect of SD-WAN contributed to the rise of SASE (secure access services edge): once you started putting SD-WAN devices at every site, you needed a way to apply security services at those sites. Fortunately, the "centralized configuration with distributed enforcement" model of SDN provides a natural way to address this issue. The SD-WAN device at the edge is not just an IPSEC tunnel terminating device, but is also a policy enforcement point to apply the security policies of the enterprise. And the central point of control for an SD-WAN system provides a tractable means of configuring the policies in one place even though they will be implemented in a distributed way. (Further complicating the picture is the fact that an SD-WAN edge device can also forward traffic to or from cloud-based security services.)

There is a lot more to SD-WAN than I have space to cover here. For example, dealing with QoS in the presence of the Internet's best-effort service turns out to be important and is one area where the commercial providers of SD-WAN equipment try to differentiate themselves. SD-WAN remains an area where open standards have yet to make much of an impact. But it certainly provides an interesting case study in how a change in the adjacent technologies can make ideas that once seemed impractical (such as central control and VPNs built with meshes of encrypted tunnels) viable again.

Bruce Davie, May 2023.

Service Mesh: SDN For Layer 7

I remember when I first heard about Service Meshes in 2017, and wondering what the big deal was. Building cloud applications as a graph of microservices was commonplace, and Telcos were hard at work inventing yet other ways to chain together virtualized network functions. Service graphs, service chains, service meshes... how many ways do we really need to talk about composing complex systems from a collection of smaller components?

It wasn't until I recognized a familiar pattern that I got it: A Service Mesh is just SDN at Layer 7. That's probably what happens when SDN is the hammer you keep hitting nails with, but I've come to believe there is value in that perspective. The figure highlights the similarities between the two scenarios, both of which include a centralized controller that issues directives to a distributed set of connectors (physical/virtual switches in one case, and a sidecar container in the other case)—based on a combination of policy intents from above and monitoring data reported from below. The primary difference is that the SDN controller on the left is controlling L2/3 connectivity and the Service Mesh on the right is controlling L7 connectivity.

Comparisons like this often break down at some point, but for me, identifying the differences between the two cases also helped me understand the opportunities in this space. In short, these two cases can be viewed as two ends of a spectrum, with each making a different performance-vs-expressibility design choice for the "connector" elements. Sidecars can run arbitrary code, and so implement any imaginable service connectivity policy, but the biggest knock on sidecars is that bouncing all traffic through an intermediate container results in a non-trivial performance hit. Physical L2/L3 switches have forwarding rates measured in terabits-per-second,

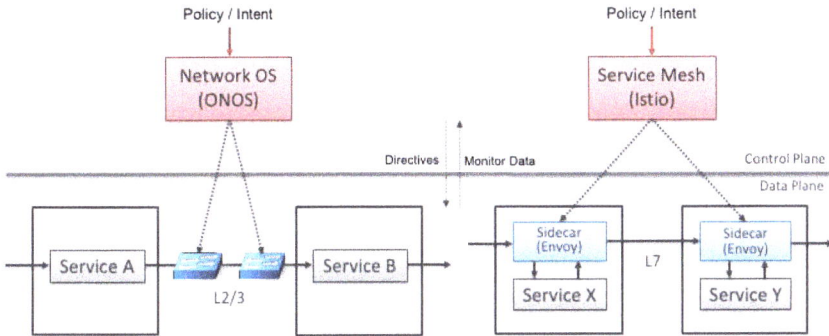

Service Mesh and SDN Similarities

but support limited/fixed functionality (e.g., coarse-grained ACLs). P4-programmable forwarding pipelines present an opportunity to offload some sidecar functionality to the switching fabric, but the best opportunity to find a best-of-both-worlds design point is in virtual switches and SmartNICs. Note also that the functionality of a sidecar generally needs to be close enough to the relevant service to see the actual RPC messages, which tends to rule out network devices that will only see encrypted traffic between hosts.

All of this brings us to a topic that is attracting a lot of attention, which is to optimize service meshes using a combination of eBPF (extended Berkeley Packet Filter) and XDP (eXpress Data Path). When used together, they provide a way to program generalized Match-Action rules in the OS kernel (as part of a virtual switch), or alternatively, on a SmartNIC. That eBPF/XDP can be viewed as an alternative implementation of OpenFlow/P4-inspired flow rules is not a coincidence; there is something fundamental about Match-Action rules as an abstraction for programming (and controlling) end-to-end connectivity. Having identified this commonality, the differences are again helpful: eBPF/XDP allows (mostly) general code, while OpenFlow defines a fixed set of Match-Actions and P4 is a restricted language for expressing the same. This is necessary when the Action must execute within a fixed cycle budget, as is the case for a switch-based forwarding pipeline. It also enables formal verification of the data plane, a promising opportunity being pursued by the research community.

It turns out I wasn't the only person to make the connection between SDN and Service Meshes—Bruce made it (in a VMware blog) two years ago, and VMware's service mesh product clearly has parallels to their other SDN offerings. In my experience, there is enormous value in recognizing commonality and defining unifying abstractions across seemingly disparate implementation artifacts. Unifying abstractions are the basis for building better systems. Acknowledging the power of a centralized policy engine (e.g., the role of the SDN controller) is one such abstraction (which we also noted in a recent security post). The fundamental nature of Match-Action rules as a way to specify forwarding behavior (e.g., the role of OpenFlow) is another. Recognizing that Envoy sidecars, eBPF/XDP kernel modules, and P4-programmed pipelines can be viewed as three implementation choices for programmable forwarding engines used to build end-to-end service connectivity is an intriguing opportunity that deserves more attention. Successful platforms build on the abstractions that have proven useful in the past. And that is a key tenet of the systems approach.

Larry Peterson, April 2021.

Service Mesh and the Goldilocks Zone

Like many people in the networking field, I learned about the 7-layer model as an established fact and I proceeded to approach networking problems by ignoring whatever was going on above or below the layer I was currently working on. For much of my early career I was able to stay focused on layers 2 through 4, occasionally cursing layer 1 when I had to polish the end of an optical fiber to improve the reliability of a SONET link.

A talk that I still remember well from those days was one given by David Clark of MIT at the 1990 SIGCOMM conference entitled "Architectural Considerations for a New Generation of Protocols". For one thing, it motivated me to become a better public speaker when I saw how much impact Dr. Clark's presentation had on the audience. But it also shook me out of my layerist comfort zone with its twin ideas of Application Layer Framing (ALF) and Integrated Layer Processing (ILP). To summarize them very briefly, ALF says that only the application really knows how its data is to be used, so it's best positioned to break a stream of data into frames. And ILP argues that just because you have a layered architecture, doesn't require you to implement layers strictly in isolation; in fact, you are likely to suffer performance problems if you do so.

In other words, this paper gave me my first experience of how to take a systems view of networks: you have to look at the overall system behavior, considering interactions among layers, all the way up to the application, to properly understand how to design and implement a system. This, along with many other interactions with "systems people", led to my embracing the systems approach. (My willingness to ignore the numerous people who insist that MPLS is a layer violation can probably also be traced back to that talk but that's a story for another day.)

With this background, I see service mesh as something of a corollary of the ALF/ILP ideas. The sidecar proxies of a service mesh run as close to the application as possible, because they need fine-grained visibility into application behavior, just as ALF argued that tasks like the construction of data frames and dealing with lost frames belong in the application layer.

Neither Too Hot Nor Too Cold

The service mesh is also an example of "The Goldilocks Zone", in that the service mesh sidecar needs to be close to the application but not too close. The Goldilocks Zone refers to the zone for habitable planets (neither too hot nor too cold), and was used as an analogy by Martin Casado and Tom Corn beginning in 2014 to explain why security features, such as distributed firewalling, should be as close as possible to an application without actually residing in the host operating system. Their idea was that security features needed to balance isolation versus context. Too close to the application and your security features would be disabled by an attacker; too far away, and there wasn't enough context to understand what was being secured, as when a firewall tries to figure out what an application is doing based only on the packets that have left the endpoint. In a network virtualization system, the virtual switch sitting in the hypervisor provides that "just right" spot that is neither in the host OS nor sitting far away in a network appliance. Endpoint detection and response (EDR) systems also took advantage of this idea.

In a Service Mesh, the tradeoff is similar. The service mesh data plane needs to be close enough to the application to have the necessary context. In particular, the sidecar needs to be able to see unencrypted traffic right at the point that it enters or leaves the microservice, because once the traffic is encrypted there is no way to tell one API request from another. Sitting next to the microservice in a sidecar allows security controls to be applied at the appropriate granularity and gives sufficient visibility of events to provide a high degree of observability.

At the same time, we don't want the service mesh functionality to reside inside the application. Here the argument differs slightly from Casado and Corn's use of Goldilocks, in that it is not about isolation so much as it is about building a general purpose platform that supports all applications. The scenario that Service Mesh avoids is one in which every application developer writes their own encryption code (or, more likely, picks up some library that then needs to be maintained), figures out how to observe events, manages certificates, etc. Instead, a service mesh provides a platform of generally useful services including traffic management, access control, encryption, observability and so on. Not only are these implemented in a consistent manner without burdening every application team, they can also be managed by a team with the appropriate expertise, i.e., a team focused on platform issues such as security rather than the application teams themselves.

There's another benefit to keeping the service mesh functionality outside of the applications, which has been memorably explained by Louis Ryan, one of the Istio project leaders. That is the challenge of maintaining old code, which he compares to opening a can of surströmming (fermented fish). The separation of service mesh from the application allows all the features required for the platform to be inserted without opening up old pieces of code, and to be maintained independently.

Finally, it's worth noting that performance issues arise in service mesh, just as they did with layered protocol processing in the 1990s. ILP was a reaction to the negative performance impact of strict layering as an implementation strategy, and the simplest implementation of sidecar proxies, which forces packets to make multiple user/kernel space traversals, suffers the same issue. This is what is driving more optimized approaches such as eBPF and the Cilium project, which is a topic we'll come back to.

At this point, I'm encouraged to see the high level of interest in service mesh, and I don't think it's just the technology flavor of the month. There is a set of solid architectural principles underpinning it and I expect its adoption among application platform teams to keep expanding.

Bruce Davie, June 2021.

────────────────────────

Closing Remarks

SDN is probably one of the best examples of how the systems approach has played out in practice. For several decades, there was an orthodox way to build networks: every router shipped with its own control plane and data plane tightly coupled, and routing algorithms were complex, distributed algorithms that only experienced experts could manage. SDN provided the opportunity to rethink the modularity of networks. The pioneers of SDN didn't just want to optimize one component of the system, they wanted to redefine the entire system architecture. Taking that big-picture view is one of the core ideas of the systems approach.

The second aspect of SDN that exemplifies the systems approach is the extent to which it has succeeded in allowing real systems to be built and deployed. Many factors led to this success, but we would point to its heavy reliance on open source software and open interfaces (such as OpenFlow and P4). Open interfaces are essential to bring more players into the ecosystem, while open source software lowers the barrier to entry for those looking to contribute to the effort through both development and deployment. And we see these trends continue to play out in the extensive open source efforts underpinning the success of service meshes.

Now, most of us won't get the chance to drive a generational change in network architecture of the scale of SDN. Nevertheless, the principles at work here, such as a re-examination of conventional wisdom, looking for an opportunity to re-modularize a system rather than just optimizing a component, and attention to key open interfaces, come into play repeatedly for system designers and implementors.

Explore Further

Nick McKeown et al. OpenFlow: Enabling Innovation in Campus Networks. SIGCOMM CCR, March 2008.

Nick Feamster, Jennifer Rexford and Ellen Zegura. The road to SDN: an intellectual history of programmable networks. SIGCOMM CCR, April 2014.

Scott Shenker. The Future of Networking, the Past of Protocols. Open Networking Summit, October 2011.

Martin Casado, Nick McKeown and Scott Shenker. From Ethane to SDN and beyond. SIGCOMM CCR, November 2019.

Gerald Popek and Robert Goldberg. Formal requirements for virtualizable third generation architectures. CACM, July 1974.

Teemu Koponen et al. Network Virtualization in Multi-tenant Datacenters. USENIX NSDI, April 2014.

Albert Greenberg et al. VL2: a scalable and flexible data center network. SIGCOMM, August 2009.

Thomas Graf. Layer 7 is the New Layer 4. Future:net 2017.

David Clark and David Tennenhouse. Architectural considerations for a new generation of protocols. ACM SIGCOMM, August 1990.

Louis Ryan. Istio: A Network for Service not Bytes. Future:net, 2018.

Centralization and De-Centralization

As people who cut their research teeth on the early Internet, we have deeply ingrained beliefs about decentralized architectures. The decentralized nature of the Internet is often cited as one of the main factors in its success, and was explicitly called out by David Clark in his 1988 paper "The Design Philosophy of the DARPA Internet Protocols". However, there have been two distinct trends towards centralization in recent years.

We contributed to one form of centralization: the use of logically centralized control in software-defined networks as we discussed previously. In this chapter, we discuss how the centralized view provided by SDN solved a long-standing problem in traffic engineering, enabling a more system-wide approach to the problem.

The other trend is one we view less positively: the centralization of many of the services that typical users of the Internet depend on, which range from social networks to content distribution networks (CDNs). We've discussed the impact of all these trends in our newsletter, and selected two posts for this chapter.

The standard criticism of centralization is that it doesn't scale well and is prone to being a single point of failure. Advances in distributed systems technologies have addressed many of those concerns, yet the Internet continues to show signs of brittleness due to over-reliance on a few centralized systems, as we discuss below.

Blockchains were once seen as a solution to excessive centralization, even by us. However, our enthusiasm for them has cooled even as the hype remains undiminished in many circles.

Finally, we have taken some concrete steps to embrace decentralization ourselves by moving our social media presence to the decentralized Fediverse. After more than two years on Mastodon we remain bullish on the prospects for decentralized social media.

How Traffic Engineering Became a Systems Problem

The systems approach has been the guiding principle for how we write, teach, and design systems for almost 30 years, and of course we get asked to define "systems approach" quite often. Sometimes it can be helpful to look at what the systems approach is not, which is the perspective that led to this post.

When trying to define the systems approach, we usually focus on the "big picture" or "end-to-end" view. (See the Introduction to this book for an example.) But it's also helpful to explain by counter-examples, where focusing too tightly on optimizing in just one dimension leads to an outcome that doesn't work well for the whole system. When I look for counter-examples from my own experience, the development of MPLS traffic engineering (MPLS-TE) comes to mind. While I was involved (1996 to about 2007) I think our approach could be more appropriately described as a series of focused optimizations than a systems approach. That was not the end of the story, fortunately, as there were significant advances in traffic engineering, largely enabled by SDN. These later approaches come closer to the systems approach, so in this post I examine the path from point optimization to systems approach as I followed the development of traffic engineering over 25+ years.

I started working on MPLS, in its pre-IETF days, when I joined Cisco in 1995, with the vague idea that there might be something in layer-2 networking (particularly popular-at-the-time ATM) that could bring benefits to layer-3 networking, which was Cisco's main business. This felt at times like mixing random ingredients together in a test-tube in the hope that something useful might emerge. The first genuinely useful idea that eventually became the core of MPLS was destination-based forwarding using labels—an idea that had, unbeknownst to us, been published by Chandranmenon and Varghese at SIGCOMM as *threaded indices* a year earlier. Not too long after we started fleshing out the details of destination-based forwarding, one of my team-mates, George Swallow (later the chair of the MPLS working group) walked into my office to pitch the idea that

MPLS could be used for traffic engineering. (In those days we were still calling it tag switching, but almost everything we did eventually got re-named—relabelled if you will—as MPLS.)

My first reaction to the idea that we could use MPLS to send packets along a path other than the one chosen by IP routing was strongly negative. The essence of destination-based forwarding was to use all the IP routing protocols we knew and loved, not the untested ones proposed as part of ATM. IP routing protocols would send packets along the shortest path to the destination. But I was missing an essential piece of context: traffic en-gineering based on mapping aggregate demand onto capacity constraints was already established with a few influential Internet Service Providers, and it was actually one of the selling features of layer-2 networking for the WAN at the time. Several ISPs in those days used either ATM or Frame Re-lay switches in their backbones to interconnect routers, and were leveraging the traffic engineering features in these switches.

As a result, we went on to recreate within MPLS a set of constraint-based routing features inspired by those L2 switches. The ISPs in general ran their backbones as a single, big link-state routing area, which meant that each backbone router had a full map of the backbone topology. By annotating the links with their capacities and flooding that information along with routing updates, each router could determine the shortest path to any destination that had enough bandwidth for the expected traffic to that destination. The value of MPLS in this scenario is that the labels can be used to force traffic to follow a certain path, even if it's not the shortest—a feature that we used to illustrate with a topology known as the "fish picture". More details on this can be found in our SDN book.

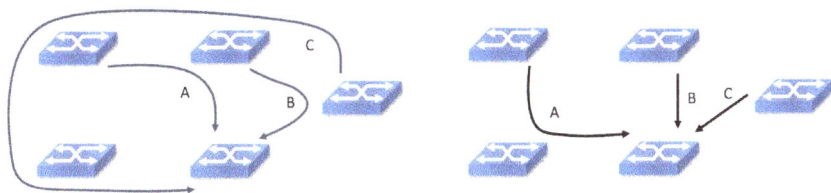

Greedy Approach to Path Placement Leads to Suboptimal Outcome

There are all sorts of challenges to be faced with this approach, and the solutions now fill a few dozen RFCs. One particularly thorny issue is that the placement of traffic in a distributed network of routers is inherently greedy. For example, suppose that in the network above we are trying to place three traffic flows of size L and that each link is also of capacity L. A greedy approach places each flow independently, which could lead to the suboptimal routes on the left rather than the much more efficient option on the right. In other cases a greedy approach could result in no feasible path being found even though a path exists. (We leave the details as an exercise for the reader.)

A partial solution to this problem is pre-emption (which was implemented as part of MPLS) but inevitably a greedy algorithm with limited coordination among the routers will run into scenarios where it either deadlocks or produces sub-optimal outcomes. At the time, our commitment to the idea that networks must not have central control meant we could only conceive of addressing this problem with ever more tweaks to the protocols, or with an offline planning tool. In the accepted wisdom of IP networking at the time, central control was forbidden. Planning tools that took a global view without directly controlling routers were OK, although far from popular. A couple of planning tools from third parties had modest success; the one I worked on did not. And that's about as far as I went with traffic engineering.

Years later, I was excited when both Google and Microsoft published new approaches to traffic engineering that leveraged the global network view enabled by SDN. These were known as B4 and SWAN respectively. In essence, SDN broke the "rule" that centralized control could not be done, thus freeing the system from greedy approaches that made only local optimizations. With SDN, the networking community imported ideas from the systems community to build logically centralized controllers that were scalable and fault tolerant, countering the arguments about single points of failure and scalability that had stood for decades. Central controllers could look at the global traffic demands and map them intelligently onto the available network capacity. This was one of the main promises of SDN: that rather than thinking about networks in terms of device-level behavior we could treat the whole network as the system to be managed.

In the absence of SDN, we viewed traffic engineering as an incremental improvement to traditional routing, leading to a cascading series of tweaks and increasing complexity for MPLS-TE. But by taking a broader view of the overall system, and particularly the use of centralized control and the separation of control from forwarding, systems such as B4 and SWAN became possible and delivered (in my view) better solutions to traffic engineering. While it's not easy to quantify the relative complexity of the systems, the performance benefits for B4 and SWAN are substantial.

There is a bit of the "innovator's dilemma" in this story. Adding MPLS to the routing hardware and software of Cisco's products was quite disruptive, but it was within the bounds of what was considered possible for a router company. Moving to centralized control, however, was viewed by most of my colleagues as too disruptive, especially as it raised the specter of commoditization of the routers themselves once enough software moved out of the routers. Combine this with a strong (and mistaken) belief that centralized control was the enemy of scale and reliability and it's not hard to see why we stuck to local optimizations and resisted the SDN-based systems approach. It took companies with sufficient resources and lack of incumbency to embrace SDN for traffic engineering.

Bruce Davie, October 2022

What Can We Learn From Internet Outages?

Now that we have had a couple of weeks to look back on the great Facebook Outage of 2021, and it's not looking like much more detail will be forthcoming, let's see if we can learn anything from what has been made public about this and some other recent outages. We've written previously about the perils of Internet Centralization. But is there more to this story than confirming what we already believed?

One of the networking talks that left a strong impression on me was given by Najam Ahmad, VP of Network Engineering at Facebook, in 2015 at the second P4 workshop. The takeaway that I have retained from that talk and passed along frequently was that software can do a better job of running networks than humans. Not that software is perfect, but using software to automate network operations is a way to avoid the configuration errors that humans are way too likely to make. Facebook was at the forefront of network automation, and it's a much more mature field now than in 2015. So when we heard that Facebook had managed to disrupt a critical piece of networking infrastructure through configuration error, I was pretty surprised. Nothing that I know about the way Facebook operates made me think they would be likely to push out an untested configuration. While the motto "move fast and break things" lives on in the popular image of Facebook, it was actually back in 2014 that Facebook embraced a new motto: "Move fast with stable infrastructure". (It doesn't have the same ring to it, as WIRED magazine noted with admirable understatement.)

What we know at this point, thanks to the blogs that came out from Facebook engineering, is that a configuration change, intended only to "assess the availability of global backbone capacity", was run through an "auditing tool", allowed to go ahead, and subsequently led to most of Facebook's DNS servers becoming unreachable. From outside Facebook, this was observed as BGP routes being withdrawn and DNS resolution requests failing. It appears there was at least one automated step: "our DNS servers disable[d] those BGP advertisements" when they lost connectivity to the backbone. These failures led to a cascading series of problems including Facebook employees being unable to gain physical access to the machines that needed to be reconfigured—the physical security system apparently depended on a working network. (Facebook refuted rumors that angle grinders were used to gain physical access to servers.)

There is certainly something to be learned here about the way distributed systems can exhibit central points of failure in spite of their designers' best intentions. DNS is a distributed system that should tolerate all sorts of failures, and BGP is the routing protocol on which the Internet depends, with lots of capabilities to route around failures. Yet a configuration error managed to take enough of Facebook's DNS offline to disable most Facebook services, both external (including WhatsApp and Instagram) and internal (e.g., physical security).

Building distributed systems that tolerate any possible failure is hard. When I worked at Nicira, our SDN product was a highly fault-tolerant, distributed system that was designed to gracefully handle the failure of any component, including a complete loss of the control plane. Yet we still managed to hit occasional corner cases that would take the system down. Similarly, Facebook apparently did have a backup path for communicating with their servers, but according to their blog "Our primary and out-of-band network access was down". So it's not that their design was flagrantly brittle (or at least, we don't have evidence that it was), but it failed in a way that was unanticipated.

Who Watches the Watchmen?

The piece of the story that really caught my attention was the mention of an "auditing tool" that allowed the offending configuration change to go ahead. I was immediately reminded of the phrase "Who watches the watchmen?" (which I'm pretty sure I learned in Latin at school). Who audits the auditors?

It seems that this is an area in which Facebook, in retrospect, could have made more investment. As we noted previously, there is a rich and rapidly growing set of tools to perform network verification. For example, you can find lots of details on how to use Batfish to test BGP configuration changes before deploying them, and it's straightforward to test assertions like "will the following prefixes be reachable after this change". It's not that Facebook wasn't trying to tackle this problem, but it seems that their in-house auditing tool wasn't robust enough to catch a really serious configuration error before it was pushed out.

As if to remind everyone that BGP configuration changes should be tested before being implemented, Telia managed to get in on the act with this outage a few days later, on Oct 7, 2021. We know less about what happened in that case but again it makes a case for testing config changes before pushing them to production.

What to take away from all of this? It seems most people have been able to confirm their existing beliefs, whether it's the perennial role of DNS in causing outages, the difficulty of getting BGP to behave, or the wisdom of separating the control and data planes. And the fact that so much of the world depends on WhatsApp does back up our earlier point about excessive centralization.

In my case, I'm refining my views on network automation. While it can reduce opportunities for human error, it can also compound errors as seems to have happened here. I am, however, more convinced than ever that we need to do a better job of verifying networks, and that includes verifying the behavior of automated systems. CI/CD with automated testing, which is commonplace for software systems, is still too rare for networks. Sure, the tools we have may not be perfect, but they provide a layer of robustness that is all too often lacking. Just as it's nearly impossible for a single "pilot error" to bring down a commercial aircraft because of all the safety checks and systems in place, we should treat networks as software systems that can be verified before we make destructive changes. And the networks of the future can be better designed to make them verifiable.

Bruce Davie, October 2021

Revisiting Blockchains

Or, How Web3 Broke My Heart

We have written a lot about the decentralization of the Internet, which could be tackled with a range of possible technologies. But it is time to admit that our thinking on blockchains, which at one point looked like a promising component for a future "re-decentralized" Internet, has moved on. It's only reasonable that our analysis of technology should evolve as the landscape changes, so let's look at how that evolution happened regarding blockchains and so-called "Web3".

I have to admit that I got some guilty pleasure reading the responses to Chris Dixon's new book on Web3, which include a withering review from Molly White (creator of the Web3 is Going Great site) and an exposé of the dubious methods by which it reached the NY Times Bestseller list from Cory Doctorow. I urge you to read White's review in its entirety because it is a delightful read. But before I get too excited about joining the pile-on, I need to admit that I have cited Chris Dixon's writing in favorable terms in the past. In an early post on re-decentralizing the Internet I linked to a Dixon blog post to back up my point about the increasing centralization of the Internet. But agreeing on the problem doesn't require us to agree on the solution. (I also like to think that citing a comic from The Oatmeal partly offset my Dixon reference.)

I really did at one point believe that blockchains could be useful for a range of purposes related to decentralization. My interest in blockchains goes back at least to 2016 when some of my colleagues at VMware Research introduced me to their work on permissioned blockchains. Unlike the majority of blockchains underpinning cryptocurrencies, permissioned blockchains such as Hyperledger don't seek to anonymize the participants. They have been positioned as suitable for "enterprise" use cases, such as clearing financial transactions among banks or settling trades on stock exchanges, where knowing the participants is important. Perhaps because my first exposure to blockchains was in this rather controlled environment, and because there was such a clear separation between this world and the Wild West of cryptocurrency speculation, NFTs, etc., I established an early optimism about the technology. (Permissioned blockchains also avoid the terrible carbon footprint problems of proof-of-work.) And it's all very clever from a computer science perspective, whether we are talking about Nakamoto consensus or scalable Byzantine Fault Tolerance (SBFT), as proposed by my VMware colleagues. Who doesn't like a clever algorithm?

In 2018 I helped to organize a VMware networking conference and I managed to persuade Gün Sirer from Cornell to come and give the keynote. Gün is a well-known distributed systems researcher who was quick to apply his expertise to blockchains. His 2013 post "Bitcoin is broken" showed that a Nakamoto-style blockchain was vulnerable to takeover by a minority of miners, contrary to popular belief (winning him few friends in the crypto world). He went on to make quite a number of contributions to the blockchain space, and his keynote holds up fairly well—one of my favorite parts is the story about 19th century virtual currencies made of big carved rocks sitting in the ocean (see Gün's Future:net video below). And he makes a good case that blockchains represent a new class of system that will have a long-term role in computing, even if we don't know yet what it will be.

The Search For Use Cases

Around the same time, VMware decided to build an enterprise blockchain based on SBFT. Being in a field role by this point, I had the chance to explain this to our customers, and this is where I started to have my first doubts about blockchain. Our pitch was that we could offer the distributed ledger infrastructure to customers and they could use it to explore use cases.

The problem for me was that the use cases never seemed to entirely stack up. For example, logistics use cases came up a lot. Wouldn't it be great if you could keep track of items being shipped around the world in a distributed, immutable ledger. But what exactly does blockchain bring to the table here? Yes, lots of different organizations might have responsibility for the package at different points in time, and maybe a distributed ledger could be used so that each organization records the location of the package as it moves through various checkpoints. But how about we just let each organization expose a REST API to a website with their view of this information? This, I believe, is how it works if I ask Amazon or Apple to track a package I've ordered. They go query the relevant API from the shipping companies and put it all together so I see the tracking history. Could I make the case that this would be more reliable with blockchain? I'm not sure I could. Even if the ledger is immutable, aren't there bigger problems such as how to avoid forged inputs, e.g., claiming that a package is somewhere when it isn't? Blockchains seem to be as vulnerable to garbage-in-garbage-out as anything else—or as I heard it, a blockchain lets you store decentralized, encrypted garbage.

Thanks to my work on the Magma mobile networking core, I learned about Helium, a decentralized mobile network that pays the providers of cellular coverage in crypto tokens, and it seemed that it might be a winning application of blockchain technology. The jury is perhaps still out on this, but the future doesn't look great for Helium (for reasons laid out in Molly White's article). Incentivizing distributed deployment of cellular radio towers with crypto tokens sounds like a clever idea, but it is looking increasingly unlikely that the economics will stand up. Which, when you consider the razor-thin margins of most cellular operators, perhaps should not come as a surprise.

Which brings us back to Web3. While we certainly agree that the centralization of almost everything on the Internet has many negative consequences, it's far from clear why a blockchain is the right solution to this problem. Would I like to see musicians fairly compensated for their work rather than being ripped off by Spotify? Yes I would, but I am struggling to see how storing music on a blockchain or paying musicians with crypto tokens for their efforts is going to play out better than the sale of bored ape NFTs.

This, I think, gets to the heart of why I have lost my faith in the potential of blockchains. The problems that they might solve, particularly those related to excessive centralization, are real. But either the problems require non-technical solutions (e.g., regulation of monopolistic tech companies who are motivated to centralize as much as they can), or the viable technical solutions don't require blockchains at all. This brings me back to one of my favorite parts of White's Web3 book review:

> *Attempts to create alternatives have all failed, [Dixon] says, before going on to describe several projects that are very much still in use, such as the RSS and ActivityPub protocols, or federated social media projects like Mastodon.*

You don't need to be deeply technical to know that RSS is how podcasts are published, which is why we so often hear the phrase "wherever you get your podcasts" and they don't just live on a single service (aside from the rare case where a streaming giant negotiates an exclusive arrangement with a podcaster).

There is a truly open, distributed system for publishing and consuming podcasts. RSS is a well-defined protocol standard that ensures that anyone can implement a publisher or subscriber of RSS feeds and that these will interoperate with each other.

Similarly, one of the reasons I remain bullish on the Fediverse is because of its foundation on the ActivityPub protocol, a W3C standard. There is an amazing amount of energy going into building servers and clients for ActivityPub, so while the Fediverse certainly has its challenges, it continues to grow in both user numbers and in functionality.

Ultimately I think that decentralization can again become a hallmark of the Internet, as its original architects intended. The answer is not to somehow insert blockchains into the Internet, but to continue the development of open, standardized protocols that support decentralized use cases, whether those use cases are logistics, podcasting, or social networking.

For me there is also a higher-level issue: much as I hate admitting I've made a mistake, it really is a good idea to change one's mind based on new information—in this case, the continued failure of blockchains to find non-speculative use cases. Funnily enough, another notable instance of my reversing my technical opinion was when I realized that centralized controllers make sense for a set of networking problems that are now addressed by SDN. But when it comes to re-decentralizing the Internet, I'm backing open protocols instead of blockchains.

Bruce Davie, March 2024

———————————————

Decentralization Strikes Back

In late 2022, we joined the masses of people leaving Twitter for Mastodon. The fact that Mastodon, building on some earlier ideas for federated social networking, is a decentralized approach, has renewed our interest in, and hope for, the decentralization of the Internet.

When Larry and I kicked off Systems Approach back in 2020, one of our first tasks was to brainstorm a list of books we'd be interested in writing. Two years later we've managed to bring three of those ideas to life, with books on SDN, Edge Cloud Operations, and TCP Congestion Control. But one book that remains on the to-do list has the working title "The Decentralized Internet". We've managed a few posts on that topic but we're still some distance away from having the material for a book. On top of that, the backlash against Web3 (quite justified in my view—see the post above) cooled my enthusiasm somewhat. But there is definitely more to decentralization than Web3, with the rapid rise in popularity of Mastodon and the Fediverse an interesting case study.

There's been a flurry of articles on the exodus from Twitter to Mastodon in both technical and mainstream publications. The underlying technology is ActivityPub, a protocol specified by the World Wide Web Consortium (W3C). ActivityPub draws on a long line of research in publish-subscribe systems going back to at least 1987. Bryan Cantrill (see below) made several good points about the benefits of decentralization as it applies to social media, including the increased opportunities for experimentation that arise when the operation of the social network is no longer the province of a single corporation. We're seeing lots of experimentation with Mastodon deployment, data is being shared, and a range of different ActivityPub implementations beyond the canonical Mastodon server (e.g. GoToSocial, Takahe) are appearing.

It's worth digging a bit deeper into what we mean by decentralization here. Twitter (now X) is not a monolith: it is a giant distributed system, made up of a large number of microservices. For example, here is a quote from a Twitter infrastructure blog:

> *We process approximately 400 billion events in real time and generate petabyte (PB) scale data every day. There are various event sources we consume data from, and they are produced in different platforms and storage systems, such as Hadoop, Vertica, Manhattan distributed databases, Kafka, Twitter Eventbus, GCS, BigQuery, and PubSub.*

Organizationally, however, Twitter is centralized. When Twitter decides to change its API, it can do so unilaterally, to the detriment of any third party apps that try to use that API. Likewise, it can (and did) unilaterally change its policies on content moderation, banning of users, etc., in a way that drove plenty of users (including me) to look for an alternative.

Conversely, Mastodon and other applications in the Fediverse are organizationally distributed. Each instance of a Mastodon server is run by a person or group who makes their own decisions both about how to run the service technically and on the policies that will apply to the instance. There are plenty of challenges on both fronts; reading a post on how to scale the performance of a Mastodon instance made me fairly sure that I don't want to run one myself for any serious purpose. Meanwhile, my "home" instance (aus.social) has been rapidly trying to onboard new volunteer moderators to deal with the sudden increase in load. I expect many other instances are doing the same.

I've seen a bit of commentary that Mastodon isn't really all that decentralized, as the distribution of users across instances follows a Zipf-like pattern (which I find unsurprising—such distributions seem to crop up everywhere). In late 2022 it was reported that 97% of Mastodon users were on the top 5 instances. I regenerated the top instance data (using instances.social) in April 2025 and the chart below shows 85% of users on the top 30 instances (which is about 0.2% of all instances). So while things are not as concentrated as they were in 2022, that's still a lot of users on a small fraction of instances.

But I actually think that graph makes the case that decentralization is working well! Yes, there are some big instances with over 1 million users. Aus.social, with around 25k users as of today, is ranked about 80th most

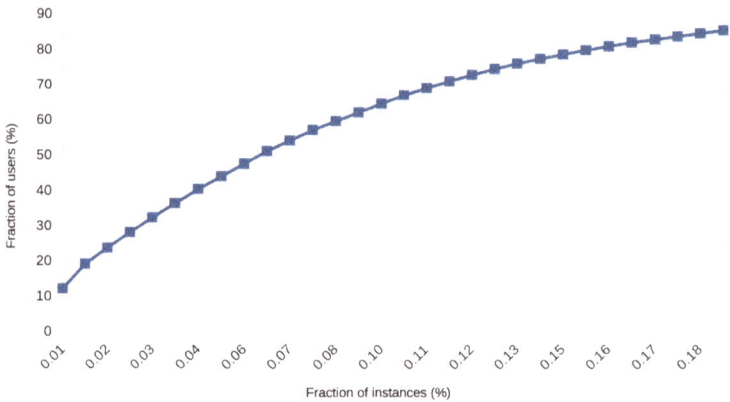

Distribution of Mastodon Users by Instance

populous instance according to instances.social. Discuss.systems, where
we maintain a Systems Approach account, has just over 3500 users (around
250th). There are thousands of active instances, with new ones coming
daily, so it's hard for me to see this as excessive centralization. It will be
interesting to see how this plays out if Mastodon continues to grow at its
current rate. Certainly many instances are experiencing growing pains, as
I've learned by following a few administrators.

Another interesting aspect of decentralization is how these instances sit
on the underlying Internet infrastructure. As we discussed previously, one
way in which the Internet has re-centralized is the heavy dependence on
a few services such as Cloudflare, Fastly and Akamai; when one of these
services has an outage, it affects huge chunks of the Internet. Here, again
the news looks fairly promising to the extent that we have data.

At least we can say from the above that there isn't a huge dependence
on a small number of ISPs, and Cloudflare doesn't appear to be responsible
for more than 10% of Mastodon instances (although we can't easily draw
conclusions about CDNs from this data). You can also see that there are
around 30k instances total in this data set, which seems pretty decentralized
to me.

One aspect of Mastodon that should help it stay decentralized is the relative ease of moving from one instance to another. Many new Mastodon
users are stressed out by the task of choosing an instance, a decision that

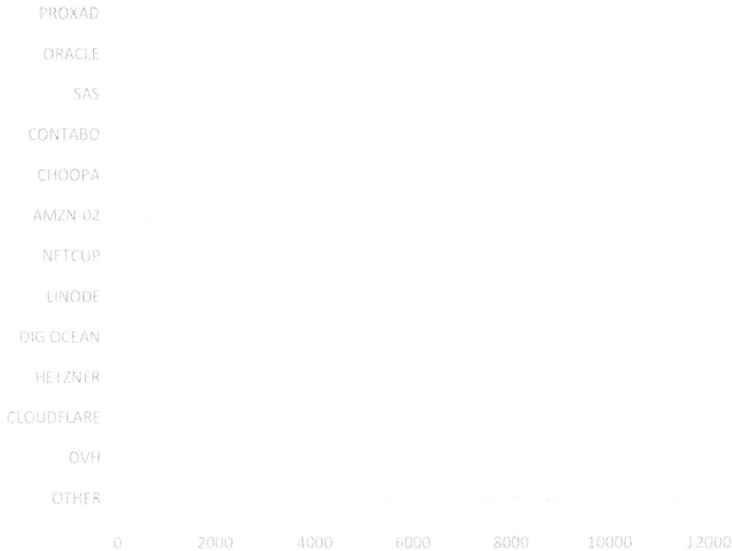

Number of Mastodon Instances by ASN
OVH and Cloudflare are the most populous with over 3000 instances each, while the total number of instances on smaller ASes (Other) is over 11000. Reported by @vanlueckn@gametoots.de.

isn't required when signing up for a typical social network. While I recommend people look at things like stability and moderation policies, there's clearly a risk of finding yourself on an instance that's unsuitable for some reason. But migrating from one instance to another, and taking all your follows/followers with you (a real pain point when leaving a traditional social network) "just works" thanks to the design of ActivityPub and the Mastodon implementation. Since users are free to move, new instances can attract users more easily, and there is no lock-in to instances that fail to perform as required.

I want to emphasize the central role that the ActivityPub protocol plays. "Mastodon" is doing a lot of work here as (a) the name for a social network (which uses ActivityPub) (b) the most common implementation of a server that implements ActivityPub, and (c) the name of a couple of mobile applications (clients) that let users talk to Mastodon instances. But just as there are lots of web browsers and web servers that implement HTTP, there are multiple ActivityPub implementations, both servers and clients. The story gets a bit complicated by the fact that some implementations of ActivityPub are offering a different service than Mastodon (e.g., Pixelfed is an image-sharing social network, BookWyrm is a social book-rating and reviewing service). But the existence of a stable, standard protocol (thanks W3C!) means that we have a solid foundation for innovation at multiple levels, be it in new clients, servers, or applications. And there is a form of resilience here: if, for example, the current Mastodon server implementation proves to be unsustainable for some reason, there's nothing stopping developers from making new (perhaps better) implementations of ActivityPub—something that is already happening as noted above.

The existence of a stable protocol cuts both ways: inside a single organization, it's easier to make substantial changes to a protocol or even replace it with something else (e.g., gRPC). Although that may not be as easy as it sounds once you have enough teams of developers trying to work independently and depending on stable APIs between components. But the history of the Internet tells us that well-specified protocols that encourage experimentation in how they are implemented and in the applications that use them can drive innovation and growth for decades. I'm optimistic that ActivityPub will be one of those protocols powering the future decentralized Internet.

Bruce Davie, December 2022 (Fediverse data updated April 2025)

Closing Remarks

The universally applicable idea that comes from our look at centralization versus de-centralization is the tension between optimization and robustness. On the one hand, centralized decision making opens the door to collecting all the data you need to make a globally optimal decision, and then having the control necessary to act on such decisions. This advantage shows up in the traffic engineering example. On the other hand, decentralized systems permit diverse and diffused decision making. This avoids the brittleness of a single entity outright failing (as we saw with the Internet outages), or failing to deliver the promised benefits we originally signed up for (as has happened with various social media applications).

From a system design perspective, the key to providing just the right amount of optimality-vs-robustness hinges on how the system is factored into components, and the interfaces used to communicate across component boundaries. The fewer assumptions that have to hold on both sides of the boundary and the more autonomy granted to the entities responsible for each side of the boundary, the more robust the resulting system tends to be.

Explore Further

David Clark. The Design Philosophy of the DARPA Internet Protocols. ACM SIGCOMM, August 1988.

Larry Peterson, Carmelo Cascone, Brian O'Connor, Thomas Vachuska, and Bruce Davie. Software-Defied Networks: A Systems Approach. Systems Approach, 2021.

Amin Vahdat, David Clark, and Jennifer Rexford. A Purpose-built Global Network: Google's Move to SDN. ACM Queue, December 2015.

Santosh Janardhan. More details about the October 4 Outage. Facebook Engineering blog, 2021.

Bruce Davie. Here's an idea: Verification for computer networks as well as chips and code. The Register, September 2021

Molly White. Review: Chris Dixon's Read Write Own. Citation Needed blog, February 2024.

Gün Sirer. Blockchains: The Promise and Challenges Ahead for Networking. Future:net conference, 2018.

Brian Cantrill. Homebrew Social Networking. Blog post, November 2022.

Social Web Working Group, W3C. ActivityPub W3C Recommendation. January 2018.

TCP: An Archaeological Dig

We started working on our first edition of Computer Networks 30 years ago. It was the first introductory networking text book to use TCP/IP to illustrate general networking concepts. Ten years before that, in the mid-1980s, Larry was in grad school when his advisor, Doug Comer, handed him a 9-track tape with the recent release of TCP/IP to be installed on the department VAX. That open source implementation of TCP/IP, first included in the BSD 4.2 release of Unix, was critical to jump-starting the Internet we know today.

Over the subsequent 40 years, TCP/IP—and hence, the Internet—has seen unparalleled success. It has done so by surviving nearly constant pressure to adapt: to increased load, to higher bandwidths, to new application domains, and so on. That journey gives us a treasure trove of information about how software systems evolve over time. A lot of the reasons for this success (and ability to adapt) can be attributed to the Internet's overall architecture, as discussed in the chapter on Architecture. This chapter takes a different tack, looking back over some of the judgement calls specific to TCP that have been made over the last four decades. It's hard to argue with TCP's success, but it's also worth taking a critical look at the decisions that have been made over the years, and the opportunity costs they incurred.

The chapter is organized around the two ideas at the heart of TCP's design: its congestion control algorithm and its reliable bye-stream semantics. In both cases, TCP is bundled with a lot of judgement (one might say, dogma) about how a transport protocol should be designed. The good thing about the passage of time, though, is that the accumulation of technical decisions tend to bend towards the right answer.

How Congestion Control Saved the Internet

Following my recent talk and article on "60 years of networking", which focused almost entirely on the Internet and ARPANET, I received quite a few comments about various networking technologies that were competing for ascendancy at the same time. These included the OSI stack (anyone remember CLNP and TP4?), the Coloured Book protocols (including the Cambridge Ring), and of course ATM (Asynchronous Transfer Mode) which was actually the first networking protocol on which I worked in depth. It's hard to fathom now, but in the 1980s I was one of many people who thought that ATM might be the packet switching technology to take over the world. ATM proponents used to refer to existing technologies such as Ethernet and TCP/IP as "legacy" protocols that could, if necessary, be carried over the global ATM network once it was established. One of my fond memories from those days is of Steve Deering (a pioneer of IP networking) boldly (and correctly) stating that ATM would never be successful enough even to be a legacy protocol.

One reason I skipped over these other protocols at the time was simply to save space—it's a little-known fact that Larry and I aim for brevity, especially since receiving a 1-star review on Amazon that called our book "a wall of text". But I was also focused on how we got to the Internet of today, where TCP/IP has effectively out-competed other protocol suites to achieve global (or near-global) penetration.

There are many theories about why TCP/IP was more successful than its contemporaries, and they are not readily testable. Most likely, there were many factors that played into the success of the Internet protocols. But I rate congestion control as one of the key factors that enabled the Internet to progress from moderate to global scale. It is also an interesting study in how the particular architectural choices made in the 1970s proved themselves over the subsequent decades.

Distributed Resource Management

In David Clark's paper "The Design Philosophy of the DARPA Internet Protocols", a stated design goal is "The Internet architecture must permit distributed management of its resources". There are many different implications of that goal, but the way that Jacobson and Karels first implemented congestion control in TCP is a good example of taking that principle to heart. Their approach also embraces another design goal of the Internet: accommodate many different types of networks. Taken together, these principles pretty much rule out the possibility of any sort of network-based admission control, a sharp contrast to networks such as ATM, which assumed that a request for resources would be made from an end-system to the network before data could flow. Part of the "accommodate many types of networks" philosophy is that you can't assume that all networks have admission control. Couple that with distributed management of resources and you end up with congestion control being something that end-systems have to handle, which is exactly what Jacobson and Karels did with their initial changes to TCP.

The history of TCP congestion control is long enough to fill a book (and we did) but the work done at Berkeley from 1996 to 1998 casts a long shadow, with Jacobson's 1988 SIGCOMM paper ranking among the most cited networking papers of all time. Slow-start, AIMD (additive increase, multiplicative decrease), RTT estimation, and the use of packet loss as a congestion signal were all in that paper, laying the groundwork for the following decades of congestion control research. One reason for that paper's influence, I believe, is that the foundation it laid was solid, while it left plenty of room for future improvements—as we see in the continued efforts to improve congestion control today. And the problem is fundamentally hard: we're trying to get millions of end-systems that have no direct contact with each other to cooperatively share the bandwidth of bottleneck links in some moderately fair way, using only the information that can be gleaned by sending packets into the network and observing when and whether they reach their destination.

Arguably one of the biggest leaps forward after 1988 was the realization by Brakmo and Peterson (yes, that guy) that packet loss wasn't the only signal of congestion: so too was increasing delay. This was the basis for the 1994 TCP Vegas paper, and the idea of using delay rather than loss alone was quite controversial at the time. However, Vegas kicked off a new trend in congestion control research, inspiring many other efforts to take delay into account as an early indicator of congestion before loss occurs. Data center TCP (DCTCP) and Google's BBR are two examples.

One reason that I give credit to congestion control algorithms in explaining the success of the Internet is that the path to failure of the Internet was clearly on display in 1986. Jacobson describes some of the early congestion collapse episodes, which saw throughput fall by three orders of magnitude. When I joined Cisco in 1995 we were still hearing customer stories about catastrophic congestion episodes. The same year Bob Metcalfe, inventor of Ethernet and Turing Award winner, famously predicted that the Internet would collapse as consumer Internet access and the rise of the Web drove rapid growth in traffic. It didn't. Congestion control has continued to evolve, with the QUIC protocol, for example, offering both better mechanisms for detecting congestion and the option of experimenting with multiple congestion control algorithms. And some congestion control has moved into the application layer, e.g., Dynamic Adaptive Streaming over HTTP (DASH).

An interesting side effect of the congestion episodes of the 1980s and '90s was that we observed that small buffers were sometimes the cause of congestion collapse. An influential paper by Villamizar and Song showed that TCP performance dropped when the amount of buffering was less than the average delay × bandwidth product of the flows. Unfortunately, the result only held for very small numbers of flows (as was acknowledged in the paper) but it was widely interpreted as an inviolable rule that influenced the next several years of router design. This was finally debunked by the buffer sizing work of Appenzeller et al. in 2004, but not before the unfortunate phenomenon of Bufferbloat—truly excessive buffer sizes leading to massive queuing delays—had made it into millions of low-end routers. The self-test for Bufferbloat in your home network is worth a look.

So, while we can't go back and run controlled experiments to see exactly how the Internet succeeded while other protocol suites fell by the wayside, we can at least see that the Internet avoided potential failure because of the timely way congestion control was added. It was relatively easy in 1986 to experiment with new ideas by tweaking the code in a couple of end-systems, and then push the effective solution out to a wide set of systems. Nothing inside the network had to change. It almost certainly helped that the set of operating systems that needed to be changed and the community of people who could make those edits was small enough to see widespread deployment of the initial BSD-based algorithms of Jacobson and Karels.

It seems clear that there is no such thing as the perfect congestion control approach, which is why we continue to see new papers on the topic 35 years after Jacobson's. But the Internet's architecture has fostered the environment in which effective solutions can be tested and deployed to achieve distributed management of shared resources. In my view that's a great testament to the quality of that architecture.

Bruce Davie, September 2023

TCP Congestion Control: Acceptable Unfairness

It's hard not to be amazed by the amount of active research on congestion control over the last 30-plus years. From theory to practice, and with more than its fair share of flame wars, the question of how to manage congestion in the network is a technical challenge that resists an optimal solution while offering countless options for incremental improvement. This seems like a good time to take stock of where we are, and ask ourselves what might happen next.

Congestion control is fundamentally an issue of resource allocation—trying to meet the competing demands that applications have for resources (in a network, these are primarily link bandwidth and router buffers), which ultimately reduces to deciding when to say no and to whom. The best framing of the problem I know traces back to a paper by Frank Kelly in 1997, when he characterized congestion control as *"a distributed algorithm to share network resources among competing sources, where the goal is to choose source rate so as to maximize aggregate source utility subject to capacity constraints."*

This is a hard problem in any computer system, but what makes it especially difficult in this case is the decentralized nature of the Internet. Not only is the Internet's approach to congestion control distributed across its millions of hosts and routers, it is fair to think of them as cooperatively trying to achieve a globally optimal solution. From this perspective, there is a shared objective function, and all the elements are implementing a distributed algorithm to optimize that function. Compounding the challenge, and arguably the reason there are so many approaches to congestion control, is the lack of consensus on the right objective function.

Of course everyone wants high throughput, low latency, stability, and fairness, but it's how you trade those off against each other that makes it a tough question to answer. To make matters worse, the problem is over-constrained, meaning that each solution must choose which constraints to give the most—and least—weight to. Fairness has been a particularly thorny issue, not only when considering a given algorithm competing against itself, but especially when comparing algorithm A with algorithm B. If A is able to measure improved throughput over B, but it does so by being more aggressive, and hence, stealing bandwidth from B's flows, then A's improvement is not fairly gained and may be discounted. In such an analysis, Jain's fairness index has historically been used as a quantitative measure of fairness.

From Fairness to Harm Reduction

Fairness arguments have been used for 30 years in favor of the incumbent algorithm (whatever it happens to be), making Ranysha Ware's recent proposal to measure harm instead of fairness a welcome breath of fresh air in this ongoing debate. Ware et al. advocate for a threshold based on harm, as measured by a reduction in throughput or an increase in latency. Intuitively, if the amount of harm caused by flows using a new mechanism B on flows using existing mechanism A is within a bound derived from how much harm A-managed flows cause other A-managed flows, we can consider B deployable alongside A without harm.

Unfortunately, replacing fairness with harm doesn't eliminate the over-constrained nature of the problem. But what might is the proliferation of purpose-built mechanisms targeted at specific usage domains. Based on my reading of a lot of the recent research, this is where congestion control algorithms seem to be headed. Data Center TCP (DCTCP) is a great example. It targets congestion within the data center, and so assumes link bandwidths are 10-Gbps or higher and RTTs are typically measured in the tens of microseconds. It doesn't have to be responsive to such a wide-range of operating parameters as the Internet as a whole. Even more importantly, because the data center is contained within a single administrative domain, it is possible to enable features like Explicit Congestion Notification (ECN) on every single switch, and optimize the algorithm to take advantage of that information.

You could argue that the data center is a special case, but I'm not so sure. Google's Bottleneck Bandwidth and RTT (BBR) mechanism is another example worth considering. It is general-purpose in that it attempts to handle the wide range of scenarios that any Internet-worthy algorithm would have to respond to, but it's not particularly fair when competing with non-BBR flows. But that doesn't matter if it's only deployed within Google's backbone, interconnecting their data centers. In that case, BBR only has to be fair to its own flows. Is it possible to generalize from this example?

Perhaps it is. In the early decades of the Internet, end-to-end meant between any two hosts in the Internet. But today, direct communication between arbitrary hosts is the exception, not the rule. Most TCP connections on today's Internet can be categorized as follows: edge-to-cloud (between an end-user device and the nearest cloud hosting center or CDN server); cloud-to-cloud (typically over a provider's backbone); or intracloud (between two servers within a data center). The second two are usage domains that already run purpose-built TCP congestion control algorithms, as covered above. And the first is well on its way to being reinvented—with the rollout of 5G (and all the spectrum-allocation algorithms 5G implies) for mobile devices, and with cloud-provider last-mile offerings for our streaming and gaming devices at home.

None of this means the resource allocation problem goes away, but it might become more tractable as the deployments become more customized. Most importantly, we won't have to agree to one universal mechanism, except as a fallback mechanism for those rare occasions when true peer-to-peer transfers are required. This may very well accelerate the rate at which congestion control papers are published, since the "it's not fair" argument is no longer relevant. Of course, if the Internet truly re-decentralizes in the coming years, congestion control might once again need to address global optimization problems, but perhaps that will happen without a single incumbent algorithm being favored by default. It seems congestion control researchers have a secure future.

Larry Peterson, October 2021

———————————————

TCP: The "P" is for Platform

The original specification for the Transmission Control Protocol (TCP) was published as RFC 793 in 1981. TCP has proven to be resilient over the intervening forty years, but hardly static. There have been so many extensions and implementation notes that it's hard to keep track of all of them, so in case you missed it, RFC 9293 was just published to address that problem. In a major milestone, RFC 793 is now officially Obsolete.

For those of us that have been around for most or all of those years, reading RFC 9293 is a walk down memory lane. From the silly window syndrome to slow start, fast retransmit, duplicate ACKs, window scaling, and much more, the history of TCP is a remarkable case study in system evolution. Proposing a clean-slate redesign is a popular pitch for researchers, and the idea of a fresh start has a certain appeal, but there is so much experience codified in TCP that any replacement has a very high bar to clear.

Taking a step back from the details and looking at the "system evolution" story, several things jump out at me. For starters, I would hate to have to implement TCP from scratch based solely on a reading of RFC 9293 (and the many RFCs it includes by reference). It's an open question as to whether doing so is even possible, since for many years it's been the case that TCP has been defined by its reference implementation; the RFCs are more descriptive than prescriptive. That's not a criticism. From the beginning, the IETF has favored protocol definitions based on implementations, where RFC 9293 is the latest update of that iterative process.

If the implementation drives the specification, then which implementation is authoritative? The answer has been the dominant open source implementation of the day. This was originally the Berkeley Software Distribution (BSD) implementation of Unix. BSD and its descendants continue to this day (notably as FreeBSD), but it was eventually overtaken by Linux, in the early 2000s, as the *de facto* open source, Unix-based OS. (It is also the case that many of today's commercial OSes are derived from either BSD or Linux.)

But the Linux version of TCP is more than a reference implementation. You could make the argument that the Linux kernel provides a platform for evolving TCP. While reading RFC 9293 I had a vague recollection of an RFC published during the heyday of TCP extensions entitled *"TCP Extensions*

Considered Harmful", so I Googled it, and it turns out to be RFC 1263. (It also turns out I was a co-author; I can only wonder what else I might have written and long since forgotten about.) The RFC describes general mechanisms for evolving TCP that would be more rational than TCP options (essentially by proposing what would today be called semantic versioning), but one takeaway that seems relevant today is a concluding statement:

> Because of lack of any alternatives, TCP has become a de-facto platform for implementing other protocols. It provides a vague standard interface with the kernel, it runs on many machines, and has a well defined distribution path.

This gets us into a murky distinction—is it TCP that serves as a platform for evolving transport functionality or is it the Linux networking subsystem—but that's a distinction without a difference. The two are effectively one and the same, with header options serving as one method for adding "transport plug-ins" to the kernel. (Here I'm using a simple definition of a platform as a tool or framework that lets us add new functionality over time.)

Congestion control is another example of how Linux TCP serves as an extensible framework. All the algorithms described in our book are available (and can be optionally activated) in the Linux kernel, where, like TCP itself, the implementation is the authoritative definition of each of those algorithms. As a consequence, an API has emerged for congestion control, providing a well-defined way to continually adapt TCP. And with a nod to feature velocity, Linux now provides a convenient and safe way to dynamically inject new congestion control logic into the kernel by supporting this API in the extended Berkeley Packet Filter (eBPF). This simplifies the task of experimenting with new algorithms or tweaking existing algorithms, side-stepping the hurdle of waiting for the relevant Linux kernel to be deployed. It also makes it easy to customize the congestion control algorithm used on a per-flow basis, as well as explicitly exposing the device-level ingress/egress queues to the decision-making process. (This is how CoDel and ECN, for example, are supported in the Linux kernel.)

That's the good news, but as a case study of how to most effectively evolve software, the results are mixed. For example, as APIs go, the Linux TCP congestion control API is not particularly intuitive and its only documentation is in the code. A second complication is that while this API makes it possible to substitute different algorithms into TCP, an ideal interface would also support reuse: making it possible for different transport protocols (e.g., SCTP, QUIC) to reuse existing algorithms rather than have to maintain a separate/parallel implementation. A third observation is while Linux has done an excellent job of making the file system replaceable (and it can now be done in a safe and high-performance way) the approach does not extend to TCP, which has too many tentacles throughout the kernel. All of this, coupled with the limitations of TCP options called out in RFC 1263, might lead us to conclude that TCP evolved over the years in spite of itself. At the very least, we are left wondering about lost opportunities.

In the meantime, the cloud has grown up around TCP, with an emphasis on improving feature velocity. Protocol standards (above the physical level) become less relevant once you have the ability to dictate what code runs on both ends of a connection, which the cloud and modern apps are well-positioned to exploit. One has to wonder if TCP as we know it today will fade into the background, not because of a clean-slate replacement, but because it is overtaken by cloud software management practices. The adoption of QUIC would seem to be a good test of this hypothesis: it both provides value that TCP does not (a well-designed and efficient Request/Reply mechanism) and a modern approach to continuously integrating and continuously deploying new features.

One plausible outcome is that the network as a whole becomes a programmable platform, improving feature velocity for everything from the transport protocols running on endpoints to the forwarding pipeline running in network switches. And the more complete and agile that platform becomes, the more likely it is that RFC-defined specifications will one day become obsolete. As we said in RFC 1263:

> We hope to be able to design and distribute protocols in less time than it takes a standards committee to agree on an acceptable meeting time.

Perhaps we are getting closer to realizing that goal.

Larry Peterson, September 2022

QUIC Is Not a TCP Replacement

In our last post about the past and future of TCP (inspired by the release of RFC 9293) we touched on the possibility that QUIC might start to replace TCP. In this post I want to argue that QUIC is actually solving a different problem than that solved by TCP, and so should be viewed as something other than a TCP replacement. It may well be that for some (or even most) applications QUIC becomes the default transport, but I believe that is because TCP has been pushed into roles for which it was not originally intended. Let's take a step back to see why I make that claim.

Back in 1995, Larry and I were working on the first edition of *Computer Networks: A Systems Approach*, and we had reached the point of writing the transport protocols chapter, which we titled "End-to-end Protocols". In those days, there were only two transport protocols of note in the Internet, UDP and TCP, so we gave each of those its own section. Since our book aims to teach networking principles rather than just the contents of RFCs, we framed the two sections as two different communication paradigms: a simple demultiplexing service (exemplified by UDP), and a reliable byte stream (TCP). But there was also a third paradigm that Larry argued we needed to cover, for which there wasn't really a well-known example of an Internet protocol: Remote Procedure Call (RPC). The examples we used to illustrate RPC in 1995 seem quaint now: SunRPC and a home-grown example from Larry's research at the time on the x-kernel. These days there are plenty of options for RPC implementations that run over IP, with gRPC being one of the most well-known examples.

Why did we feel the need for a whole section on RPC, when most other networking books would have just covered TCP and UDP? For one thing, RPC was one of the key research areas in the distributed systems community at that time, with the 1984 paper of Nelson and Birrell spurring a generation of RPC-related projects. And in our view, a reliable byte stream is not the right abstraction for RPC. The core of RPC is a request/reply paradigm. You send a bunch of arguments from the client to the server, the server does some computation with those arguments, and then it returns the results of the computation. Yes, a reliable byte stream might help get all the arguments and results across the network correctly, but there is more to RPC than that. Leaving aside the problem of serializing the arguments for transmission over a network (which we also covered later in the book), RPC is not really about transferring a stream of bytes, but about sending a message and getting a response to it. So it is a bit more like a datagram service (as provided by UDP or IP) but it also requires more than just unreliable datagram delivery. RPC needs to handle lost, misordered, and duplicated messages; an identifier space is required to match requests and responses; and fragmentation/reassembly of messages must be supported, to name a few requirements. Out-of-order delivery, which a reliable byte stream prevents, is also desirable for RPC. There may be a reason why so many RPC frameworks came into existence in the 1980s and 1990s—distributed systems people needed an RPC mechanism, and there wasn't anything readily available in the standard TCP/IP protocol suite. (RFC 1045 actually does define an experimental RPC-oriented transport, but it never seems to have caught on.) It also wasn't obvious then that TCP/IP would become as dominant as it is today. So some RPC frameworks (DCE for example) were designed to be independent of the underlying network protocols.

The Need For a Third Transport Paradigm

The lack of support for RPC in the TCP/IP stack set the stage for QUIC. When HTTP came along in the early 1990s, it wasn't trying to solve an RPC problem so much as an information sharing problem, but it did implement request/response semantics. The designers of HTTP, lacking any obviously better options, decided to run HTTP over TCP, with famously poor performance in the early versions due to use of a new connection for every "GET". A variety of tweaks to HTTP such as pipelining, persistent connections, and the use of parallel connections were introduced to improve the performance, but TCP's reliable byte-stream model was never the perfect fit for HTTP. With the introduction of transport layer security (TLS) causing another set of round-trip exchanges of cryptographic information, the mismatch between what HTTP needed and what TCP provides became more and more clear. This was well explained in the 2012 QUIC design document from Jim Roskind: head-of-line blocking, poor congestion response, and the additional RTT(s) introduced by TLS were all identified as problems inherent to running HTTP over TCP.

One way to frame what happened here is this: the "narrow waist" of the Internet was originally just the Internet Protocol, intended to support a diversity of protocols above it. But somehow the "waist" began to include TCP and UDP as well. Those were the only transports available. If you only wanted a datagram service, you could use UDP. If you needed any sort of reliable delivery, TCP was the answer. If you needed something that didn't quite map to either unreliable datagrams or reliable byte streams, you were out of luck. But it was a lot to ask of TCP to be all things to so many upper layer protocols.

QUIC is doing a lot of work: its definition spans three RFCs covering the basic protocol (RFC 9000), its use of TLS (9001) and its congestion control mechanisms (9002). But at its heart it is an implementation of the missing third paradigm for the Internet: RPC. If what you really want is a reliable byte stream, such as when you are downloading that multi-gigabyte operating system update, then TCP really is well designed for the job. But HTTP(S) is much more like RPC than it is like a reliable byte stream, and one way to look at QUIC is that it's finally delivering the RPC paradigm to the Internet protocol suite. That will certainly benefit applications that run over HTTP(S), including, notably, gRPC, and all those RESTful APIs that we've come to depend on.

When we wrote about QUIC previously, we noted that it was a good case study in how to rethink the layering of a system as the requirements become clearer. The point here is that TCP meets one set of requirements—those of a reliable byte stream—and its congestion control algorithms continue to evolve in service of those requirements. QUIC is really meeting a different set of requirements. Since HTTP is so central to the Internet today—indeed it has been argued that it is becoming the new "narrow waist"—it could be that QUIC becomes the dominant transport protocol, not because it replaces TCP exactly, but because it meets the needs of the dominant applications above it.

Bruce Davie, September 2022

It's TCP vs RPC All Over Again

We've written previously about the fact that the Internet seems to be missing a standard protocol for the request/response paradigm, with repeated attempts to force-fit TCP leading to inevitable mismatches. Sometimes we feel that we are the only people who think this way, with our networking book being one of the few to suggest a third paradigm beyond datagrams (UDP) and byte streams (TCP). But a lively debate on the topic—spurred by Ivan Pepelnjak's recent blog post raising objections to John Ousterhout's position paper *It's Time to Replace TCP in the Datacenter*—has reassured us that we are not alone.

But it's John's rebuttal to Ivan's post that convinced me to revisit the debate. To put it bluntly, I have never understood why the Internet has worked so persistently to adapt TCP in support of request/reply workloads instead of standardizing an RPC transport protocol to complement TCP. Their exchange gives me a reason to revisit that question (apropos of Groundhog Day, I suppose).

Before getting to that, I want to be clear that John does not need anyone's help defending his work. His original position paper and follow-on response are clearly argued and backed by as much data as he could lay his hands on. That does not surprise me. I remember the first paper I saw his research group present. It was at the 10th SOSP, entitled "A Trace-Driven Analysis of the UNIX 4.2 BSD File System", and it is worth mentioning because two years later he came back to the 11th SOSP with Caching in the Sprite Network File System, describing a system that addressed the problems the analysis revealed. At the time (the mid-to-late 1980s), Sprite was one of a handful of distributed operating systems built around fast RPC mechanisms. Dave Cheriton's V kernel and Andy Tanenbaum's Amoeba were two others. This work happened at the same time TCP was starting to get attention, in no small part because it was released as part of UNIX 4.2 BSD. To close the loop on this story, I found Sprite's RPC mechanism to be compelling, and so adapted it to my own research on the x-Kernel. That line of research later formed the basis of the RPC Section in our textbook. I was pleased to see Sprite RPC reincarnated in the Homa protocol.

RPC is Everywhere

It was important to me to put RPC on equal footing with TCP when we wrote the first edition of our book, in part because of the central role it played in distributed computing, and in part because you didn't have to look far to find RPC-like behavior in the Internet: SMTP was a purpose-built RPC for email; SNMP was a purpose-built RPC for network management; DNS was a purpose-built RPC for name resolution; and then several years later, HTTP was introduced as purpose-built RPC for web resources. That we have since turned HTTP into the Internet's de facto RPC protocol (and then now realizing that it is suboptimal, are trying to optimize it by collapsing all the layers into the new QUIC protocol), is only a testament to how small a role technical rationale plays in what happens in industry. Or maybe it's more about NIH, in as much as the Internet and distributed systems communities were largely disjoint for many years. (I can count on one hand the people I saw at both SOSP and SIGCOMM during the years I actively attended both.)

Another explanation is that the Internet has unnecessarily coupled the transport protocol with the rest of the RPC framework. Conflating the two naturally follows from the purpose-built examples I just gave: SMTP is bundled with MIME; SNMP is bundled with MIB; and HTTP is bundled with HTML. But the idea of promoting a self-contained and general-purpose request/reply transport protocol as a peer of TCP goes back to 1988, and the (ultimately) thwarted attempt to standardize VMTP, which was based on experience with the V kernel.

But coming back to the specific question of RPC vs TCP in the datacenter, it still has me scratching my head about why it hasn't happened. The datacenter is a unique and self-contained environment. One explanation is that TCP is a chameleon protocol, or as I described it in another post, as much a platform as it is a protocol. You want individual messages instead of a byte-stream? TCP has an option for that. In contrast, RPC is natively message-oriented. You want multiple outstanding calls without head-of-line blocking? TCP can do that by opening multiple connections. In contrast, RPC protocols decouple "logical channels" from request/reply message pairs. You want congestion control? TCP can give you one version tuned for the wide-area and another version tuned for the datacenter. In contrast, perhaps the biggest contribution of Homa is to challenge the premise of TCP's flow-centric approach to congestion control for datacenter workloads. You want a low-latency network stack? Well that's a challenge TCP has a 40-year history of trying to optimize away, and when that falls short, ultimately looking to SmartNICs to solve. In contrast, RPC was designed from the start to optimize round-trip performance in low-latency networks. It's difficult for me to imagine TCP ever doing better.

Maybe it comes down to a matter of judgment. Do you prefer multiple specialized tools or a single general-purpose tool? Creating the latter is the holy grail of system design, but when you consider how dominant the request/reply message exchange is in cloud computing, I find the argument for a transport protocol optimized for that use case to be more compelling. Or said another way, maybe RPC is the general-purpose tool, and we've been stubbornly trying to adapt a niche tool for far too long, creating what my former student Sean O'Malley once called a Swiss army knife with a jacuzzi blade.

But my original question was to ask why that hasn't happened. The only answer I can come up with is that judgment often reflects biases. If you've been taught that TCP covers every use case (with UDP providing an escape hatch for the rare exceptions that might arise), then it's difficult to see a request/reply transport protocol as an equally viable alternative. The emergence of QUIC lends credibility to the latter perspective, with Homa representing a second design—one that's been optimized for the datacenter (and not limited to HTTP's five operations).

Larry Peterson, February 2023

TCP vs RPC (Redux)

Reposts of our recent TCP vs RPC article generated considerable commentary, and some of the feedback was quite helpful. (Some comments on other sites reminded us why we don't spend a lot of time reading comment threads.) The considerable interest in the topic convinced me that a follow-up post would be worth doing. I have three observations, which for your reading convenience, are filtered to exclude all ad hominem flamethrowing.

The first observation is that there has long been a "parallel universe" in which the High Performance Computing (HPC) community has created their own networking substrate—from communication hardware (Infini-Band) to end-to-end software (MPI, Active Messages)—without being overly concerned about broad interoperability (which is the hallmark of Internet technology). The goal is simple: maximize throughput and minimize latency, under the simplifying assumption that you have full control over both sides of the communication. This approach started on purpose-built multiprocessors, but as those architectures gave way to cloud-based commodity hardware, solutions like RDMA (Remote DMA) over Converged Ethernet (RoCE) started to get traction.

RDMA gives the sender (caller) the ability to directly address memory on the receiver (callee). This requires tight coupling between the two parties, as would be the case in a parallel program, but is less generally applicable when building distributed systems since (a) someone else is likely responsible for the service you're calling, and (b) you can't be sure if that service runs on the same server, another server in the same datacenter, or in a datacenter across the country. RDMA was originally included as part of InfiniBand; RoCE is a variant of that idea suitable for running over commodity ethernet. It runs on top of UDP, sacrificing performance (compared to InfiniBand) in return for supporting commodity cloud deployments.

The second observation is that there is a feature of QUIC that I had not appreciated. Christian Huitema pointed out that QUIC can be used without HTTP/3, and as a consequence, could serve as a general-purpose request/reply protocol underpinning any RPC framework. It is reassuring to see the request/reply protocol decoupled from the application domain. That's a major step forward, and caused me to wonder if it might be possible to fold some of Homa's latency optimizations into QUIC, giving Homa an alternative path to wider adoption. But I see two issues that will need to be addressed.

The first is that a claimed advantage of QUIC is that it runs in user space, and if that remains its dominant deployment scenario, it negates some of Homa's latency improvements—those that are due to being kernel-resident. While QUIC can also be implemented in the kernel (for example see the work of Peng Wang, et al), it's not clear why retrofitting Homa-inspired techniques into QUIC is an improvement over natively running Homa in the kernel. There's more to say on this topic, but I'll save it for my third observation. The second issue centers around Homa's approach to congestion control, which I consider its main contribution. Debates about congestion control seldom turn out well for the new kid on the block, but QUIC does do a good job of modularizing congestion control (particularly when it runs in user space), and so it may offer a viable deployment path.

Looking For Generality

Saving the best for last, my third observation is the consequence of an exchange between David Reed and John Ousterhout. David argued that "RPC was one big reason for creating UDP as a datagram *'process addressing' support layer"* and that *". . . argument passing and waiting for a return was way too high level for a transport protocol."* John's response was to call out the distinction between "RPC transport" and things like "argument processing [that] fit pretty naturally at the application level." These two positions are consistent with the overall framing I laid out in my original post, and worth a closer look.

On the one hand, both the End-to-End Argument and Application-Layer Framing (ALF)—two stalwart Internet design principles—point to the endpoint (with the application process being the ultimate end-point) as knowing best. On the other hand, good system design is always looking for opportunities to carve out common functionality that can be packaged as a general-purpose tool and pushed down into the underlying platform. (The e2e paper acknowledges this tension, albeit from a performance perspective.) Doing so both frees applications from having to reinvent the wheel, and perhaps more importantly, makes sure complex functionality is implemented correctly.

Let's apply that tradeoff to TCP and RPC. No one would argue that implementing a reliable byte stream service, bundled with a fair congestion control algorithm, should be left to the application. (Unless, of course, the application is real-time multimedia, which is exactly the use case that motivated ALF.) So why is an RPC transport any different? I don't see how it is: Its complexity is on par with TCP's, ensuring (enforcing) well-behaved congestion control is important, and the set of applications it supports is substantial. It's a nearly perfect example of an end-to-end networking substrate that your OS should provide. Of course an RPC transport can always be implemented on top of UDP, but the same is true of TCP.

If we weren't assuming a monolithic kernel, we might be able to have a different discussion. For example, an Exokernel would let me run Homa in my LibraryOS, TCP in your LibraryOS, and perhaps RoCE or QUIC in yet another LibraryOS. But that's not the world we live in. Someone has to decide what functionality does and does not get to run in privileged mode (and by extension, in the SmartNIC or IPU), and that decision impacts performance—especially latency—which is at the heart of the case for RPC in the datacenter. The HPC community realized this years ago, and deviated from Internet standards in response. My view of Homa is that it tries to achieve similar performance in low-latency environments, but in a more interoperable way. After 40 years, it makes sense that a second design point—a request/reply transport protocol, perhaps some variant of Homa/QUIC—sits side-by-side with TCP in the kernel.

But that's just my opinion, and I don't have a vote. What I find fascinating is questions about how systems evolve over time, and the Internet is fertile ground for such an archaeological dig (especially as it relates to the OS kernel). Given all the competition TCP/IP has faced over the years—in a battle for survival of the fittest—I now better appreciate the symbiotic role UDP played in its success. If you're going to promote a take-over-the-world substrate, pair it with a minimal side-kick as a way of avoiding discussions about alternative designs.

Larry Peterson, March 2023

Closing Remarks

Taking a close look at TCP, one of the essential building blocks of the Internet, illustrates how successfully the Internet architecture was built to support evolution. An obvious example is that fact that TCP had no congestion control in its initial design, and since the introduction of the first congestion control mechanisms in the late 1980s, it has continued to evolve and provide fertile ground for research. So the principle of "design for evolvability" gets good support from these essays.

Another aspect of the Internet's evolution that is illustrated here is how support for remote procedure call (RPC) has been developed over the decades. We were a bit outside the mainstream in 1995 when we published a networking book that covered RPC, but the intervening decades have demonstrated a recurring need for the request/response paradigm to be supported over the Internet. QUIC can be viewed as one of the latest responses to that requirement. The decision to split TCP and IP in the early design of the Internet was another great example of a decision about modularity that reflects the systems approach, leaving open the path for new transport protocols, meeting evolving requirements, to be developed in the future.

Explore Further

David Clark. The Design Philosophy of the DARPA Internet Protocols. ACM SIGCOMM, August 1988

Van Jacobson. Congestion Avoidance and Control. ACM SIGCOMM, August 1988.

Lawrence Brakmo and Larry Peterson. TCP Vegas: End-to-End Congestion Avoidance on a Global Internet. IEEE Journal on Select Articles on Communications, October 1995.

Frank Kelly. Charging and Rate Control for Elastic Traffic. European Transactions on Telecommunications, 1997.

Raj Jain, Dah Ming Chiu, and William Hawe. A Quantitative Measure of Fairness and Discrimination for Resource Allocation in Shared Computer Systems. DEC Research Report TR-301, 1984.

Ranysha Ware, *et al*. Beyond Jain's Fairness Index: Setting the Bar for the Deployment of Congestion Control Algorithms. ACM SIGCOMM HotNets, November 2019.

RFC 793. Transmission Control Protocol. September 1981.

RFC 9293. Transmission Control Protocol (TCP). August 2022.

RFC 1263. TCP Extensions Considered Harmful. October 1991.

RFC 9000. QUIC: A UDP-Based Multiplexed and Secure Transport. May 2021.

Ivan Pepelnjak. Is it Time to Replace TCP in Data Centers? ipSpace Blog, January 2023.

John Ousterhout. It's Time to Replace TCP in the Datacenter. January 2023.

Andrew Birrell and Bruce Nelson. Implementing Remote Procedure Calls. ACM Transactions on Computer Systems, February 1984.

Behnam Montazeri, Yilong Li, Mohammad Alizadeh, and John Ousterhout. Homa: A Receiver-driven Low-latency transport protocol Using Network Priorities. ACM SIGCOMM, August 2018.

RFC 1045. VMTP: Versatile Message Transaction Protocol. February 1988.

Jerome Saltzer, David Reed, and David Clark. End-to-End Arguments in System Design. ACM Transactions on Computer Systems, November 1984.

David Clark and David Tennenhouse. Architectural considerations for a new generation of protocols.. ACM SIGCOMM, September 1990.

Peng Wang, et al. Implementation and Performance Evaluation of the QUIC Protocol in the Linux Kernel. Proceeding of the 21st ACM International Conference on Modeling, Analysis, and Simulation of Wireless and Mobile Systems, October 2018.

Dawson Engler, Frans Kaashoek, and James O'Toole Jr. Exokernel: an Operating System Architecture for Application-level Resource Management. ACM Symposium on Operating System Principles, December 1995.

Bufferbloat project website.

Security: A Negative Goal

We have had some coverage of security topics in our main networking text since the first edition of 1996, although it wasn't until the second edition that we decided to elevate security to its own chapter. From the very beginning we have been a little less comfortable writing about security than most other networking topics. We mostly attribute this to the fact that some people have devoted their entire careers to becoming security experts, whereas we are definitely still amateurs in that field. But we also find ourselves wondering periodically "Is Security Different?" For example, it is often noted that security is a *negative goal*: you are trying to stop all possible avenues of attack, so you can never quite be sure that you are done. This issue of what makes security different inspired a few of the posts in this chapter.

One thing that makes security a productive area for us is that it definitely merits the "systems approach" treatment. That is, ensuring the security of networked systems requires one to consider the interactions among a large set of components in order to have some chance of achieving a reasonable outcome. There is also a substantial area of intersection between SDN (a topic that we know a fair bit about) and security, thanks largely to the work on microsegmentation that SDN enabled.

In spite of our relative lack of security expertise, we've had security on the list of topics that we could tackle in a specialized Systems Approach book for about as long as we've been writing books. We made considerable progress on that book in 2024, and reported on some of our key findings in the newsletter. The following essays give some sense of where we are heading with that book, which we aim to finish in 2025.

Learning From Our Mistakes

Lessons in Security

I recently went hiking in the Little Desert, a lovely little piece of wilderness about 4 hours drive West of Melbourne. One of my hiking companions is a big storyteller, and very well read; he seems to have an endless supply of material to pass the hours on the trail. At one point he launched into a discussion of a book he was reading on Bletchley Park, the famed home of cryptanalysts during WWII. In an effort to hold up my end of the conversation I mentioned my current work on a network security book, and made the observation that many of the ideas around cryptography and cryptanalysis developed at that time remain in use today. As you can imagine, it is non-stop fun when I go hiking!

After the hike I went back to refresh my memory on the details of the Enigma machine and the success of the Bletchley park team in decrypting its messages. It makes for fascinating reading. There are examples of known plaintext attacks and brute force attacks using parallel computation, as well as some lessons about how often to change keys and the perils of keys that are not truly random. The Enigma machine also embodies Kerckhoffs's principle from 1883—that a system should remain secure even if all the mechanism is known to an adversary but the key is not. The history of cryptography and secure communication goes way back.

One of the first news items I read on my return to civilization from the desert was an update on the hacking of a large number of Snowflake customers. As Brian Krebs reported, a man has been arrested in connection with the hacks. The article is full of interesting details, including the fact that the person in question appears to have been communicating with Krebs for some time before his arrest. But what jumped out to me was the fact (also reported previously) that this hack impacted more than 160 customers of Snowflake, all of whom chose to protect sensitive information in a cloud service using only a username and password. These companies include household names like AT&T and Ticketmaster, who apparently believed that multi-factor authentication (MFA) wasn't required for their customer data. This is rather mind-boggling to me as I try to recall the last time I accessed a sensitive corporate resource without MFA.

I think there was a time in 1990 or so when, in my first post-PhD job at Bellcore, it might have been possible to log in remotely to our systems with only username and password. Around that time, my colleagues Neil Haller and Phil Karn developed a system of one-time passwords known as S/key, which eventually became an Internet Standard. S/key was based on an idea from Lamport published in 1981 that used repeated applications of a one-way hash to generate a sequence of one-time passwords from a single long-lived secret. Unlike a password, the user's long-lived secret never leaves their machine, and is not stored on the remote server; the user's machine responds to a challenge by performing a cryptographic operation that only an entity with possession of the secret can successfully complete. Even though the architecture is different, S/key shares some of the desirable characteristics of passkeys. At some point S/key support was dropped at Bellcore and we moved to the one-time passwords provided by physical RSA tokens, but I missed S/key for its elegance and the fact that I didn't need to carry an extra device around.

In every job since I left Bellcore in 1995 I have had to use something like an RSA token as my second authentication factor, so I think it's about 30 years since I used a simple username/password to access corporate systems. That is, whenever I've tried to access something from outside the corporate firewall, I have used MFA. (See the Zero Trust essay below for why this isn't sufficient.) So I find it hard to accept that there exist modern corporations that don't enforce MFA. I mean, AT&T, the company from which Bellcore was spun out in 1984—how can they have missed the need for MFA in 2024?

In my time at VMware, the network virtualization product that I worked on, NSX, eventually became a security product, thanks to the realization that microsegmentation provided its most compelling use case. As security became a bigger part of our business, we started talking to customers about best practices in security. MFA was always mentioned in the list but hardly discussed because it didn't seem to need repeating. Of course we also pushed microsegmentation as a best practice, which was self-serving but also good advice in my view. But I am beginning to think we didn't emphasize MFA enough.

Learning Best Practices From Experts

I picked up some of my personal security "best practices" from listening to those with more security expertise than I, including my former VMware colleague Guido Appenzeller. Guido, well known for his SDN work, had founded a security startup (Voltage) before joining VMware and later would go on to a role at Yubico, maker of the Yubikey hardware tokens. (Thanks to him I have a good supply of Yubikeys around the house.) And I have to thank him for putting me onto password managers as one of the simplest and most effective ways an individual can improve their personal security. I'm an avid fan of 1password, my chosen password manager, for a variety of reasons. One feature I love is that it tells you about accounts where MFA is available and you have no second factor configured.

I hope that I am mostly preaching to the choir, since I imagine most of our readers have a better appreciation of security than the average person on the street. Given the 165+ instances of Snowflake password compromises that could have been prevented with MFA, however, I figure it is worth a bit of coverage here. I also note that getting a code sent to your phone by SMS is one of the worst ways to implement MFA, because of the relative ease of SIM hijacking. I love my Yubikeys, although support could be a lot better among the consumer-facing businesses for which I need passwords, and I try to use TOTPs (time-based one-time passwords), such as those produced by an authenticator app on a phone, in preference to SMS-delivered codes.

I try not to be too harsh on those who fail to get everything right when it comes to setting up their security systems and processes. Security is hard. My experience in writing about security suggests that it's a field best left to the experts. I introduced an error into our first edition's coverage of MD5-based authentication—it took two editions before it was pointed out to us—and I discovered last week that our coverage of keyed-hash message authentication codes (HMACs) has been wrong (or at least oversimplified to a fault) since the 4th edition (i.e., for about 15 years). At least we are catching these mistakes as we plug along on our new security book. That said, our rate of progress is limited by our need to triple-check our work for correctness given the difficulty of being certain in this field. But there is a difference between knowing how message authentication codes are calculated and recognizing that MFA is no longer an optional feature.

There is another post below entitled "Is security getting worse or better?" In some dimensions, security is improving because we now have a set of principles that have stood the test of time, and we know enough to apply them. We keep referring back to the 1975 paper by Schroeder and Saltzer, *"The Protection of Information in Computer Systems,"* which includes MFA (by another name) among its design principles. But as my AI professor said to me in 1985, there is a difference between having knowledge and using knowledge. As educators currently writing a book on security, we still have work to do.

Bruce Davie, November 2024.

Why Security is Different (or is it?)

More Thoughts on How to Write About Security

Inspired by Bruce's musings on our struggles to write clearly about network security, I started to ask myself what, if anything, is unique about security as a systems topic. We're the first to admit that our initial efforts to cover security weren't as "systems approach" as our other writing. Is there something about security that explains our challenges? Or, to put it another way, is there anything about security that makes it fundamentally different from scalability, availability, or any other design requirement when we talk about large systems such as the Internet?

One refrain you often hear is that security must be built in from the ground floor; that retrofitting security to an existing system is the source of design complications, or worse, outright flawed designs. While it is the case that the early Internet was largely silent on the question of security (as Vint Cerf, Dave Clark, and others have explained), I suspect "retrofitting" is often used pejoratively. Certainly there have been convoluted (and short-sighted) attempts to improve security—especially when we wrote the first version of our security chapter—but the Internet has also evolved to include a sound architecture for securing end-to-end communication. Focusing on stopgap mechanisms is never a good recipe for understanding the underlying principles, no matter what aspect of a system one is talking about.

In a similar vein, it is worth remembering that the early Internet came up significantly short on other requirements. On scalability, for example, it was originally assumed that all host-to-address bindings could be managed using a centralized hosts.txt file that every system admin had to download once a week, and EGP assumed a simple, loop-free "catenet" model of inter-network routes. These, and similar limitations, were corrected over time, for example, with DNS and BGP, respectively. And today it is straightforward to explain the system design techniques—e.g., aggregation and hierarchy—that were then applied. The question to ask is: what are the analogs for security?

This example highlights a second straw-man that I will set up and then knock down: That security is uniquely hard because you have to get it right over and over again, at every layer of the system. Of course the same is true of every other system requirement. There's no such thing as getting scalability or availability right in just one place, and then you're done. You have to make sure your system scales and survives failure at every layer and in every component. It takes only one bottleneck or single point of failure to defeat the system. Security has introduced the idea of Defense-in-Depth (DiD) to capture this idea. DiD says (in part) that you need to build multiple, possibly overlapping defenses, but this is essentially what someone building a reliable system has to do as well. (DiD has other implications, which I'll return to in a moment.)

This suggests the next possibility, which is that security is harder because we've set it up as an absolute requirement under all conditions, whereas we sometimes cut ourselves some slack on scalability and availability. For example, we may allow for an upper bound in the workload we expect to serve (e.g., 2x the last flash crowd event) or the unlikely failure scenarios that we can safely ignore (e.g., a transatlantic cable cut). In contrast, we assume an adversary always finds the weakest link and exploits it, so there must be no weak links. But cost/risk calculations are exactly the same in all three cases: for security, you decide what parts of the system to trust, what threats you understand, what resources your adversaries can bring to their side, and what resources you are able to spend defending against those threats. My takeaway is that for all systems topics, but especially security, the starting point has to be a clear articulation of requirements and assumptions.

A Negative Goal

This brings me back to the idea of DiD, which is broader than just saying all layers/components of the system must be secured. It also implies that any single defense might be penetrated, but it will be hard to penetrate all of them. Saltzer and Kaashoek make this point succinctly when they talk about security being a negative goal, the point being that it is extremely difficult to prove something cannot happen. Building highly available systems has a similar negative goal, but somehow security feels qualitatively different. Perhaps because we know our adversaries are actively plotting against us, whereas our hardware fails passively (except, of course, when it doesn't, pointing to the fuzzy line between security and availability).

Another seemingly unique aspect of security is the centrality of cryptographic algorithms. My initial (and by no means exhaustive) survey suggests that many books and courses explain security through the lens of cryptography. This is understandable, because without these algorithms we could not build the secure systems we have today. But cryptography is a means, not an end. It is a necessary building block, but you still need to construct end-to-end systems around those building blocks, which depends on many other components (and assumed technologies) as well. Get the overall architecture wrong, and even the most powerful cryptographic algorithms provide no value. From the systems perspective, the key is to abstract the algorithm in such a way that you can then design a system that builds upon it.

This is a familiar theme. In our work to bring a systems perspective to 5G, I found that the lion's share of attention in standard treatments of 5G is placed on the coding algorithm and underlying information theory (e.g., OFDMA), with the rationale for the architecture of the communication system built around that algorithm often lacking. Other complex algorithms show up in large systems (e.g., Paxos for consistency, weighted fair queueing for packet scheduling, and so on), but those algorithms only work when the overall system has been factored into the right set of interdependent components. Get the factoring wrong, and you've unnecessarily coupled policy and mechanism, baked in unnecessary assumptions, or in some way limited how your system can evolve over time. That's not to say today's security systems are poorly designed, but in describing those systems, em-

140

phasis should also be put on the design that is able to take advantage of the algorithms.

Exploring these possible reasons why security might be unique has served to identify four criteria for how we ought to talk about security: (1) understand the rationale for individual mechanisms, and not just their current implementation choices; (2) recognize that systems evolve, and sometimes in the middle of that evolution it's difficult to see the forest (architecture) for the trees (today's mechanisms); (3) be as thorough and detailed as possible about requirements and assumptions a system makes, along with the risks that follow; and (4) decompose the system into its elemental components and explain how they all work together in an end-to-end way. These last two points seem to be the key: being explicit about assumptions is essential for coping with a negative goal, and once you've done that, separating concerns and requirements, unbundling features, and teasing apart related concepts is the cornerstone of the systems approach. This seems especially relevant to security, where I am still searching for the clarity that should be possible.

Larry Peterson, February 2024.

Security is an Architectural Issue

I've been interested in architecture—of the physical building variety, as distinct from computer or network architecture—for as long as I can remember. So I was pretty excited when I got to work in a Frank Gehry-designed building at MIT in the late 2000s. As it turns out, the building is something of a case study in the perils of high-profile architecture, with a litany of defects including mold, ice falling on passers-by from the roof, and a conference room that made people (including both me and Frank Gehry) sea-sick. While MIT eventually settled a lawsuit against Gehry and the builders, it was never entirely clear how many of the issues were a matter of design versus implementation. But it was pretty clear that architectural decisions have significant implications for those who have to live with them.

Which brings us to the Internet and its architectural shortcomings. While the Internet has been hugely successful in almost every dimension, even

No Ice Falling Off the Stata Center

those most closely associated with it have pointed out that it lacked a solid architectural foundation on the matter of security. Vint Cerf, for example, argued that the Internet's original architecture had two basic flaws: too little address space, and no security. David Clark, the "architect of the Internet", suggested that how we apply the principle known as the "end-to-end argument" to the Internet should be rethought in the light of what we now know about security and trust (among other things).

To paraphrase the concerns raised by Internet pioneers, the Internet has done really well at connecting billions of people and devices (now that the address space issues are dealt with in various ways), but it remains quite flawed in terms of security. The original design goal of making it easy for a distributed set of researchers to share access to a modest number of computers didn't require much security. The users mostly trusted each other, and security could be managed on end-systems rather than being a feature of the network. In 1988, the Morris Worm famously illustrated the limitations of depending on end-system security alone. So today we have an architecture where the default is that every device can talk to every other device, and any time we want to enforce some other behavior, we need to take some specific action—like inserting a firewall and explicitly blocking all traffic except some specified subset. And that approach of adding point fixes, like firewalls, has led to a proliferation of security devices and technologies, none of which really changes the architecture, but which does increase the overall complexity of managing networks.

A few significant developments in the last decade give me reason to think there may be cause for optimism. One is the emergence of "zero trust" approaches to security, which pretty much inverts the original security approach of the Internet. The term was coined at Forrester in 2009 and can be thought of as a corollary to the principle of least privilege laid out by Saltzer and Schroeder in 1975:

> *Every program and every user of the system should operate using the least set of privileges necessary to complete the job.*

Rather than letting every device talk to every other device, zero trust starts from the assumption that no device should be trusted a priori, but only after some amount of authentication does it get access to a precisely scoped set of resources—just the ones necessary to complete the job.

Zero trust implies that you can no longer establish a perimeter firewall and let everything inside that perimeter have unfettered access to everything else. This idea has been adopted by approaches such as Google's Beyond Corp in which there is no concept of a perimeter, but every system access is controlled by strict authentication and authorization procedures. From my perspective, the ability to enforce zero trust has also been one of the major benefits of software-defined networking (SDN) and network virtualization.

In the early days of network virtualization, my Nicira colleagues had a vision that everything in networking could eventually be virtualized. At the time I joined the team, the Nicira product had just virtualized layer 2 switching and layer 3 routing was about to ship. It took a little while after the VMware acquisition of Nicira for us to make our way up to layer 4 with the distributed firewall, and in my mind that was the critical step to making a meaningful impact on security. Now, rather than putting a firewall at some choke point and forcing traffic to pass through it, we could specify a precise set of policies about which devices (typically virtual machines in those days) could communicate with each other and how. Rather than operate with "zones" in which lots of devices that didn't need access to each other nevertheless could communicate, it was now a relatively simple matter to specify precise and fine-grained security policies regarding how devices should communicate.

A similar story played out with SD-WAN. There are lots of reasons SD-WAN found a market, but one of them was that you no longer had to backhaul traffic from branch offices to some central firewall to apply your security policy. Instead you could specify the security policy centrally but implement it out at the branches—a significant win as more and more traffic headed for cloud services rather than centralized servers in a corporate data center.

This paradigm of specifying policy centrally and having software systems that implement it in a distributed manner also applies to securing modern, distributed applications. Service meshes are an emerging technology that applies this paradigm, and a topic that we go deeper on in the SDN chapter.

So while it is too early to declare success on the security front, I do think there are reasons for optimism. We don't just have an ever-expanding set of point fixes to an architectural issue. We actually have some solid architectural principles (least privilege, zero trust) and significant technological advances (SDN, intent-based networking, etc.) that are helping to reshape the landscape of security.

I'm indebted to my former VMware colleague Tom Corn for inspiring much of the thinking that went into this post. An example of his work is listed below.

Bruce Davie, April 2021.

Security and the Internet Hourglass

Early in 2024 we assembled the founders of Systems Approach for an offsite lunch in Tucson and talked about our plans for a security book. Whereas a topic such as software-defined networking comes naturally to us—we both worked on the development of SDN systems for close to a decade—security is proving to be more of a challenge. It's a notoriously complex field, and our involvement has always been more peripheral. That said, we have learned something about network security since we first started covering that topic in our textbook in the 1990s. And the way we think about security today has a lot to do with how the architecture of the Internet has evolved, which provided the inspiration for this post.

In reading Larry's recent comments about the Internet Hourglass, I was struck by the observation that the decision to build a network architecture without any security features is an example of late binding—delaying complex decisions and features until late in the design process. It's common to look back at the lack of security as an "obvious" flaw in the Internet architecture, and you can find quotes from luminaries such as Vint Cerf and David Clark to back up that thinking. But it is going too far to suggest that security was just overlooked. Cerf commented that, while hindsight might suggest that security should have been given more attention, "getting this thing to work at all was non-trivial". And Clark was very much aware of security issues, saying "it's not that we didn't think about security... we thought we could exclude [untrustworthy people]." This seems eminently reasonable to me when you consider that the initial remit of the ARPANET was to interconnect a few dozen computers, all of which sat in research labs accessed by relatively limited groups of people. Of course, this perspective became untenable because of the Internet's enormous success in connecting first millions and then billions of users.

Prior to his work on the Internet, Clark was involved in the development of the Multics operating system, one of the most heavily scrutinized systems from a security perspective. I was absolutely fascinated by a retrospective article about the security of Multics, published in 2002, almost 30 years after a vulnerability analysis of the operating system was conducted by the US Air Force. It's worth reading the article in its entirety, but one takeaway from the audit was that Multics, in spite of being the most secure operating system of its day, was not considered secure enough for use in an "open" environment, i.e., one in which anyone could run code on it. Yet today's operating systems are run in just such an open environment, and it's hard to argue they are more secure than Multics. They are certainly more complex (the 2002 paper makes this case by comparing SELinux with Multics). The Multics authors argued for a more secure follow-on version of the OS, but that work ultimately did not proceed.

This foray into the ancient history of operating systems security was prompted by the efforts to frame our discussion of network security for the upcoming book. The way Larry and I came to think about network security was in the context of how it was being introduced to the Internet in the 1990s. As I wrote previously, looking at a series of mechanisms as they were proposed for inclusion in the RFCs defining Internet standards led to a rather piecemeal view of security. As I aim to take a more "systems approach" view of security, I have found that looking at operating systems security is particularly helpful. The end systems that the Internet connects have always been part of the security landscape, and the early focus on end-system security, of which the Multics work is just one example, reminds us of the importance of taking an end-to-end view of security. The famous end-to-end paper makes the similar point that end systems must be involved in functions such as encryption and authentication if the requirements of applications are to be fully met.

Securing the Whole System

It is clear to me that we'd be in a much better position today if the advice of the Multics team to invest in OS security had been taken more seriously. Operating system security is hard, and it's much harder if you are trying to fix deficiencies in a system that was never designed to be secure in the first place. I recall that, as a networking person in the 1990s, OS security seemed out of scope: as long as we could get end-to-end encryption and authentication designed and deployed, we'd have a secure network: problem solved. But it's the nature of the systems approach that you don't stop when you have optimized a single part of the system: you have to look at the entire system, which in this case includes the hosts, both hardware and software.

This "whole system" view is common across our Systems Approach books, and will be central to the new one.

The importance of end-system security to the Internet was made painfully apparent by the Morris Worm, one of the first widespread examples of Internet malware. It was the presence of multiple weaknesses in a common host operating system, coupled with the default "accept any packet" posture of the Internet itself, that enabled it to spread (with a bug in the worm code itself greatly exacerbating the impact).

Clearly a book on network security needs to cover topics such as encryption, authentication, and message integrity. As soon as you start sending packets over a highly decentralized network such as the Internet, you need to be concerned about sensitive information being read by unintended recipients (hence the need for encryption) or modified in flight (hence message integrity and authentication). But these are just some of the building blocks of secure systems, and ultimately our book needs to cover not only the building blocks but also the systems principles that can be applied to building such systems.

Today there are constant reminders that "perfect" security is not possible, and this needs to be part of our thinking when developing an approach to system security. The xz backdoor has highlighted just how much we depend on code from a wide range of sources that are not entirely trustworthy. The "GoFetch" attack on Apple silicon, which leverages microarchitectural features of recent CPUs, is an example of how a cascading set of weaknesses can be exploited by an attacker, and illustrates the challenges in making end systems that are truly robust in open environments—just as stated by the Multics authors decades ago.

It is tempting to throw up one's hands in the face of these sophisticated attacks, but they do reinforce the importance of various principles of system design, such as least privilege, and the importance of reducing the size of the components that we need to trust. I've written previously about the application of the principle of least privilege to networking (using network virtualization). "Design for iteration" is another principle (described by Kaashoek and Saltzer) that remains timely: assume that you will get things wrong and that you will need to iterate as you find the flaws. In a sense, the narrow waist design of the Internet followed similar principles: keeping the functionality of the ubiquitous IP layer as small as possible, and facilitating iterative development of other functions such as reliability and end-to-end encryption. As we continue to work towards a more secure Internet, our best hope is to apply the systems principles developed over many decades. These principles don't stop at the network boundary, but apply to end systems as well. Identifying and describing these principles, and showing how they apply in the networking context, is the central task for our new book.

Bruce Davie, April 2024.

Is Zero Trust Living Up to Expectations?

A topic that seems to keep coming up in our work is the importance of security for APIs. In particular, I hear the term "zero trust" increasingly being applied to APIs, which led to the idea for this post. At the same time, I've also noticed what might be called a zero trust backlash, as it becomes apparent that you can't wave a zero trust wand and instantly solve all your security concerns.

Zero trust has been on my radar for almost a decade, as it was part of the environment that enabled Network Virtualization to take off. We've told that story briefly in our SDN book—the rise of microsegmentation as a widespread use-case was arguably the critical step that took network virtualization from a niche technology to the mainstream. In fact the term goes back at least to 2009 when it was coined by Forrester analyst John Kindervag and it is possible to draw a line back from there to the principle of least privilege as framed by Saltzer and Schroeder in 1975. As noted above, that principle states:

> *Every program and every user of the system should operate using the least set of privileges necessary to complete the job.*

Whereas the Internet was designed following another of Saltzer's principles—the end-to-end argument, which he formulated with David Clark and David Reed—least privilege didn't really make it into the Internet architecture. In fact, as David Clark pointed out some 20 years after the end-to-end paper, he and his co-authors assumed that end-systems were willing participants in achieving correct behavior, an assumption that no longer holds true. Whereas the goal of the early Internet was to interconnect a handful of computing systems running in research labs around the U.S. (initially), a substantial subset of the end-systems connected to the Internet today are actively trying to harm other systems—inserting malware, launching DoS attacks, extracting sensitive information, and so on. The last 20+ years of networking have seen an ever-expanding set of attempts to deal with the lack of security in the original Internet.

For me, the easiest way to conceptualize zero trust is by considering what it is not. Perimeter-based security (as provided by perimeter firewalls for example) is a good counterexample. The idea of a firewall is that there is an inside and an outside, with systems on the inside being "trusted" and those outside being "untrusted". This division of the world into trusted and untrusted regions fails both the principle of least privilege and the definition of zero trust. Traditionally, a device on the inside of a firewall is trusted to access lots of other devices that are also inside just by virtue of its location. That is a lot more privilege than needed to do its job, and contrary to this description of zero trust provided by NIST:

> Zero trust... became the term used to describe various cybersecurity solutions that moved security away from implied trust based on network location and instead focused on evaluating trust on a per-transaction basis.

(As someone who has been involved in plenty of documents produced by committees, I have to say that the NIST Zero Trust Architecture is remarkably clear and well written.)

VPNs are another example of an approach to security that fails to meet this definition, because, even though modern VPN technology lets you connect to a corporate network from anywhere, it still creates the sense of an inside that is trusted and an outside that is not. The Colonial pipeline ransomware attack is an example of a compromise of a VPN with dire consequences because of the broad range of systems that were reachable once the attacker was "inside" the VPN.

Narrow And Specific Trust

My theory about the occasional backlash that I've seen around zero trust has two parts. First, the name is an oversimplification of what's going on. It's not that you literally trust nothing. But rather, trust is not assumed just because of a device's (or user's) location, and nor does an entity gain wide access to resources just because it was able to authenticate itself for a single purpose. So "zero-trust" might be better termed "narrow and specific trust after authentication" but that's not very catchy.

Second, there is a lot of work to be done to actually implement zero trust comprehensively. So while a vendor might say "my product/solution lets you implement zero trust", the reality is that there are a lot of moving parts to a comprehensive zero trust implementation, which is unlikely to be solved by one or two products.

When we were developing microsegmentation as part of our network virtualization solution at VMware, we were quick to point out that it helped with zero trust implementation by allowing fine-grained firewalling of east-west traffic. Distributed firewalls enabled us to move beyond zone-based trust (as provided by traditional firewalls) to an approach where an operator could specify precise rules for communication between any pair of virtual machines (VMs), and the default could be that no VM could communicate with any other VM. That default, applied to VMs even if they sat in the same zone (relative to traditional firewalls), was what enabled us to claim a "zero trust" approach. While that was quite a breakthrough in 2014, the granularity of control is limited by what is visible to the distributed firewall, and so it doesn't really achieve the "per-transaction" evaluation of trust described above. If communication between applications is encrypted (as it should be in many if not most cases) then the granularity at which the firewall would have to operate is the TCP port, with no deeper visibility into the type of transactions happening.

Which brings us to securing APIs. As we discussed in our earlier post, the unit of infrastructure is no longer the server or the VM but the service (or microservice) and so the API to the service becomes the point of security enforcement. This is why we see things like API Gateways and service meshes becoming increasingly important: we need new classes of tools to manage the security of APIs, providing fine-grained control over exactly which API requests can be executed by whom. This is further discussed in the Software-Defined Networking chapter.

A final observation is that we are now reaping the rewards of the SDN architectural approach that combines central control with distributed data planes. Like many networking people of a certain era, I grew up learning that the end-to-end argument was the basis for all good architecture, and I was unimpressed with the rise of firewalls and other "middle-boxes" because they clearly didn't adhere to the end-to-end principle. But over time I came to realize that firewalls were appealing because they offered a central point of control, and that was important for those operators who needed to secure the network after the fact. What we saw with the rise of distributed firewalling, and SDN more broadly, was that we could have centralized control (with the benefits that provides for operators) and a distributed implementation that pushed the necessary security functions closer to the end points, where they were more effective. Service meshes are the next step in that journey: effectively SDN for a world where APIs are the primary form of communication.

Bruce Davie, June 2022.

Can Passkeys Replace Passwords?

As part of our work on the forthcoming book *"Network Security: A Systems Approach"* I have been playing around with Passkeys, or as they are formally known, discoverable credentials. Passkeys are defined in the Web Authentication (WebAuthn) specification of the W3C (World Wide Web Consortium). This work evolved from several prior efforts including those of the FIDO alliance (FIDO = Fast Identity Online).

My quick take on passkeys is that they are a good idea and if we could convince the world to use them instead of passwords we would all be much better off. Phishing in particular should take a big hit if they are widely adopted. But I fear that this isn't likely to happen, for reasons that I will explain in a moment. In the perennial quest to create more secure systems that are also user-friendly, some significant implementation issues are apparent. My experience reinforces my belief that a systems view of security is necessary and user interactions with the system must be carefully thought through.

The basic idea behind passkeys is straightforward enough: a user (or more likely, a device owned by the user) creates a private/public key pair specifically for a single web site and provides the public key to the site.

The user proves their identity to the web site using some other method such as a previously established user name and password, maybe some other factors as well. The web site stores the public key for subsequent use. The next time the user wants to authenticate to the web site, the site issues a challenge to the user, who uses the locally stored private key to sign their response to the challenge. The web site uses the stored public key to authenticate the user.

Public Key Cryptography: This Time For Sure

Passkeys, in other words, replace passwords with public key cryptography. Because the user's private key never leaves their device it should be much harder for a phishing attack to succeed. Phishing normally relies on getting a user to divulge their password by entering it into a bogus site. (Sophisticated attacks sometimes get users to divulge their second factor, such as a one-time code from their phone, as well.) Passkeys, as well as remaining local to the user's device, are unique to a particular site—implementations verify a certificate from the designated site before the relevant private key is used to respond to a challenge. So you can't accidentally use a passkey on a bogus site. Similarly, the problems of password reuse across sites are avoided. Password reuse often means that a breach on one site can be used to gain access on others. None of that with passkeys.

There remain a few weaknesses. The process is bootstrapped by getting the user to authenticate using a traditional approach (such as user name and password) which remains open to traditional attacks. One way to mitigate this is to require multi-factor authentication (MFA)—and there are better options than one-time codes sent over SMS, which I will get to. There is no getting away from the fact that public keys always need some sort of bootstrap process. (Remember PGP key-signing parties?) But if a website adopts passkeys without disallowing subsequent login attempts by password, then the system remains roughly as vulnerable to phishing attacks as it was before. A savvy user might detect that they are being phished if they are suddenly being asked for passwords after using passkeys for a long time, but any time we rely on the judgment of users to detect security attacks we are bound for disappointment. It bothers me to read blog posts from seemingly credible sources that don't address the fact that passkeys are being added in addition to passwords but not (yet) replacing them. Maybe the time will come when passwords are the exception, but I see no way to get there on the current trajectory.

There are two broad categories of passkey implementation. One approach binds the key to a specific piece of hardware, such as a USB key (e.g., Yubikey). Or a passkey might be stored on a mobile phone and require biometric authentication (e.g., facial recognition) before the passkey can be accessed.

The second class of passkey implementation allows the credentials to be copied among multiple devices, typically using some sort of password manager to keep the credentials secure and synchronized across devices. In this case, the private/public key pair is stored in the password manager and then is made available to the user across different devices (laptops, mobile phones, etc.) when they need the passkey.

Hardware tokens make phishing attacks almost impossible (if they replace passwords, see above), since the only way to get access to the user's credential is to have physical access to the key. A password manager, on the other hand, is a piece of software that normally has some cloud service behind it to handle synchronization across devices. If an attacker manages to get access to the credentials necessary to log in to the cloud service, then they have access to the passkeys stored within it. For this reason (among others) password managers are generally secured with some sort of multi-factor authentication. One of those factors might be biometric, or even a hardware token.

As an aside, I would note that there is considerable variation in the security of different password manager implementations. Lastpass, for example, apparently made some poor design decisions that meant a breach was much more serious than it needed to be. By contrast, 1password's description of system security suggests that the only way the passwords (or passkeys) in their password manager can be accessed by anyone is if they have access to all your authentication factors (which in my case includes a hardware token).

My last concern about passkeys is that the implementation seems to have failed the "make it easy for users" test, which in my view is the whole point of passkeys. I have been using public key cryptography for 30+ years. (My first boss insisted his managers use PGP to encrypt emails containing sensitive information about employees—ah, those were the days.) Surely the reason for yet another technology based on public key cryptography is to simplify its use. If I find passkeys confusing to use, it doesn't bode well for more typical users. Let me walk through an example.

Competing For Attention

I decided to try to add a passkey to my WordPress.com account. So I log in using my existing password and second factor (a hardware token). I navigate to the security page; there is no mention of passkeys, so I click "2-factor authentication" then "add a security key". OK, I'm not going to replace a password with a passkey here; instead I am going to add a security key as a second factor. And for the sake of this example, let's say I want to store it on my Yubikey. When I click "add key", three different bits of software compete for my attention. First up is the password manager, offering to store a passkey. (This is the first time passkeys have shown up in this process—you can begin to see how a casual user might be getting confused.) I don't want the password manager to be involved in this case, so I dismiss the window. Next up, a window appears from MacOS asking me if I would like to use TouchID to "sign in" (to what?—I am already signed in to the website) and to save a passkey. Again note the different terminology. When I dismiss that window it is time for the browser to have a go, offering me four (!) ways to save a passkey, including (finally) the option to store it on the hardware token. I insert the USB key and proceed.

I think we can all agree that this is a confusing experience, with three different systems fighting to be the One True Place To Store Passkeys, along with the inconsistency of terminology (passkeys or security keys) and use cases (password replacement or strong second factor?). It's like every piece of software wants to "help" but there is no-one looking at the system-level behavior where these different bits of software interact with each other and the end user. I've encouraged my wife (a social scientist not a computer scientist) to adopt a password manager and 2FA, and she's very willing to follow my lead, but the confusion of terminology and bewildering arrays of options frequently (and understandably) leads to complete frustration on her part.

There is a longstanding tradeoff between security and usability. It's important to take a systems approach to security and that should, I believe, include viewing the user as part of the system. If you can't make a security technology sufficiently easy for users, then it's unlikely to provide good security.

Passkeys and the WebAuthn specification were intended to make public key cryptography accessible to average users, rather than just the domain of the tech-savvy. If done right, they could seriously improve security on the Web. There is a well-defined API to allow a broad choice of authentication devices (such as FIDO keys or password managers) to manage the creation and use of private/public key pairs. But unless things get a lot more consistent and smooth for the end user, I fear this will end up just like PGP or client certificates in TLS: a technically valid solution that has minimal impact on the majority of users.

Bruce Davie, October 2024.

Is Security Getting Worse or Better?

Working on a book about network security has led to us paying a lot more attention to reports on the latest security breaches. It's easy to assume that the situation is only getting worse since we see so many stories of attacks. But a recent article from The Economist suggests that, in economic terms, the worst days of cyber-attacks might be behind us. There is probably no simple way to resolve this question but our recent focus on security principles and technologies has led us to have a degree of optimism.

Security breaches are now a standard risk of connecting any system to the Internet, and it is rare for a week to go by without news of some new attack. Verizon conducts an annual review of the state of cyber-attacks; in 2024 they reached a milestone with over 10,000 incidents, such as ransomware and phishing attacks, covered in the report. Measured by number of attacks then, it seems that things are getting worse. By contrast, The Economist argues that, in terms of economic damage, the worst era for attacks was 2003—2004 by a large margin.

There are certainly some respects in which security is improving. This can be attributed both to greater awareness of the need for strong security whenever important information is being handled, and the development of new techniques that enable better security practices.

In the process of researching material for our new book on network security, we've been looking at a number of classic old papers on systems security. One of our favorites is *"The Protection of Information in Computer Systems"* by Saltzer and Schroeder (1975). It lays out a number of general principles of system security, such as least privilege, open design, and fail-safe defaults. Interestingly, the way they describe fail-safe defaults is almost the exact opposite of how the Internet was designed: whereas Saltzer and Schroeder argue that the correct approach is where "the default situation is lack of access", the default in the Internet has long been that any device could send packets to any other device. Any restriction of access was initially implemented in the end-system (which follows another important systems design principle, the end-to-end argument). Firewalls came later and only presented barriers to communication at specific choke points (e.g., the ingress/egress of a corporate network).

One thing that I find encouraging is that the principles outlined in 1975 are much closer to being followed today than they were when the Internet was first designed. In part that is because we've come to realize that network security can't just be left to the end systems (as the Morris Worm demonstrated) and in part it is because new technological developments have made it much easier to follow some of the Saltzer and Schroeder principles.

Better Security Technology

One example of a technology development that improved security implementations is software-defined networking (SDN). SDN enabled the approach to providing isolation among systems known as microsegmentation. We noted above that this was a way to bring least privilege to networking. And it also supports the implementation of fail-safe defaults.

Microsegmentation stands in contrast to traditional approaches to segmenting networks, in which large sets of machines are placed in a "zone" and firewalls filter traffic passing between zones. While this makes for relatively simple network configuration, it means that lots of machines are in the same zone even if there is no need for them to communicate. Furthermore, the complexity of firewall rules grows over time as more and more rules need to be added to describe the traffic allowed to pass from one zone to another.

By contrast, SDN allows for the creation of precisely defined virtual networks—microsegments—that determine both which machines can communicate with each other and how they can do so. For example, a three-tier application can have its own microsegmentation policy which states: machines in the web-facing tier of the application can talk to the machines in the application tier on some set of specified ports, but web-facing machines may not talk to each other. This is a policy that was difficult to implement in the pre-SDN era; instead all the web-facing machines would sit on the same network segment, free to communicate with each other.

The complexity of configuring segments was the reason that machines from many applications would often sit on the same segment, creating opportunities for an attack to spread from one application to another. The lateral movement of attacks within datacenters has been well documented as a key strategy of successful cyberattacks over many years.

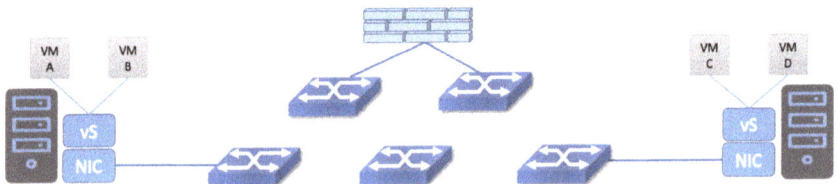

A Conventional (Not Distributed) Firewall

The situation in the above figure, taken from our SDN book, shows the main idea. Suppose that we wanted to put VM A and VM B in different segments and apply a firewall rule for traffic going from VM A to VM B. We have to prevent VM A from sending traffic directly to VM B. To do this, would have to configure two VLANs in the physical network, connect A to one of them, and B to the other, and then configure the routing such that the path from the first VLAN to the second passed through the firewall. If at some point VM A was moved to another server, we'd then have to make sure the appropriate VLAN reached that server, connect VM A to it, and ensure that the routing configuration was still forcing traffic through the firewall. This situation may seem a little contrived, but it demonstrates why microsegmentation was generally too challenging to implement before the arrival of SDN. By contrast, SDN allows the firewall function to be implemented in each virtual switch (vS in the figure). Thus, traffic from VM A to VM B passes through the firewall inside the vswitch without any special routing configuration. It is the job of the SDN controller to create the appropriate firewall rule to enforce the desired isolation between VM A and VM B (and deal with movements of VM A and VM B if they occur). There is no magic, but SDN, with a central controller pushing policies to distributed vswitches, gave us a new tool to make a finer degree of isolation much easier to manage.

The development of microsegmentation over the last decade was one of the major drivers of SDN adoption in the enterprise. It became the basis for a best practice in security known as "zero-trust" networking. Zero trust means that, as much as possible, every system in the network is assumed to be untrusted, and hence should be isolated from all other systems aside from precisely those systems it needs access to in order to do its assigned job. It is a form of least privilege for networking.

The importance of the Internet in the running of critical systems and as the underpinning for much of the world's commerce has made it an attractive target for hackers. At the same time it drives home the need to develop and adopt best practices such as zero-trust networking. When we read of breaches today, it is often the case that some best practice has not been followed. For example, there appears to have been a comprehensive effort to attack customers of Snowflake who failed to use multi-factor authentication (MFA) on their accounts. (The defense-in-depth principle certainly argues in favor of MFA). The Verizon data breach report noted below provides some helpful analysis of the common issues that lead to breaches.

Another issue that we have noticed repeatedly in our research for the new book is the fact that "security is a negative goal". That is one reason it is nearly impossible to declare success: we can only be confident that we prevented the attacks we knew about, while a new vector for attack may be just around the corner. But the security principles that have been developed since the 1970s still apply, and at least we have more awareness of them and better techniques to apply them now than we did in the early days of the Internet.

Bruce Davie, June 2024.

───────────────────────

Closing Remarks

It is often said of network security that an attacker only needs to be right once but defenses need to be correct 100% of the time. With security having been added to the Internet piece-by-piece rather than "baked in" from the beginning, it can be tempting to view security as a never-ending set of point solutions striving to plug all the holes but lacking a coherence architecture. However, our efforts to take the systems approach to security as we develop a new book have shown that there are architectural principles to draw on, and the adoption of such principles is improving the state of network security.

The early work of Saltzer and Schroeder on establishing principles of information security has held up extremely well, with ideas such as "least privilege" continuing to find application today. And advances in networking technology such as SDN and network virtualization have eased that task of applying those principles to the modern Internet in spite of the lack of built-in security in the original Internet architecture. Similarly, the success of the Web as the dominant Internet application platform has enabled the widespread roll-out of well-known technologies such as public-key cryptography, even if (as in the case of passkeys) implementation and usability issues sometimes hamper adoption.

One of the central challenges in dealing with security is the sense that one can never declare success. With security being a negative goal, we can only say that no weaknesses in our defenses have been found *so far*, not that none exist. While this is sometimes cited as something that makes security unique, we note that similar issues arise for other system properties such as availability, and it precisely because of the difficulty of plugging all the gaps in our defenses that principles such as "defense in depth" are so important.

Explore Further

Jerome Saltzer and Michael Schroeder. The Protection of Information in Computer Systems. In Proceedings of the IEEE, 1975.

Jerome Saltzer and Frans Kaashoek. Principles of Computer System Design: An Introduction. Chapter 11. Morgan Kaufmann Publishers, 2009.

Sue Halpern. Weaponizing the Web.. The New York Review of Books, April 2021.

Tom Corn. Intrinsic Security. VMworld, 2019.

Paul Karger and Roger Schell. Thirty Years Later: Lessons from the Multics Security Evaluation. ASCAC, 2002.

Scott Rose, et al. Zero Trust Architecture. NIST, August 2020.

Dan Goodin. Passkey technology is elegant, but it's most definitely not usable security. Ars Technica, December 2024.

Unexpectedly, the cost of big cyber-attacks is falling. The Economist, May 17 2024.

2024 Data Breach Report. Verizon, 2024.

5G: Comparative Architecture

We have been arguing—in both our books and our newsletter—that 5G represents a transformative change in mobile cellular networks. It goes beyond simply providing higher bandwidth rates, to also embracing a cloud native design. This is being done in large part to position the mobile network to offer more than just a broadband connectivity service. But the result is to put the mobile network on an "architectural collision course" with the Internet, which serves as the networking substrate for today's cloud.

The "collision" part of this claim is rooted in the fact that the mobile cellular network and the Internet represent two completely independent networking architectures that evolved in parallel over the last 40 years. The Internet treated the mobile network as "yet another access network" and the global cellular network treated the Internet as "yet another backbone", with business interests ensuring there was virtually no visibility across this boundary. With 5G, that boundary is being erased, or said another way, the mobile network is being consumed by the cloud.

Three-Letter Acronyms (TLAs) Galore

We expect readers with a technical background will be familiar with the challenge of wading through acronym-filled prose. But for those (like us) familiar with Internet terminology, venturing into the parallel universe of the Mobile Cellular Network introduces a whole new level of jargon. You'll need to read our 5G book to parse all of it, but for the purpose of this book, it's enough to understand who is defining all those acronyms. There are two standards organizations of note, which is interesting in its own right.

The first is 3GPP, the original standards body that was created to de-

> *fine 3G; the PP in 3GPP stands for "Partnership Project" indicating that it represents seven existing telecom organizations (each with its own four-letter acronym). While "3G" stood for third generation, 3GPP continues to standardize current generations of mobile technology such as 5G and 6G. Through the years, 3GPP has become dominated by a handful of vendors, most notably Nokia, Ericsson, and Huawei. This has resulted in vendor lock-in, making it difficult for Mobile Network Operators (MNOs) to change suppliers, but at a more fundamental level, to even steer the direction of the technology. In response to this situation, two of the biggest operators—AT&T and China Mobile—created the Open RAN Alliance (O-RAN) to define open interfaces and open source software for the Radio Access Network. In many ways, this was seen as an attempt to bring SDN to the RAN. Whether this effort will be successful is still an open question.*

As students of network architecture, this collision offers a unique opportunity to compare two different approaches to providing global connectivity. However, we can't claim to be 100% neutral in this comparative analysis: one architecture adheres to the system design principles we highlight in our Systems Approach writing, and the other grew out of the telephony ecosystem. Those who have been around long enough will recognize this as the next skirmish in the "Net-Heads vs Bell-Heads" war.

This chapter documents and comments on some of the technical challenges we have encountered while trying to build open source systems right at this architectural boundary. The challenges point to different design decisions made by the two architectures, as well as the consequences of those decisions in how easy or hard it is to operate the resulting network. Spoiler alert: when an architecture is designed by companies that call themselves "operators" you can be fairly certain the barrier to entry for being able to operate the network will remain high.

Why 5G Matters

Over the last month I undertook a detailed review of a new book in the Systems Approach series, *5G Mobile Networks: A Systems Approach* by Larry Peterson and Oguz Sunay. Talking to people outside the technology world about my work, I soon found myself trying to explain "why does 5G matter" to all sorts of folks without a technical background. At this point in 2020, we can generally assume people know two things about 5G: the Telcos are marketing it as the greatest innovation ever; and conspiracy theorists are having a field day telling us all the things that 5G is causing or covering up (which in turn led to more telco ads making fun of the conspiracy theories). By the end of reviewing the new book from Larry and Oguz, I felt I had finally grasped why 5G matters. I'm not going to bother debunking conspiracy theories, but I do think there is something quite important going on with 5G. And frankly, there is plenty of hype around 5G, but behind that hype are some significant innovations.

What is clear about 5G, technically, is that there will be a whole lot of new radio technologies and new spectrum allocation, which will enable yet another upgrade in speeds and feeds. If you are a radio person that's quite interesting—there is plenty of innovation in squeezing more bandwidth out of wireless channels. It's a bit harder to explain why more bandwidth will make a big difference to users, simply because 4G generally works pretty well. Once you can stream video at decent resolution to your phone or tablet, it's hard to make a case for the value of more bandwidth alone. A more subtle issue is bandwidth density—the aggregate bandwidth that can be delivered to many devices in a certain area. Think of a sporting event as a good example (leaving aside the question of whether people need to watch videos on their phones at sporting events).

Lowering the latency of communication starts to make the discussion more interesting—although not so much to human users, but as an enabler of machine-to-machine or Internet-of-things applications. If we imagine a world where cars might communicate with each other, for example, to better manage road congestion, you can see a need for very low latency coupled with very high reliability—which is another dimension that 5G aims to address. And once we start to get to these scenarios, we begin to see why 5G isn't just about new radio technology, but actually entails a whole new mobile network architecture. Lowering latency and improving availability aren't just radio issues, they are system architecture issues. For example, low latency requires that a certain set of functions move closer to the edge—an approach sometimes called edge computing or edge clouds.

Architecture, Not Just Speed

The high points of the new cellular architecture for 5G are all about leveraging trends from the broader networking and computing ecosystems. Three trends stand out in particular:

1. 5G networks are architected much like modern public clouds, leveraging lots of related technologies such as virtualization and microservices architectures.

2. The actual networking part of 5G is largely based on software-defined networking, the dominant paradigm for networking in modern data centers and clouds.

3. The entire cellular architecture has been disaggregated—that is, what used to be vertically integrated systems from a single vendor are now broken apart into components that can be realized using a selection of components from a much wider ecosystem of vendors, including open source components.

None of this matters to the end user unless it provides some compelling benefit to them. Fundamentally, I believe this new architecture will unleash a whole lot of innovation and we don't yet know exactly what apps will be enabled. This is precisely where the Internet succeeded 25 years ago, when it was not obvious that it would become the dominant networking technology. It was the most general-purpose architecture out there, with the greatest flexibility to support new applications, and in the end the rich diversity of applications was what made the Internet a success. By contrast, the cellular network has historically been optimized for a few well-understood applications (voice calls, SMS, etc.) and it is only with 5G that it really becomes a general purpose platform for innovation. This is one of the reasons it can be challenging for Telcos to market 5G: they have to show us its potential when we (and they) don't know what the "killer apps" will be.

If you want to know more about the architecture of 5G, the application requirements that are driving it, and how it will enable innovation, you should go read the book as I did!

Bruce Davie, December 2020

What's in a Name?

It has been said that the principal function of an operating system is to define a number of different names for the same object, so that it can busy itself keeping track of the relationship between all of the different names. (David Clark, RFC 814)

As I've come up to speed on the mobile cellular network, it's been interesting to learn about the design decisions made over the years. And it's natural (for me) to compare those decisions to how the Internet addressed similar problems. Being a student of system design, I can't resist the opportunity to compare two similar systems that evolved in parallel over the same 40-year time period. My favorite example is global identity management, which puts me in mind of the most influential paper I read as a grad student many years ago: Jerry Saltzer's Lecture Notes on Naming and Binding of Objects (which he later amended with RFC 1498).

For starters, I'll assume everyone understands how IP addresses serve as a globally unique identifier for every device that wants to send and receive packets on the Internet, and how routers "interpret" these identifiers to carry out the process of packet delivery. (For simplicity, I'm ignoring NAT in this summary.) A critically important design decision is that these unique identifiers are independent of any addresses used by the underlying networking technologies (802.3 and 802.11's 48-bit addresses being the canonical example), with each network technology providing an IP-to-Physical address mapping mechanism (e.g., ARP).

In the mobile cellular network, the objective is to build a global Radio Access Network (RAN), where any two RAN-connected devices can communicate, no matter where they are currently located and how often they move. And to support this global connectivity, each device is assigned a globally unique identifier, called an IMSI (International Mobile Subscriber Identity). This IMSI, which is "burned" into the device's SIM card, is a 64-bit, self-describing identifier that is commonly represented as a 15-digit decimal number. For example, the following is an interpretation we use in a Private 5G implementation:

- MCC: Mobile Country Code (3-digit decimal number).

- MNC: Mobile Network Code (3-digit decimal number).

- ENT: Enterprise Code (3-digit decimal number).

- SUB: Subscriber (6-digit decimal number).

The first two fields (MCC, MNC) uniquely identify the MNO (Mobile Network Operator), while the last two fields are one example of how an MNO might use additional hierarchical structure to uniquely identify every device it serves. (When providing 5G connectivity to enterprises, an ENT field makes sense, but other MNOs might assign the last 9 digits using some other structure.) The MCC and MNC play a role in roaming: when a device tries to connect to a "foreign network" those fields are used to find the "home network", where the rest of the IMSI leads to a subscriber profile that says whether or not roaming is enabled for this device. It's then the responsibility of the Mobile Core to "interpret" IMSIs in support of global connectivity.

There are two equally valid views of the Mobile Core. The Internet-centric view is that each local instantiation of the Mobile Core (e.g., serving a metro area) acts as a router on the global Internet. In this view, IP addresses serve as the unique global identifier that makes it possible for any RAN-connected device to communicate with any Internet addressable device or service. The 3GPP-centric view is that a distributed set of Mobile Cores (interconnected by one or more backbone technologies, of which the Internet is just one example) cooperate to turn a set of physical RANs into one logically global RAN. In this perspective, the IMSI serves as the global identifier that makes it possible for any two mobile devices to communicate with each other.

Both of these perspectives are correct, but since broadband communication using Internet protocols to access cloud services is today's dominant use case, taking the Internet-centric perspective of the Mobile Core makes sense. But the 3GPP-perspective is still there, making it worth a closer look at its underlying design rationale and the consequences of those decisions as the two networks become increasingly integrated.

Identity or Identifier?

For starters, a careful reader will likely have already objected to my use of the term "identity" instead of "identifier" since we're talking about devices and not principals. But the word "identity" is explicitly part of an IMSI because the assumption is that it uniquely identifies a subscriber (the "S" in both SIM and IMSI). The device and the customer using the device have been conflated in the 3GPP architecture, which of course breaks down when there could be tens or hundreds of IoT devices for every person, with no obvious association among them. Accounting for this problem is the first "architecture alignment" fix we had to make when trying to provide Private 5G Connectivity as a managed cloud service.

Once you think of an IMSI as the mobile network's equivalent of a 48-bit MAC address, the design makes more sense. This includes how addresses are assigned to ensure uniqueness: (MCC, MNC) pairs are assigned by a global authority to every MNO, each of which then decides how to uniquely assign the rest of the IMSI identifier space to devices. This approach is similar to how network vendors are assigned a unique prefix for all the MAC addresses they configure into the NIC cards and WiFi chips they ship, but there is a big difference: It is the MNO, not the device vendor, who is responsible for assigning IMSIs to SIM cards. This makes the IMSI allocation problem closer to how the Internet assigns IP addresses, but unlike DHCP, the IMSI-to-device binding is static.

This is important because, unlike 802.11 addresses, IMSIs are also intended to support global routing. (Here, I am using a liberal notion of routing, and focusing on the original 3GPP-perspective of the global RAN in which the Internet is just a possible packet network that interconnects Mobile Cores.) A hierarchically distributed database maps IMSIs onto the collection of information needed to forward data to the corresponding device. This includes a combination of relatively static information about the level of service the device expects (including the corresponding phone number and subscriber profile/account information), and more dynamic information about the current location of the device (including which Mobile Core instance, and which base station served by that Core, currently connects the device to the global RAN).

There are, of course, many more details—including how to find a device that has roamed to another MNO's network—but conceptually the process is straightforward. (As a thought experiment, imagine how you would build a "logically global WiFi" using just 802.11 addresses, rather than depending on the additional layer of addressing provided by IP.) The important takeaway is that IMSIs are used to locate the Mobile Core instance that is then responsible for authenticating the device, tracking the device as it moves from base station to base station within that Core's geographic region, and forwarding packets to/from the device.

Two other observations about the relationship between IMSIs and IP addresses are worth highlighting. First, the odds of someone trying to "call" or "text" an IoT device, drone, camera, or robot are virtually zero. It is the IP address assigned to each device (by the local Mobile Core) that is used to locate (route packets to) the device. In this context, the IMSI plays exactly the same role in a physical RAN as an 802.11 address plays in a LAN, and the Mobile Core behaves just like any access router.

Second, whether a device connects to a RAN or some other access network, it is assigned a new IP address any time it moves from one coverage domain to another. Even for voice calls in the RAN case, ongoing calls are dropped whenever a device moves between instantiations of the Mobile Core (i.e., uninterrupted mobility is supported only within the region served by a given Core). This is typically not a problem when the RAN is being used to deliver broadband connectivity because Internet devices are almost always clients requesting a cloud service; they just start issuing requests with their new (dynamically assigned) IP address.

So what have we learned? Certainly that reconciling identifiers across network architectures is a tricky exercise, especially when one of those architectures conflates device identifiers with principal identity, and is not able to dynamically reassign said identifiers when devices move. More importantly, though, this case study is a great reminder that while technology changes frequently, system design principles such as those articulated by Saltzer stand the test of time. We can expect the Internet's IP addressing scheme, which embodies many of these principles, to define the global identifier that matters, while IMSIs may be reduced to providing value only within a physical RAN, similar to 48-bit MAC addresses in a physical LAN.

Larry Peterson, November 2022

TCP x 5G: Mind the Gap

As we tie up the loose ends in the TCP Congestion Control book, I found myself reviewing the literature on optimizing TCP for wireless networks, and wondering if 5G is going to change the equation. The short answer, I believe, is yes, but the reason for that (and the history behind that reason) is fascinating. The place you have to start is to recognize that the mobile cellular network and the Internet evolved in parallel, with each treating the other as an opaque box. Each generation of the cellular network admitted a few more Internet-based mechanisms into its internal structure, but 5G is now embracing some of the best practices in building scalable Internet services. That puts us on the cusp of finally being able bridge the gap between these two global networks. By applying a systems view to the increasingly common case where TCP runs over wireless links, we can stop treating the Internet and 5G as distinct worlds, and improve the end-to-end performance of the overall system.

Both networks provide global connectivity, with the Internet traditionally treating the cellular network as an opaque last-hop technology, and the global cellular network using the Internet as a backbone interconnecting RAN aggregation points around the world. From the perspective of the TCP congestion control algorithm trying to find the available end-to-end bandwidth, the RAN has always been problematic. This is for three main reasons: (1) the wireless link has typically been the bottleneck in the end-to-end path due to the scarcity of radio spectrum, (2) the bandwidth available in the RAN can be highly variable due to a combination of device mobility and environmental factors, and (3) this environmental variability can also lead to the basestation retransmitting corrupted segments, which results in variable latency.

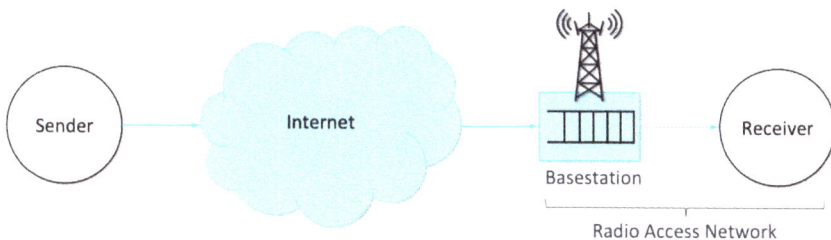

Basestation Packet Queue on the End-to-End Path

To further complicate matters, the internals of the RAN have been largely closed and proprietary, with vendors treating their radio scheduling algorithms as a critical piece of their intellectual property. Researchers have experimentally observed that there is significant buffering at the edge, presumably to absorb the expected contention for the radio link, and yet keeping sufficient work "close by" for whenever capacity does open up. (For example see a paper by Haiqing Jiang and colleagues in the 2012 CellNet Workshop.) This large buffer is an instance of bufferbloat, which is problematic for TCP because it causes the sender to overshoot the actual bandwidth available on the radio link, and in the process, introduces significant delay and jitter.

Other researchers, notably the authors of the BBR congestion control algorithm, have observed that the scheduler for the wireless link actually uses the number of queued packets for a given client as an input to its scheduling algorithm, rewarding senders for building up a queue by increasing the bandwidth they receive. BBR attempts to take advantage of this incentive in its design by being aggressive enough to queue at least some packets in the buffers of wireless links (but that aggression is not universally fair).

Given this fundamental tension between the RAN scheduler needing to keep the packet buffer full so it can exploit capacity that becomes available (as part of a ~1ms control loop) and the TCP congestion control mechanism pacing transmissions to match the available end-to-end bandwidth (as part of a ~100ms control loop), an optimal solution is likely not attainable. But is there an opportunity to do better? I believe the answer is yes.

There are three specific reasons for that optimism (which I'll get to in a moment), but they all hinge on acknowledging that the opaque wall between the Internet and the mobile cellular network is an anachronism. In particular, with TCP traffic now being such an important use case for 5G, the focus needs to shift to delivering end-to-end goodput and maximizing the throughput/latency ratio, rather than focusing solely on maximizing the utilization of the radio spectrum. The latter is, of course, important, but it is a means to an end; not the ends, itself. Now to the three specific changes on the horizon.

First, with open software-based implementations of the RAN becoming a reality (see our companion 5G and SDN books for more details), it will soon be possible to take a cross-layer approach to congestion control, whereby the RAN provides an interface that give higher layers of the protocol stack visibility into what goes on inside its queues and scheduler. Incumbent vendors will likely be hesitant to reveal too much information (which I discuss in a related post), but high-level signals that support Active Queue Management should be sufficient to make a difference.

Second, 5G deployments are promising to support network slicing, a mechanism that isolates different classes of traffic. Each slice will have its own queue, and that queue can be sized and serviced in traffic-specific ways. As a consequence, long-distant TCP flows need not be scheduled in the same way as, say, local IoT traffic. Moreover, assuming there is sufficient opportunistic traffic to keep spectrum utilization high, it should be possible to reduce the variability in the bandwidth set aside for TCP traffic, especially those flows with high round-trip times. One caveat is that support for slicing is still mostly aspirational, but this use case is an example of how it might provide value.

Third, it will become increasingly common for 5G-connected devices to be served from a nearby edge cloud rather than from the other side of the Internet. This means TCP connections will likely have much shorter round-trip times, which will make the congestion control algorithm more responsive to changes in the available capacity in the RAN. As we discussed in a recent post, this "segmentation" of the end-to-end path is already starting to happen, but we expect it to become even more pronounce as on-premises edge clouds start to host both the RAN's central elements and application end-points. (See Aether for an example of a 5G-enabled edge cloud.)

There are no guarantees, of course, and there will be other variables in play (e.g., small cells will likely reduce the number of flows competing for bandwidth at a given basestation), but these factors point to there being ample opportunities to tune congestion control algorithms well into the future. The big takeaway, though, is that these opportunities are the consequence of taking a big-picture (systems) approach to the problem, working across traditional boundaries instead of myopically trying to optimize one narrow aspect of the system as a whole.

Larry Peterson, December 2021

Private 5G: As Easy as Wi-Fi*

*Your Mileage May Vary

Our Private 5G book is informed by our experience designing and implementing an open source Kubernetes-based edge cloud that hosts—among other edge workloads—a managed 5G connectivity service. Edge applications can take advantage of local breakout, meaning they can communicate directly with IoT devices (and the like) without their packets ever leaving the enterprise. This local Connectivity-as-a-Service is then offered as a managed cloud service (rather than a traditional Telco service), including an API and Dashboard that makes it easy to monitor and control connectivity at runtime. The hope is that Private 5G will be as easy to deploy and use as Wi-Fi is today. (For the reader prepared to argue that Wi-Fi is sufficient for all edge use cases, we leave the 5G vs. Wi-Fi debate for another time.)

It should come as no surprise that designing/implementing Private 5G is not exactly the same as deploying/operating Private 5G, and since the main goal of the Aether OnRamp tutorial is to help readers with the latter, we decided to take the system we had built out for a test drive. But there's an important qualifier before we get to that. The system we're talking about, Aether, is not a collection of isolated components that leaves the dirty work of operationalization to someone else. Aether includes all the integration glue needed to bring up an operational system in support of live traffic—a topic we've covered in other posts and written an entire book about—but that doesn't mean it's easy for ivory tower architects like Bruce and myself to bring up Aether without a little friction. Some of the challenges were our missteps, but some point to the inherent difficulty in the Telco-to-Cloud transition Aether is trying to catalyze.

Step one is getting your hands on a 5G small cell radio, and they aren't exactly available today at Best Buy. We're using the Bridgestone Indoor 5G Sub-6G Small Cell from Sercomm. We also have experience with Sercomm's 4G counterpart (which is less expensive and easier to find). You'll also need a starter set of UEs, and while several smartphones support CBRS (e.g., iPhone 11, Google Pixel 4, or newer), our recommendation is to include a 5G dongle that can be attached to a Raspberry Pi. Acquiring the 5G hardware is still a problem today, but that's probably a short-term situation. The other bit of hardware you'll need is a server (or VM) to run Aether on, but the requirements aren't too steep (Quad-Core, 12GB RAM, running Ubuntu 20.04 or 22.04). Note that the approach I'm describing uses CBRS spectrum that is allocated in the US; other countries are in different stages of establishing similar allocations.

Step two is where 5G is the most unfamiliar to anyone who has installed a Wi-Fi AP: Configuring the small cell radio. There are three parts to this. The first part is setting the RF-related parameters, which I am wholly unqualified to do. Their names are cryptic (e.g., FreqSsb, Arfcn), their settings seemingly arbitrary (e.g., 3609120, 643356), and the formulas to compute them... not exactly intuitive.

$$\text{FreqSsb} = \text{SSBOffset2PointA} + \text{CenterFreq} - (\text{PrbNum} * \text{SCS} * 12)/2$$

$$\text{OffsetToPointA} * 12 * 15 + k_{SSB} * 15 + 10 * 12 * \text{SCS}$$

absoluteFrequencySSB   carrierBandwidth(N_{RB})

15kHz for FR1, 60KHz for FR2   subCarrierSpacingCommon

Parameters Required to Configure 5G Radio

These (and other) parameters are related to the control the operator has over how the available frequency band is used, which is part of the value 5G brings. I clearly have more to learn, but fortunately, the out-of-the-box defaults work. The second part is connecting the small cell to the local network, which is straightforward, complicated only by the fact that the radio has two 802.3 ports: one known as WAN (but labeled 2.5G on the Sercomm 5G small cell) and the other know as LAN (but labeled 1G on the Sercomm 5G small cell). The WAN port is how the small cell connects to the Internet (indirectly via the Mobile Core, which we'll get to in a moment). The LAN port is for connecting the radio to a management network, which is worth mentioning because you'll eventually need to learn TR-069/TR-098 (in place of SNMP/MIB, respectively), since you'll technically be managing on-prem Telco equipment instead of IETF-specified Internet devices. There's also an O1 Management interface, which is the O-RAN approach to managing RAN elements, but I have not yet had an opportunity to use it. It's probably better to have too many programmatic interfaces than too few, but I was able to do everything I needed to through the dashboard, which is enough to get started. The third part is configuring the Spectrum Allocation Server (SAS), which is responsible for managing access to the three tiers of the CBRS spectrum. You'll need to familiarize yourself with the SAS requirements and get credentials from a SAS provider (we use Google) if you want to get past the "turn it on and see if it boots up" stage. (You'll also need to connect a GPS antenna, which the radio needs so it can tell the SAS its precise location.)

Step three is interesting because it's related to how you assemble a system out of building-block components. As I discussed previously, the mobile cellular network defines a global naming scheme that makes it possible for any two RAN-connected devices to communicate with each other. You need to configure both the small cell radio and the Mobile Core software stack so they know how to plug into that global network. This means defining the Mobile Country Code (MCC) and Mobile Network Code (MNC) that you plan to use. This MCC/MNC pair forms a Public Land Mobile Network (PLMN) code, where we've used two different ids in different settings: 315010 constructed from MCC=315 (US) and MNC=010 (CBRS), and 00101 constructed from MCC=001 (TEST) and MNC=01 (TEST). And since you'll technically be the MNO responsible for the Private 5G network you bring up, you'll also need to burn the SIM cards that are to be inserted into all the UEs. The SIM cards include a unique identifier (called an IMSI), which is a 15-digit number with the PLMN code as its prefix. (You can buy a 5G SIM writer on Amazon, where one product description reads:

PLS Kindly Note: The cards be provided to professional engineers, PLS be professional, you need have knowledge about sim cards, if you don't have, PLS do not buy it!)

Finally, in step four, you'll be back in familiar IP-land, but your ability to juggle IP subnets, Linux bridges, and iptable rules will be taxed to the max. I won't go through all the details, and your mileage will vary depending on how deeply you want to integrate the RAN into your enterprise network, but by my count, there are as many as seven subnets in play. This is in part because the Mobile Core is implemented in Kubernetes (with its own set of intra-cluster and service-visible addresses), in part because the backhaul that connects the small cell radios to the Mobile Core is an overlay network (for example, running on top of your local enterprise network), and in part because the forwarding plane of the Mobile Core—the User Plane Function

(UPF) running as a Kubernetes-hosted microservice—is itself an IP router that forwards packets between the RAN and the rest of the Internet. You'll certainly find that having access to diagnostic tools such as ping, traceroute, and tcpdump to be essential (which is one reason we recommend connecting at least one Pi+Dongle UE).

I'm pretty sure Wi-Fi configuration was never this complicated. To some extent, this may be due to where the line is drawn between the customer and the provider: Telcos have strived to keep the end-system they sell subscribers simple, but have accepted operational complexity in the network devices (such as base stations) that they manage. In contrast, anyone who purchases a Wi-Fi AP from a vendor assumes it will be straightforward to install. One would expect that, with time, small cells deployed in enterprises (and maybe even homes) can be pre-configured before they are shipped or auto-configured after they are installed, but our goal with the book is to demystify 5G, including all the configuration steps. If you're an enterprise system admin (or a hobbyist who wants to try out the technology at home) you will need to know about all of this. That's why we wrote the book! It's also why it's important to have access to open source implementations of all this technology.

Larry Peterson, April 2023

Democratizing 5G

Bringing Technology to a Wider Audience

I recently attended SIGCOMM for the first time in many years, and was immediately reminded of the standard salutation when you run into someone at an academic conference: *"What are you working on?"* I wasn't prepared with a succinct-yet-meaningful response, but quickly settled on *"Democratizing 5G"*. It wasn't the expected research-focused answer, but it did have the quaint advantage of not directly involving AI/ML. It seemed to do the trick, but also got me thinking about how common the word "democratizing" has become in our technical jargon.

I believe the first time I heard the word being used in a technical setting was in 2004, when Mike Freedman and colleagues published "Democratizing Content Publication with Coral" at the first Usenix Symposium on Network System Design and Implementation (NSDI). And if the meaning wasn't already intuitive, the paper gave a definition that nicely captures the spirit of what it means to democratize something technology-related:

> CoralCDN replicates content in proportion to the content's popularity, regardless of the publisher's resources, in effect democratizing publication.

The Internet (like the printing press centuries before) is widely regarded as playing a central role in the democratization of knowledge—making information readily available among the wider population. CoralCDN focused specifically on the publishing side of the equation, making it easier for the wider population to also disseminate information. That's now taken for granted with the explosion of various platforms (e.g., blogs, social media) that include built-in content distribution mechanisms, but was novel at the time. It also highlights the idea that there are multiple barriers to lower; in this case, both acquiring and disseminating content. Less obviously, it points to the role "access to resources" plays in the equation. CoralCDN was only able to democratize publication because it ran on a publicly-funded infrastructure, in this case PlanetLab.

My use of the word democratization in the context of 5G focuses more on the underlying network infrastructure—with the intended audience being people who build and operate that infrastructure—than on end-users who benefit from that infrastructure. I tend to think of it as lowering the barrier to innovation, but it also shares much with the idea of Freedom to Tinker, where know-how is essential to crafting good policy. Either way, it's about broadening the set of people able to participate in technologies that impact our lives.

For 5G, democratization turns out to be a multi-faceted challenge. A necessary condition is access to open source implementations of both the RAN and the Mobile Core, which, thanks to various open source organizations (ONF's Aether and OAI for example), now exist. But a quick perusal of the Git repos for those and similar projects will immediately convince you that the mere existence of open source software is not sufficient; users also need the wherewithal to deploy and operate the code if they have any ambition to take advantage of it. My experience is that "wherewithal" maps onto a combination of tooling and documentation, with the latter being the "long pole". The result—our Private 5G book, which includes a tutorial guiding the reader through the OnRamp deployment toolset—is now available.

A Mountain of Configuration

I've written about that topic before, so won't rehash the challenges here, except to make two observations. The first is that in our haste to implement new functionality, we have created a nearly impenetrable mountain of configuration variables needed to manage that functionality; YAML files layered on top of Jinja2 templates overlaid on still other YAML files layered on top of JSON... I'm sure it's not the intention to obfuscate the underlying code, but that is the practical effect. It's almost as though we've created a problem only AI will be able to help us solve. The other option is to be a well-resourced company with a team of experienced engineers, but of course that flies in the face of our goal, which is to democratize access to that know-how.

The second observation, which follows from my experience trying to bring up a 5G small cell, is that the mobile cellular technology has operational complexity baked into its design. This makes sense (in a perverse way) when you consider that the technology was defined by MNOs that built businesses around their ability to operate the network on behalf of their subscribers. But this creates additional barriers that need to be lowered if you want to broaden participation. For example, programming a SIM is a required step to establishing a secure 5G connection, but being able to do that in turn requires having the necessary credentials (plus the know-how to correctly specify another few hundred lines of YAML). Fortunately, the broader ecosystem includes players that help on that front, but the main takeaway is that there is much more to the democratization of technology than initially meets the eye.

Why Are We Doing This?

But that all raises the question—typically following immediately after "What are you working on?"—which is: "Why should I care?" It's a good question. If you're going to put the effort into lowering the barrier-to-entry, there ought to be something important on the other side of those barriers. Again, there are a couple of parts to the answer.

The first part is to simply acknowledge that Internet access is going to be dominated by mobile wireless connectivity. Nearly 60% of all web traffic already comes from mobile devices, and that doesn't yet take into account the tens of billions of IoT devices that are expected to connect to the Internet over the next few years. We've spent 40 years building the Internet out of open and accessible technologies, but going forward, democratizing Internet infrastructure is meaningless without also democratizing wireless access. That the mobile cellular industry has been so closed and proprietary for so long makes that goal all the more relevant.

The second part is to zero in on 5G vs other wireless technologies, most obviously Wi-Fi. At the coding and modulation level, Wi-Fi 6 and 5G's New Radio (NR) are converging on OFDMA. The difference is how the available spectrum is allocated by the two systems, which Bruce and his Magma collaborators discuss in depth in their NSDI paper on Magma. Digging deeper, 5G scheduling includes the ability to dynamically change the size and number of schedulable resource units, including scheduling intervals as short 0.125ms. This opens the door to making fine-grained scheduling decisions that are critical to predictable, low-latency communication. The 5G scheduler also allocates some of the available spectrum to a light-weight over-the-air-interface that is simple enough for IoT devices to implement. These devices are not particularly latency-sensitive or bandwidth-hungry, but they often require long battery lifetimes, and hence, reduced hardware complexity that draws less power.

There's reason to be skeptical, but as Bruce discusses in a previous post, the application of cloud best-practices to 5G is a game changer. The hype around 5G has certainly gotten out in front of the reality, but it's only just now the case that 5G is becoming viable in the enterprise (aka Private 5G). For example, the Aether project has only recently been able to certify a commercially available small cell radio, with ubiquitous 5G devices (other than smartphones) still to follow. Until these components become ubiquitous, many of these advantages outlined above will not be realized.

Bringing this discussion back to the question of what democratization means in the technical world, a personal takeaway is that I now see a direct line between "Democratizing X" and "X: A Systems Approach". The systems approach always looks at technology through the lens of deployed systems, using real implementations to explain the design decisions. Democratizing access to technologies is an almost inevitable consequence of how we help readers to understand them—by first deconstructing them into their elemental components and then showing how all the pieces are assembled into a coherent whole.

Larry Peterson, October 2023

Closing Remarks

The mobile cellular network is fertile ground for learning about the design and implementation of large, complex systems. For most of its history, dominated by large telcos and a handful of incumbent vendors, it was perhaps a better example of what the systems approach is *not*. For example, the fact that every major change to coding and modulation in the radios, from 3G to 4G to 5G and so on, has also entailed a complete redesign of the network architecture, strikes us as the antithesis of a well-architected system that allows for evolvability. Consider, by contrast, the relative ease with which the Internet has accommodated a rich diversity of link technologies that didn't exist at the time of its design.

The more positive view that we take, however, is that 5G represents a significant shift from the past, with the cellular architecture becoming more evolvable while also opening itself up to a broader set of players for both implementation and deployment. Probably the best example of this is the arrival of private 5G, the subject of our latest book on cellular networks. While still not for the faint of heart, deploying a private 5G network is now within the reach of small organizations thanks to the availability of open source components and leverage of a standard set of cloud native software tools. This should be applauded as a sign that the systems approach is taking hold at last in cellular networking.

Explore Further

RFC 1498. On the Naming and Binding of Network Destinations. August 1993.

Haiqing Jiang, et al. Understanding Bufferbloat in Cellular Networks. 2012 CellNet Workshop, August 2012.

Jim Gettys. Bufferbloat: Dark Buffers in the Internet. IEEE Internet Computing, April 2011.

Neal Cardwell, et al. BBR: Congestion-Based Congestion Control. Communications of the ACM, February 2017.

5G Tools for RF Wireless.

O-RAN Alliance. O-RAN Architecture Overview.

Michael Freeman, Eric Freudenthal, and David Mazieres. Democratizing Content Publication with Coral. USENIX NSDI, March 2004.

Center for Information Technology Policy. CITP Blog (Formerly Freedom to Tinker).

Shaddi Hasan, et al. Building Flexible, Low-Cost Wireless Networks with Magma. USENIX NSDI, March 2023.

Larry Peterson, Oguz Sunay, and Bruce Davie. Private 5G: A Systems Approach. Systems Approach, 2023.

SmartNICs, IPUs and DPUs

There has been a surge of interest in SmartNICs and the specialized hardware that powers them, which goes by various names such as Infrastructure Processing Units (IPUs) or Data Processing Units (DPUs). SmartNICs sit at the boundary between the network and the end-systems, and offer a range of functions including hardware support for software-defined networking. They also represent a target for P4 programs, extending the impact of P4 from switches to computing infrastructure.

Our own interest in SmartNICs goes back a long way, to a collaboration on Gigabit network testbeds in the 1990s. That collaboration not only produced our first joint paper, it laid the foundation for our decision to team up on the first edition of *Computer Networks: A Systems Approach*. One reason we have come back to writing about SmartNICs in recent years is because they are a great illustration of how the systems approach plays out in the real world.

One of the recurring themes of the systems approach is the importance of deciding where to place various functions within a system. The end-to-end argument is a classic of systems thinking because it lays out how to address this issue in a methodical way. The programmability of smartNICs allows us to explore tradeoffs in the design space for moving functions closer to the network or to the host, which is why we find them deserving of our attention.

The Accidental SmartNIC

The moment when the current generation of SmartNICs really captured my attention was during a demo at VMworld 2019. At the time, VMware's

ESXi hypervisor was formally supported on x86 processors only, but there had been a skunkworks project to run ESXi on ARM for several years. Since most SmartNICs have an ARM processor, it was now possible to run ESXi on it. I do remember thinking "just because you can do something doesn't mean you should" but it made for a fun demo.

This certainly wasn't my first exposure to SmartNICs. As a member of the networking team at VMware, I was periodically visited by SmartNIC vendors who wanted to offer their hardware as a way to improve the performance of virtual switching. And AWS had been subtly incorporating them into their EC2 infrastructure since about 2014 (depending on exactly how a SmartNIC is defined). But as I looked more closely at SmartNIC architectures, I realized that I had actually been involved in an earlier incarnation of the technology in the 1990s—not that we called them SmartNICs then. Even the term NIC was not yet standard terminology. Below is a slightly prettified diagram from a paper I published in SIGCOMM in 1991.

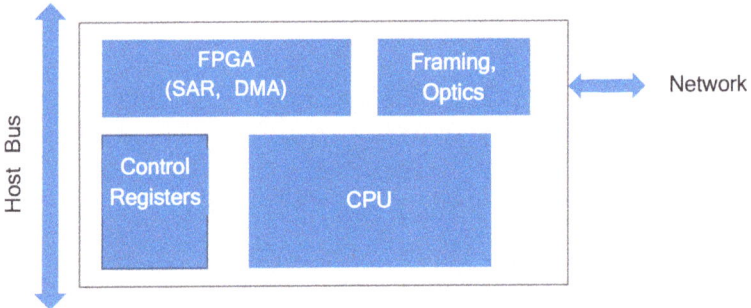

SmartNIC Block Diagram

If you compare this to the block diagram of a current generation SmartNIC, you will see some pretty remarkable similarities. Of course you need to connect to a host bus on one side; that's likely to be PCIe today. (That choice was much less obvious in 1990.) And you need the necessary physical and link layer hardware to connect to your network of choice; today that's invariably some flavor of Ethernet, whereas in 1990 it still seemed possible that ATM would take off as a local area network technology (it didn't). In between the host and the network, there's one or more CPUs, and some programmable hardware (FPGA). It's the programmability of the system, delivered by the CPU and FPGA, that makes it "Smart".

To be clear, I definitely didn't invent the SmartNIC. The earliest example that I can find was described by Kanakia and Cheriton in 1988. Other researchers around this time took a similar approach. There was a reason we gravitated towards designs that were relatively expensive but highly programmable: we didn't yet know which functions belonged on the NIC. So we kept our options open. This gave us the ability to move functions between the host and the NIC, to experiment with new protocols, and to explore new ways of delivering data efficiently to applications. This was essentially my introduction to the systems approach to networking: building a system to experiment with various ways of partitioning functionality among components, and seeking an approach that would address end-to-end concerns such as reliability and performance. I was fortunate to be influenced in the design of my "SmartNIC" by David Clark, the "architect of the Internet" and co-author of the end-to-end argument, and this work also led to my collaboration with Larry Peterson.

The 1990s, in retrospect, was a time when a lot of questions about networking were still up for debate. As we tried to achieve the then-crazy goal of delivering a gigabit per second to a single application, there was a widespread concern that TCP/IP would not be up to the task. Perhaps we needed completely new transport protocols, or a new network layer (e.g., ATM). Perhaps transport protocols were so performance-intensive that they needed to be offloaded to the NIC. With so many open questions, it made sense to design NICs with maximum flexibility. Hence the inclusion of a pair of CPUs and some of the largest FPGAs available at the time.

By the 2000s, many of these networking questions were addressed by the overwhelming success of the Internet. TCP/IP (plus Ethernet) became the dominant protocol stack. There turned out to be no problem getting these protocols from the 1970s to operate at tens of gigabits per second. Moore's law helped, as did the rise of switched Ethernet and advances in optical transmission. As the protocols stabilized, there wasn't so much need for flexibility, and hence fixed-function NICs became the norm.

Jump ahead another ten years, however, and fixed-function NICs became a liability as new approaches to networking emerged. By 2010 NICs frequently included some amount of "TCP offload", echoing one of the concerns raised in the 1990s. These offloads left hosts free to transfer large chunks of data to or from the NIC while the NIC added the TCP headers to segments on transmit and parsed them on receipt. This was a performance win, unless you wanted anything other than a simple TCP/IP header on your packets, such as an extra encapsulation header to support network virtualization. The optimization of performance for the common case turned into a huge handicap for innovative approaches that couldn't leverage that optimization. (My colleagues at Nicira found some creative solutions to this problem, ultimately leading to the GENEVE encapsulation standard).

As networking became more dynamic with the rise of SDN and network virtualization (and the parallel rise of software-defined storage) it started to become clear that once again the functions of a NIC could not be neatly tied down and committed to fixed-function hardware. And so the pendulum swung back to where it had been in the 1990s, where the demand for flexibility warranted NIC designs that could be updated at software speeds—leading to what we might call the second era of SmartNICs. This time, it's the need to efficiently support network virtualization, security features, and flexible approaches to storage that demands highly capable NICs. While all these functions can be supported on x86 servers, it's increasingly more cost-effective to move them onto a SmartNIC that is optimized for those tasks and still flexible enough to support rapid innovation in cloud services. This is why you see projects like AWS Nitro, Azure Accelerated Networking, and VMware's Project Monterey all moving functions that you expect to see in a hypervisor to the new generation of SmartNICs.

Why did I title this post "The Accidental SmartNIC"? Because I wasn't trying to make a SmartNIC; there was just so much uncertainty about the right way to partition our system that I needed a high degree of flexibility in my design. (It's also a nod to the excellent film "The Accidental Tourist".) Determining how best to distribute functionality across components is a core aspect of the systems approach. Today's SmartNICs exemplify that approach by allowing complex functions to be moved from servers to NICs, meeting the goals of high performance, rapid innovation, and cost-effective use of resources. Building a platform that supports innovation is a common goal in systems research and we see that playing out today as SmartNICs take off in the cloud.

Bruce Davie, June 2021.

IPUs: Balancing Generality and Specialization

The recent announcements from Intel about Infrastructure Processing Units (IPUs) have prompted us to revisit the topic of how functionality is partitioned in a computing system. As we noted in "The Accidental Smart-NIC", there is at least thirty years' history of trying to decide how much one should offload from a general purpose CPU to a more specialized NIC, and an equally long tussle between more highly specialized offload engines versus more general-purpose ones. The IPU represents just the latest entry in a long series of general-purpose offload engines, and we're now seeing quite a diverse set of options, not just from Intel but from others such as Nvidia and Pensando. These latter firms use the term DPU (data processing unit) but the consensus seems to be that these devices tackle the same class of problems. A continuum can be drawn from fixed-function NICs through SmartNICs to DPUs and IPUs (see Further Reading below).

There are several interesting things going on here. The first is that there is an emerging consensus that the general purpose x86 (or ARM) server is no longer the best place to run the infrastructure functions of a cloud. By "infrastructure functions" we mean all the things that it takes to run a multi-tenant cloud that are not actually guest workloads: the hypervisor, network virtualization, storage services and so on. Whereas the server used to be the home of both guest workloads and infrastructure services, these functions are increasingly viewed as "overhead" that is only taking cycles away from guests. One oft-cited paper is Facebook's "Accelerometer" study, which measures overhead within Facebook's data centers as high as 80%, although this may not be generalizable to cloud providers. More plausibly, Google reported in 2015:

> "Datacenter tax" can comprise nearly 30% of cycles [. . .], which makes its constituents prime candidates for hardware specialization in future server systems-on-chips.

Amazon Web Services presumably saw the same issue of overheads cutting into the revenue-generating workloads, and started to use specialized hardware for infrastructure services when it acquired Annapurna Labs in 2015, laying the groundwork for its Nitro architecture. The impact was to move almost all infrastructure services out of the servers, leaving them free to run guest workloads and little else.

Once you decide to move a function out of the general-purpose CPU complex into some sort of offload engine, the question is how to retain the appropriate level of flexibility. These offloaded functions are not static, so putting them into fixed-function hardware would be a short-sighted move. This is why we have seen NICs move in recent years from fixed-function offloads such as TCP segmentation to the more flexible architecture of Smart-NICs. So the goal is to build an offload system that is more optimized for the offloaded services than a general-purpose CPU, yet still programmable enough to support innovation and evolution of offloaded services.

Intel's IPU family contains several entrants, which take different approaches to delivering that flexibility, including both FPGA- and ASIC-based versions. The Mount Evans ASIC is particularly interesting as it includes both ARM CPU cores and programmable networking hardware (from the Barefoot Networks team) that is P4-programmable. This is a subject dear to our hearts here at Systems Approach, as the P4 toolchain is central to much of the technology that we wrote about in our SDN book.

Putting a P4-programmable switch in an IPU/DPU makes lots of sense, since the networking functions that are likely to be offloaded include those of a virtual switch. And one thing we learned at Nicira and later in the NSX team at VMware was that if you want to move the vswitch to an offload engine, that engine needs to be fully programmable. If a NIC is insufficiently general to implement the whole vswitch, you can only move some subset of the vswitch functionality to the offload engine. Even if you could move 90% of the functionality, that remaining 10% that you have to keep doing in the CPU is likely to be a bottleneck. So a P4-programmable offload engine based on PISA (Protocol Independent Switching Architecture) provides the required level of flexibility and programmability to make offloading of the whole vswitch possible. Combine this with some other programmable hardware (such as ARM cores) and you can see how the entire set of infrastructure functions, including the hypervisor, storage virtualization, etc., can be offloaded to the IPU.

One way to view the latest generation of DPUs/IPUs is that the efforts of the SDN movement to create more programmable switches has enabled innovation in a new space. SDN initially promised to drive control plane innovation by decoupling the switching hardware from the software that controlled it. Network virtualization was one of the first applications of

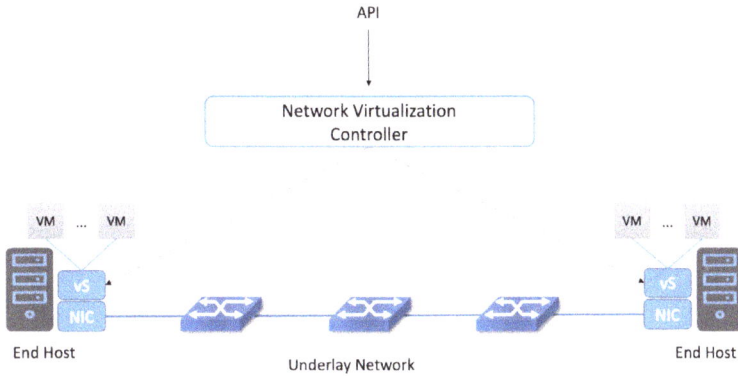

Virtual Switch of a Network Virtualization System is a Candidate for Offloading

SDN to take off, with the separation of control and data planes and highly flexible software switches enabling networks to be created entirely in software (on top of a hardware-based underlay). PISA and P4 led to a more flexible form of switching hardware and a new way to define the hardware-software interface (improving on the earlier efforts of OpenFlow). All of these threads—control plane innovation, network virtualization, and flexible, programmable switch hardware—are now being brought together in the creation of IPUs and DPUs.

We can also view the development of IPUs/DPUs as a continuation of the trend in which processors are both highly flexible and yet specialized for certain tasks. GPUs and TPUs are really flexible, being used for everything from crypto-mining to machine learning to graphics processing, but are nevertheless quite specialized compared to CPUs. (GPUs were even used for packet processing in an era before we had PISA and P4.) DPUs and IPUs now seem well established as a new category of highly programmable devices that are optimized for a specific set of tasks that need to be performed in a modern cloud data center. With that greater specialization comes greater efficiency, while flexibility remains high enough to support future innovation.

Bruce Davie, November 2021

Always in the Kitchen at Parties

Separating Guests From Infrastructure

Late in 2021 I gave a keynote at the Euro P4 Workshop, and I took the opportunity to revisit a topic that has held my attention for much of my career: the appropriate partitioning of functionality in networked systems. This talk was an opportunity to reflect on what has (and hasn't) changed since I was accidentally building SmartNICs in the 1990s, and to talk about Infrastructure Processing Units and Data Processing Units (IPUs/DPUs). After my earlier post on that topic, Guido Appenzeller, my former colleague at VMware and at the time an Intel executive, reached out to raise a point that I had missed in my first crack at the topic. This point concerns the role of IPUs in separating the guest workloads in a data center from infrastructure functions—those tasks performed by the cloud operator that are important to running the cloud but strictly not a concern of a guest. Guido used the analogy of kitchens in a hotel being off-limits to guests, reminding me of a minor synth-pop classic from the 1980s, "You'll always find me in the kitchen at parties", and I took that as the title for my keynote. As a result of this interaction, along with others I've had in recent weeks, I'm forming the view that IPUs/DPUs are a bigger deal than I first realized.

Whereas I had previously thought of IPUs as just an extension of the trend to move more and more functionality out of the server onto the NIC, there is another way to think about them. In the computing era before clouds, we might move some function to a NIC because it was more efficient to do it there. But in the cloud era, there are really two distinct classes of function: those that belong to guests (or users, tenants, or customers) and those that are the responsibility of the cloud service provider. And so a helpful way to think about the IPU is that it's not just a sort of offload engine, but instead it is a way to fully separate those two classes of workload—those of guests and those of operators—into two separate types of computing system. The guest workloads run on traditional servers (x86 or ARM) while the infrastructure functions run on hardware optimized for that task: infrastructure processing units.

While I previously viewed this as a performance optimization (as have others) there is more to it than performance. There are a number of significant consequences that follow from isolating these two sets of functions into separate hardware subsystems. For example, a spike in the processing load on the IPU will not affect the performance of the guests (unless it were to affect the data path of the IPU, on which we have more to say later). Furthermore, this separation opens up interesting options for what actually runs on the guest system. For example, the guest need not necessarily have a hypervisor at all: we could dedicate an entire host to a bare-metal operating system, which includes the possibility of running something like Kubernetes on bare metal for the guest. Or the guest can "bring their own" hypervisor, which is effectively what VMware does when running VMware cloud on AWS. VMware's hypervisor (and other software) runs on the server, while the AWS infrastructure (provided by Nitro) manages things like resource allocation and virtual networking. Guido also pointed out that your guest doesn't have to be a traditional server either: it could, for example, be a bunch of GPUs.

Composable Infrastructure

I spoke to Kostadis Roussos (a VMware principal engineer) on this topic and he observed that these sophisticated interfaces to the servers can be thought of as "programmable wires": a foundational building block for composable infrastructure. For example you can compose a server with networking and storage connected via the IPU, without being constrained by the networking or storage capabilities of any physical server. This again is more than a performance optimization—it's giving us new capabilities to deliver services in a cloud.

As noted by both Intel and AWS, moving these infrastructure functions out of the servers and onto IPUs (or Nitro in the case of AWS) means that servers can be 100% allocated to guests. While this sounds like a good thing—stop wasting those precious x86 cycles on overhead, allocate them to real work—it's only really a win if the new home of the infrastructure functions can do those tasks efficiently. The last thing we want is a new bottleneck, or an expensive piece of hardware doing a job that used to be done perfectly well on x86.

For this reason, the architecture of an IPU must provide high performance and achieve it at reasonable cost and power consumption. And this is where the role of P4, or more generally, a highly programmable and fast data path, becomes apparent. Just as the PISA architecture for switching is a new sweet spot for networking hardware that is both programmable and high-performance, the P4-programmable data plane in an IPU such as Intel's Mount Evans ASIC also aims to find the right tradeoff between performance and flexibility. This enables the IPU to meet the evolving requirements of infrastructure functions such as network virtualization, storage, encryption and so on, without becoming a bottleneck, and in a way that is more efficient than simply performing those functions on the x86 servers where they previously lived.

For those of us who have been watching the evolution of SDN for over a decade, it is intriguing to see IPUs as another step along the path to making everything software-defined. Rather than seeing them as just another incremental tweak on SmartNICs, there is a case to be made that IPUs are an important strategic control point in the future of cloud architecture. By pulling IPUs out of the servers, operators gain a new central point of control over their infrastructure whose benefits include security, isolation, and the chance to innovate faster in their cloud services.

Bruce Davie, January 2022.

Closing Remarks

Function placement—whether it be in the kernel versus in user space, in the network or at the edge, on the host processor or in the NIC—is a theme that crops up over and over in system design. Sometimes there are security implications (only trusted functions belong in a trusted kernel). Sometimes the end-to-end argument helps you decide (there's little value in implementing a function inside the network that also has to be applied at the edge). But in many cases, it comes down to a cost-benefit analysis, with different classes of resources in a system having different capacities, capabilities, and costs. SmartNICs and IPUs demonstrate the thinking that goes into a design, and how that thinking potentially shifts over time as technology changes.

Beyond the examples given in this chapter, we are likely to continue encountering similar questions, especially as the cloud expands to the edge.

Does a service belong on-premises or in a remote datacenter? What computations should be done on a user device versus in the cloud? Knowing how to answer questions like these, and recognizing that the cross-over points are constantly moving, is an integral part of the systems approach.

Explore Further

Peter Druschel, Larry Peterson and Bruce Davie. Experiences with a high-speed network adaptor: a software perspective. ACM SIGCOMM, August 1994.

Kit Colbert. Announcing Project Monterey — Redefining Hybrid Cloud Architecture. VMware Blog, 2020.

Patrick Kennedy. DPU vs SmartNIC and the STH NIC Continuum Framework. Serve the Home blog, May 2021.

Amazon Web Services. AWS Nitro System.

Salvatore Salaaming. IPU Chip Offloads Networking and Some Security Tasks from CPUs. Network Computing, October 2022.

Network Management Is Now Cool

The print copy of the latest edition of our Computer Networks book is 817 pages. That's enough pages to cover multiple networking technologies (from Ethernet to WiFi to SONET), the protocols needed to interconnect those networks into a global communication substrate (from IP to ARP to BGP), the transport protocols needed to support distributed applications (from TCP to RPC to RTP), and several network applications (from the web to email to VoIP).

All hard problems worthy of study, to be sure, but the book includes only six pages on what turns out be an equally challenging endeavor: how to actually deploy the hardware and software that implement the network into the field, keep it running 24/7 in the face of failures and malicious attacks, and upgrade it over time as technology improves and more capacity is required. This is the problem of *network management*, which has historically been left to the system admins and network technicians who operate the network. Introductory networking textbooks—not just ours—have largely ignored the topic.

This is in part because management has been considered boring, but also because it has long been an ad hoc practice. There were few principles or abstract concepts to teach; what Tracy Kidder refers to as *"secrets and mysteries of the trade"* in the book *House* (see our chapter on Judgement). That situation is rapidly changing, however, as best practices in building clouds start to "trickle down" into the underlying network. These practices include the commoditization of the hardware (devices can be treated like "cattle" rather than "pets"), the softwarization of network functionality (of which SDN is an important advancement), and the adoption of DevOps and GitOps engineering practices.

That transformation has not come easily, and it is far from complete. The clash between traditional network management practices and cloud practices is substantial, and includes the question of how far one can go in replacing human operators with automated processes. This makes the overall problem space ripe for applying the systems lens. This chapter does exactly that by touching on several inter-related topics. But it starts with a look back to gain a better appreciation of why management and operations are so important in the first place.

Read Section 8

If (like me) you were a CS graduate student who cut your teeth on Berkeley Unix—complete with the first open source implementation of TCP/IP—you know Section 8 as the cryptic System Maintenance Commands section of the Unix User's Manual. (Not to be confused with the Section 8 that was a recurring theme in M*A*S*H.) It was obvious (to me) that this concluding section warranted a closer look because the introduction warned: *"Information in this section is not of great interest to most users."* Judging by my taste in research problems over the years, reading Section 8 turned out to be a pretty good investment.

But before getting to Section 8, you first learned about the rest of Unix, where you discovered how empowering it is to be able to build new Internet applications. Anyone interested in how targeted investments in open source software, coupled with affordable hardware, can spur innovation should study the role of BSD (Berkeley Software Distribution) in the success of the Internet. It's easy to assume the Internet as we know it today was inevitable, but at the time BSD Unix happened, it was not at all clear the incumbent Telcos could be disrupted. We've commented on the power of APIs many times, but the impact of the Socket API (Section 2) on enabling innovation on top of the Internet cannot be overstated. With that stable fixed-point in the architecture, a thousand flowers bloomed... and we have (thankfully) moved well beyond the telco vision of B-ISDN.

Section 8 was the second half of the story. In addition to describing how to shutdown and boot a system, it defined the process for managing long-running daemon processes, the Unix equivalent of today's microservices. If you had responsibility for configuring and managing system services on your department's server, which came with superuser privilege, you needed not only to know how to program Unix, you also needed to understand the ins-and-outs of operating Unix. As a grad student, the lessons I learned while being responsible for sendmail(8) on a live multi-user system were immeasurable. Every mistake instantly sent the faculty into the hallway looking for the responsible idiot. (In my defense, this was at a time when email addresses contained percent (%) and bang (!) operators in addition to at (@), and their precedence was not well-defined.)

BSD also provided me with an early lesson in the power of having many eyeballs on the lookout for security vulnerabilities. Looking at the source code for Sendmail, for example, revealed a backdoor, whereby one could Telnet to port 25, type the magic "wizard" command, and fork a root shell. So I made my counterparts at Berkeley and other Universities aware of that vulnerability by doing exactly that. Others probably did too, but it was a different time, and the lesson didn't initially take hold. With debugging convenience and a naive sense of community trumping security, the backdoor remained open by default in Sendmail until the Morris Worm used it as one of its attack vectors a few years later. (For a full account of that watershed moment, Cliff Stoll's *The Cuckoo's Egg* is must reading.)

Management as Research Inspiration

Gaining this sort of practical experience is obviously valuable if your plan is to become a system administrator, but it has long been my experience that an opportunity to manage systems that deliver services to actual users is a great source of systems research problems, as well as fertile ground for platform innovations. My PhD dissertation, born out of frustration with sendmail, turned out to be on naming and addressing; later, real-world experience running a CDN on PlanetLab generated a sequence of systems papers (as Vivek Pai and I reported in a 2007 CACM article); and most recently, our experience operating an edge cloud has led to an appreciation for the state management problem inherent in DevOps (as well as our latest book). And my experience is far from unique: many of the cloud tools we take for granted today—Kubernetes is a great example—started as someone's response to an operational point-of-pain.

This all leads me to believe that an open operations platform (as documented in Section 8) is just as important as an open programming platform (as documented in Section 2) for democratizing innovation. Would BSD Unix have had the same impact in the 1980s and 90s if the University Computer Center had supported it rather than the CS department letting its grad students take ownership of the operations problem? We can ask a similar question today. The value of being able to create new cloud applications is abundantly clear, but is there also value in having open access to the tools used to manage and operate the cloud (rather than delegating the latter to the cloud providers)?

To me, the answer is clearly yes. It comes down to the virtuous cycle of solutions being enabled by platforms on the one hand, and platforms being reshaped with the experience of usage on the other. Stable platforms with well-defined APIs surely allow a thousand flowers to bloom, but eventually, disruptive refactoring of those platforms is what leads to the next round of innovation. Software-Defined Networking is a famous example of disruptive refactoring, but it only works if we have sufficiently sophisticated tooling to assemble all the components into a coherent—and manageable—system. Orchestration and Lifecycle Management have become the dominant operational issues because (a) many smaller parts have to be assembled, and (b) these individual parts are expected to change more frequently. They are essential parts of what we might call the Cloud OS.

Certainly not everyone who writes programs—whether it's running on a personal server or in the cloud—also needs to know how to keep that program running 24/7, but from the perspective of empowering more people to participate in the creation of new systems, the operations platform needs to be kept open and accessible to anyone who wants to invest the time in it. Fortunately, there are a plethora of open source components available today that can be used to operate and lifecycle-manage a cloud. We've documented a roadmap for using them in *Edge Cloud Operations: A Systems Approach* (a sort of "Section 8" for the Cloud). We're hoping there are still a few people who are just crazy enough to give it a try.

Larry Peterson, January 2022

If GitOps is the Answer, What's the Question?

It's not hard to form the impression that building and deploying cloud native systems is rapidly becoming a solved problem, with GitOps providing the roadmap. The approach revolves around the idea of configuration-as-code: making all configuration state declarative (e.g., specified in Helm Charts and Terraform Templates); storing these files in a code repo (e.g., GitHub); and then treating this repo as the single source of truth for building and deploying a cloud native system. It doesn't matter if you patch a Python file or update a config file, the repo triggers a fully automated CI/CD pipeline.

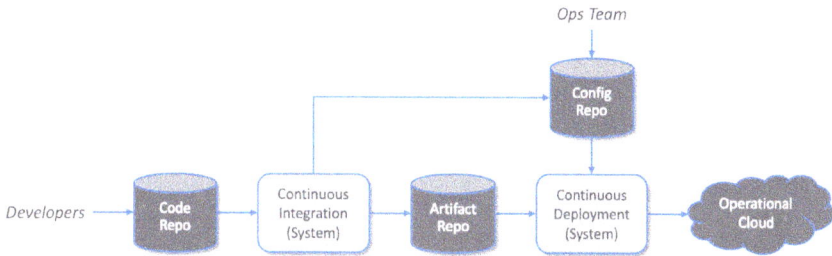

Continuous Integration (CI) / Continuous Deployment (CD) Pipeline

   Having built cloud native systems using this model (for example, see the Aether Project, a Private 5G Edge Cloud), the power of this GitOps model is clear—it provides a straightforward approach to the thorny problem of managing configuration state. But like any seemingly straightforward solution, there's more to the story. As others have already pointed out, GitOps isn't a silver bullet. In our experience, there are at least three considerations that lead us to this conclusion. All hinge on the question of whether all state needed to operate a cloud native system can be managed entirely with a repository-based mechanism.
   The first consideration is that we need to acknowledge the difference between people who develop software and people who build and operate systems using that software. DevOps (in its simplest formulation) implies there should be no distinction. In practice, developers are often far removed from operators, or more to the point, they are far removed from design decisions about exactly how others will end up using their software. For example,

software is usually implemented with a particular set of use cases in mind, but it is later integrated with other software to build entirely new cloud apps that have their own set of abstractions and features, and correspondingly, their own collection of configuration state. (This is true for Aether, where the Software Defined Mobile Core was originally implemented for use in global cellular networks, but is being repurposed to support private 4G/5G in enterprises.)

While it is true such state could be managed in its own GitHub repo, the idea of configuration management by pull request is overly simplistic. There are both low-level (implementation-centric) and high-level (application-centric) variables; in other words, it is common to have one or more layers of abstraction running on top of the base software. In the limit, it may even be an end-user (e.g., an enterprise user in Aether) that wants to change this state, which implies fine-grained access control is likely a requirement. None of this disqualifies GitOps as a way to manage such state, but it does raise the possibility that not all state is created equal—that there is a range of configuration state variables being accessed at different times by different people with different skill sets, and most importantly, needing different levels of privilege.

The second consideration has to do with where configuration state originates. For example, consider the addresses assigned to the servers assembled in a cluster, which might originate in an organization's inventory system. Or as in the case of a 5G service like Aether, there are unique identifiers assigned to mobile devices that are managed in a global subscriber database. In general, systems often have to deal with multiple—sometimes external—sources of configuration state, and knowing which copy is authoritative and which is derivative is problematic. There is no single right answer, but situations like this raise the possibility that the authoritative copy of configuration state needs to be maintained apart from any single use of that state. Building into all components the assumption that they are not the authoritative source for any configuration parameters they use is a good place to start. The idea of a "single source of truth", while attractive, misses some of the complexity we find in real deployments.

The third consideration is how frequently this state changes, and hence, potentially triggers restarting or possibly even re-deploying a set of containers. Doing so certainly makes sense for "set once" configuration parameters, but what about "runtime settable" control variables? What is the most cost-effective way to update system parameters that have the potential to change frequently? Again, this raises the possibility that not all state is created equal, and that there is a continuum of configuration state variables.

These three considerations point to the distinction between build-time configuration state and runtime control state. We emphasize, however, that the question of how to manage such state does not have a single correct answer; drawing a crisp line between "configuration" and "control" is notoriously difficult. Both the repo-based mechanism championed by GitOps and runtime control alternatives provide value, and it is a question of which is the better match for any given piece of information that needs to be maintained for a cloud to operate properly.

Runtime State vs Configuration State

Configuration state is reasonably well-defined, but what do we mean by Runtime State? In general, runtime state is more dynamic. If we take the example of Kubernetes, the configuration is declared in a YAML file, but runtime state is handled by controllers that must respond quickly to events such as the failure of a pod. No-one imagines that spinning up a new pod after a failure would be handled by a GitOps pull request; but the YAML file to declare how many pods should be running is an example of configuration state that sits well in the GitOps framework. In this example the distinction between configuration and runtime state is fairly obvious, but in practice it can be more of a continuum.

Maintenance of runtime state requires an appropriate control mechanism (as in the preceding example). We are building such a control mechanism for Aether, and without getting into the details, the central idea is to leverage a network device configuration micro-service, re-targeted at virtual devices (aka, software services). Such mechanisms have several nice properties: (1) they use YANG as the declarative specification language, and so come with a rich toolset for defining and manipulating data models; (2) they support versioning, so state changes can be rolled forward and backward; (3) they are agnostic as to how data is made persistent, but are typically paired with a cloud native key/value store; and (4) they support role-based access controls (RBAC), so different principals can be given different visibility into and control over the control/configuration parameters.

Apart from being designed to manage more dynamic runtime control state, the Control API that can be auto-generated from the YANG data model has delivered two advantages in our environment: (1) RBAC helps support the principle of least privilege, and (2) it provides an opportunity to implement early parameter validation and security checks (thereby catching errors closer to the user and generating more meaningful error messages). Effective data models have proven invaluable, a topic that we'll return to in a later post.

So is there a single best mechanism? Almost certainly there is a need for both, decided on a case-by-case basis: Runtime Control maintains authoritative state for some parameters and the code repos maintain authoritative state for other parameters. We just need to be clear about which is which, so each backend component knows which "configuration path" it needs to be responsive to. Is there a big takeaway from all this? Only that no one said state management was going to be easy, and you should beware of anyone who claims otherwise!

Larry Peterson, June 2021

The Source of Truth Moves to the Edge

The most rewarding experience of my 30+ year research career was building and running PlanetLab, which I reflected upon when we decommissioned it last year. Of the many lessons it taught me, appreciating the challenge of operationalizing an Internet-scale distributed system that runs continuously—through hundreds of bug fixes, security patches, feature enhancements, software upgrades, and hardware refreshes—is at the top of the list. That's now the core job description for thousands of DevOps engineers responsible for cloud infrastructure, but at the time we started PlanetLab in 2002, our small team was flying blind... and we often ran into obstacles, sometimes repeatedly, before figuring out how to get past them.

The tooling available today is light years ahead of where we were 15+ years ago, thanks in large part to open source made available by the cloud providers that were on a similar (but certainly higher-stakes) journey. A great example is Google's Borg begetting Kubernetes, which then catalyzed a vibrant ecosystem of provisioning, integration, deployment, and management tools. Many times over the years (with both PlanetLab and commercial edge clouds I've worked on), we've decided to abandon a home-grown mechanism because a better community-supported and widely-adopted solution had become available.

Everyone Gets a Lesson in Operations

Keeping PlanetLab running was not just an operational challenge for Larry and the PlanetLab ops team, but it also exposed a generation of system researchers to real-world operational issues that are inevitable when you're running Internet services. Researchers who had been safely working in their labs were suddenly exposed to all sorts of unexpected user behavior, both benign and malicious, not to mention the challenges of keeping a service running under varied network conditions. There were a lot of lessons learned under fire, with unexpected traffic bursts (immediately followed by email from upset University system admins), a common rite of passage for both grad students and their advisors.

Today, Larry is not surprised when visiting cloud operators and catching up with former PlanetLab users to hear that they now spend most of their time worrying about operational problems. Suddenly, network management has become cool.

This is something I've been thinking a lot about recently, as edge clouds gain momentum in the marketplace. Operating a cloud is fundamentally about balancing feature velocity against service stability, and even though the tooling continues to improve, the underlying problem hasn't gotten any easier. More importantly, the design principles that we came to understand when we were trying to make progress with duct tape and baling wire remain unchanged. Sometimes those principles are easy to overlook when your tools become more powerful and complex, but they are what's enduring.

As a result of that experience, I've come to view the challenge of operationalizing a cloud as a classic systems problem of managing state—configuration state, but a collection of state variables nonetheless. This reduces to controlling who gets to write each variable, ensuring that every component that needs to read a variable eventually does, synchronizing access among multiple readers and writers, recovering from partial failures, and so on. That's the academic in me reducing the problem to first principles—which I realize is of little comfort to a practitioner in the middle of a git merge that will trigger a re-deployment—but I have found this systems lens is helpful (if not essential) when trying to tease apart the many factors that are so easily conflated.

One lesson that we kept learning (and relearning because the root problem manifests in different ways) is the importance of establishing a single source of truth for every configuration variable. This forces you to think critically about (a) the distinction between variables that are written by humans and those that are derived from other variables, and (b) who is allowed to write each "source" variable. There are several best practices that follow from this focus on the source of truth, such as: making the variables explicit rather than burying them in the middle of scripts; version controlling the source variables, so it is possible to roll back to previous values; maximizing the state that is derived, which minimizes the state humans are responsible for setting/changing; recognizing that schema and model definitions are a kind of configuration state; making operations on configuration state idempotent; and programming components to assume they are not the source of truth. This is by no means an exhaustive list, but we have started the process of documenting these lessons.

There are many pragmatic issues that influence implementation choices, such as how frequently a given variable is likely to change, but these are secondary to correctness (the goal is to deploy the intended configuration every time) and repeatability (it should be possible to update and redeploy the system continuously). This brings me back to the available tooling, which by its nature, comes with baked-in engineering decisions. Many of those tools encourage best practices—the Configuration-as-Code paradigm championed by Helm and Terraform is a great example—but (1) it's not easy to select the right tool for the situation when there are so many to choose from, and (2) there are hard problems that no amount of tooling can correct for. These were on my mind while writing the first draft of our *Edge Cloud Operations: A Systems Approach* book.

Navigating Through The Tool Space

On the first point, there are (at least) several dozen DevOps-related open source projects available, and navigating the project space is one of the biggest challenges we faced in putting together the cloud management platform we used as a case study in the book. This is in large part because these projects are competing for mindshare, with both significant overlap in the functionality they offer and implicit dependencies on each other. Keeping in mind that there is no single tool that solves all problems (despite what you might read in the project description), the ultimate challenge is to assemble the available parts into a coherent end-to-end system. It turned out that the book is a retrospective on that decision-making process. For example, one of the tools we started with, Rancher, ended up playing a much smaller role than we originally expected it to. That's not a unique example, as we integrated over 20 narrowly targeted components. Deciding what features of each tool not to use happened over and over.

On the second point, the problem remains hard (and the solution elusive) for several reasons. In some cases, there are variable settings that originate in external systems, which is to say, the single source of truth is sometimes a process (or service) that you have to query. These sources need to be incorporated into an end-to-end solution rather than treated as exceptions. This happened in the 5G-capable edge cloud we've been building, for example, because it's necessary to call a remote Spectrum Access Service (SAS) to learn how to configure the radio settings for the small cells you've deployed. Naively, you might think that's a variable you could pull out of a YAML file stored in a git repository. In other cases, it's problematic to not take UX requirements into account, for example, by assuming a component-specific config file is the source of truth, when in fact a class of end-users expect to be able to change a subset of the configuration variables at runtime.

The bottom line is that there are many moving parts involved in operationalizing a cloud, and while dealing with that complexity has largely been left to the hyperscalers, the migration of the cloud into enterprises and other edge locations brings the problem front-and-center for many. The reality is that embedding the cloud in edge environments exposes it to many local variables, all of which have the potential to be the source of truth. Using an open source edge cloud as a case study, we have undertaken to provide a tour of the available tools and document the design principles that should be brought to bear on that challenge.

Larry Peterson, November 2021

Boundary Conditions: A Systems Approach

I recently attended the kickoff workshop for the FlexNet Project, where research on building more dynamically programmable networks was framed as a sort of Maslow's Pyramid. This is a diagram Amin Vahdat originally presented at ONF Connect 2018 to convey the importance of *Availability* in everything Google does when building cloud infrastructure. It's the foundation you have to get right before worrying about anything else, and no new feature or improvement higher in the pyramid is introduced unless it preserves or improves availability. Similarly, *Manageability* and *Feature Velocity* follow, in that order of priority. *Performance* improvements (shown at the top of the pyramid) are the least important consideration. (*Stranding* could be labeled "Efficiency" in the sense that it's about making sure you have the right kind of capacity in the right place.)

Amin was talking about cloud infrastructure, but it strikes me that the idea also applies to computing systems in general, which, like infrastructure, often involve platforms that others (e.g., app developers) can build upon. Even *Capacity Delivery* is a consideration when we're talking about scalable systems, although most of the time we're focused on virtual rather than physical resources, in which case spinning up additional capacity is clearly part of the system's management machinery. I realized this approach can be generalized to the sorts of systems I've been involved with over my career.

First, and most directly, the pyramid is a great visualization of the "systems approach" that we talk about all the time—in the sense that every system addresses a set of requirements, but the real challenge is understanding how to trade those requirements off against each other. Individually, no one can argue with the virtue of Manageability or Velocity or Availability (or

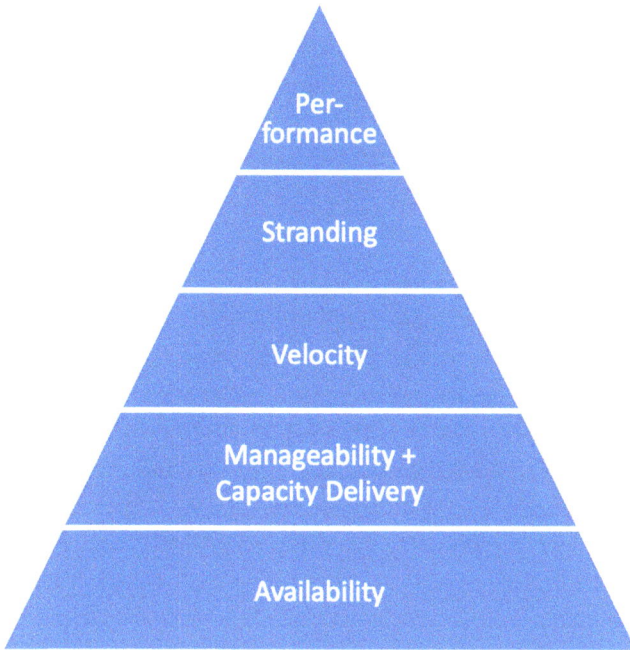

Maslow's Pyramid Applied to Cloud Priorities

whatever your favorite set of -ities might be), but each system should have a clear set of priorities. In the case above:

Availability > Manageability > Velocity > Stranding > Performance

And as a corollary, any obsession on just one dimension of the design might succeed in optimizing to reach a local maximum, but be rendered irrelevant (or worse, counterproductive) in the larger scheme of things. This is just "System Design 101", but worth repeating.

Second, while the systems research community has long been focused on Performance and Availability—in part because both lend themselves to quantitative evaluation, but also because those experiments are easy to control by isolating the problem and ignoring the rest of the pyramid—Velocity is now also getting its fair due. Coming up with good metrics is still a challenge, but "Software-Defined Anything" is now widely accepted as a credible research agenda. And new efforts like FlexNet take that a step further by trying to make software-defined systems even more dynamically upgradable. (Now if only we could go back and introduce more dynamicity into our most mature software-based platform—the OS—we'd have real progress. Maybe eBPF is the answer, but that's probably a discussion for another time.)

Velocity vs. Manageability

Third, what I find most interesting is this: once you've prioritized your requirements, how do you manage the boundaries and interactions between them? Here are two examples at the interplay between Velocity and Manageability, which are often in conflict. The first is one I encountered over a decade ago while working at a CDN startup. (I've come to think of a CDN as a PaaS for content providers, who both publish content and program how it is delivered.) In any startup, feature velocity is paramount, and in practice (even if not in principle) it is often prioritized over manageability. This leads to the following all-too-common scenario: Customer asks for feature X; Engineers implement feature X; Operators are unable to change the cryptic config-file for feature X without help from Engineers. That's an approach to manageability that does not scale, but either you prioritize "plumbing" every feature through to a well-defined management interface, or you pay for your architectural debt at some point down the road. (More on that after my second example.)

The other example is one that's recently emerged due to SDN, and we've had to address it while building private 5G Connectivity-as-a-Service for enterprises. Suppose you have a programmable data plane, and perhaps have even figured out how to reprogram it on-the-fly with no negative impact on current packet flows. If you add a new feature, you likely also need to upgrade the control plane. The joint development of P4 (for programming the forwarding pipeline) and tooling around P4Runtime (to auto-generate the control API) is a huge step forward on this front. But if you update the control plane, you may also need to update the management plane, and this needs to be coordinated across all three planes. This is where the challenge is the same as in the first example: We need a well-defined management API.

Part of the solution comes in the form of modern DevOps tooling. The availability of declarative configuration specs such as Kubernetes CRDs,

Helm Charts, and Terraform Templates is an improvement over having to deal with dozens of one-off config files, but they assume it's an operator who will be responsible for managing the system. If it's an end-user of a multi-tenant, cloud-managed platform service (for example, a content provider in the case of a CDN or an enterprise admin in the case of a managed connectivity service), then management directives need to be codified in a programmatic API. And most importantly, this API has to be updated in sync with all the layers below it. There is no standard P4/P4RT-equivalent for doing this, but from my experience, a reasonable approach is to define a data model for the abstract service you are trying to provide (e.g., using a language like YANG), around which you build tools to auto-generate the Platform-as-a-Service API. This approach is the focus of one of the chapters in our Edge Cloud Operations book.

There's one final lesson we can take away from these two examples that applies to the general challenge of managing the boundary between Manageability and Velocity. It's one that we touch on in the next post about Observability (an aspect of Manageability). A common refrain you hear is frustration about needing to "plumb the feature through to the API so it can be controlled" and needing to "instrument the feature so it can be observed". The frustration comes from both sides: from operators who need to control and observe the system and from developers who have to deal with the burden of making it so (often at the expense of the next feature on their todo list). Acknowledging the friction at this boundary is the first step, but to me this challenge looks like an opportunity to build a platform. Management is clearly a first-class property of any system you build, but I would argue it can (and should) also be a platform in its own right, one that provides value by making it easier to "control and observe" new features. Service meshes such as Istio do exactly that, but whatever your mechanism of choice, the goal should be to support feature velocity by streamlining how those features are managed.

Larry Peterson, October 2022

———————————————

Observability Joins the List of Essential Properties

While working to complete the Monitoring and Telemetry chapter of our Edge Cloud Operations book, I couldn't help but notice all the hype on the Internet about observability, and especially how many sites were eager to explain to me why observability is so much more than monitoring. The message is clear: anyone who is satisfied with just monitoring their cloud services will miss the boat. But what isn't clear is exactly why.

None of those sites described observability as another of the set of "-ities" (qualities) that all good systems aspire to—alongside scalability, reliability, availability, security, usability, and so on—but that's where I would start. Observability is simply the property of a system that makes visible the facts about its internal operation needed to make informed management and control decisions. That leads to the obvious question: How? What are best practices and techniques in achieving observability?

At a mechanistic level, the answer is straightforward: instrument your code to produce useful facts that are then collected, aggregated, stored, and made available (via query) for display and analysis. Where the problem starts to become interesting is in answering the question: What data is useful? Again, the answer seems to be well-understood, at least at a high level, with three types of telemetry data typically identified: metrics, logs, and traces. (I would add a fourth—being able to query the flow-level state in the network data plane using Inband Network Telemetry (INT)—which I'll return to at the end.)

Metrics are quantitative data about a system. These include common performance metrics such as link bandwidth, CPU utilization, and memory usage, but also binary results corresponding to "up" and "down". These values are produced and collected periodically (e.g., every few seconds), either by reading a counter, or by executing a runtime test that returns a value. These metrics can be associated with physical resources such as servers and switches, virtual resources such as VMs and containers, or even end-to-end cloud services.

Logs are the qualitative data that is generated whenever a noteworthy event occurs. This information can be used to identify problematic operating conditions (i.e., it may trigger an alert), but more commonly, it is used to troubleshoot problems after they have been detected. Various system components—all the way from the low-level OS kernel to high-level cloud services—write messages that adhere to a well-defined format to the log. These messages include a timestamp, which makes it possible for the logging stack to parse and correlate messages from different components.

Traces are a record of causal relationships (e.g., Service A calls Service B) resulting from user-initiated transactions or jobs. They are a form of event logs, but provide more specialized information about the context in which different events happen. Tracing is well understood in a single program, but in a cloud setting, a trace is inherently distributed across a graph of network-connected microservices. This makes the problem challenging, but also critically important because it is often the case that the only way to understand time-dependent phenomena—such as why a particular resource is overloaded—is to understand how multiple independent workflows interact with each other.

For each of these types of telemetry data, the central challenge is to define a meaningful data model, so there is agreement across the many components that go into an end-to-end solution. Now we've dug down to the essential technical problem, and while there may one day be universal agreement about those data models—active open source efforts like OpenTelemetry are working toward such definitions—as a practical matter, cloud services are built from components pulled from many sources, each of which have adopted a different instrumentation practice. So today the state-of-the-art is to write filters that translate one format into another (and to hope that components outside your control are well instrumented).

If all of this sounds obvious, it is only so in retrospect. Hype about the latest hot topic is largely an exercise in creating the illusion of differentiation and uniqueness. There is little value in finding commonality. Returning to the question of monitoring vs observability, how you answer it depends on how you define terms. My view is that there are two broad use cases for telemetry data: (1) proactively watching for warning signs of trouble (e.g., attacks, bugs, failures, overload conditions) in a steady-state system; and (2) reactively taking a closer look to determine the root cause and resolve an issue (e.g., fix a bug, optimize performance, provision more resources, defend against an attack) once a potential problem is flagged. I tend to refer to the overall problem space as "monitoring", but if we call the first use case monitoring and the second use case troubleshooting, then no one would suggest that monitoring without troubleshooting is a viable approach. Observability is simply a prerequisite for both.

One thing that does seem to be happening under the "observability banner" is to recognize that "always on" tracing is an essential part of troubleshooting. This should not come as a surprise; a paper describing Google's experience with the Dapper tracing tool dates back to 2010, and Microsoft described their Sherlock tool for debugging enterprise networks in a 2007 SIGCOMM paper. Tracing requests through a microservice architecture is in many ways the cloud's version of profiling, a practice with a long history in both debugging and performance tuning. It is certainly the case that diagnostic scenarios that benefit from tracing and profiling are among the thorniest a DevOps team will ever encounter (he said from experience).

Aligning Incentives

Having access to the right data is essential, and every attempt should be made to achieve observability, but it is also important to acknowledge that troubleshooting is an inherently human-intensive and context-dependent process. You often need to be an expert to know what questions to ask, which means it's difficult to fully "platform-tize" the problem away. I suspect this also contributes to the reluctance of some developers to embrace a one-size-fits-all observability framework. If we're going to try to convince developers to always use the best possible tools, we just as well start by asking them to program in a strongly typed language like Standard ML or Haskell. Not going to happen. An equally sticky problem is that component developers are motivated to make sure their components are correct (get past the "it runs on my box" stage), but have less stake in end-to-end operational behavior, especially when it's someone else's deployment. There is a crack in the DevOps storyline, where incentives are not always aligned.

So beyond best-effort observability, what are our options? A couple of related ideas come to mind. One is service meshes, discussed in our SDN chapter, which are increasingly being positioned as a tool for observability. A large part of the appeal of service meshes is that they sit close enough to an application to see in detail what is coming in and out of it (e.g. API requests and responses) without requiring the application developer to insert additional code to achieve that visibility. Examples of this can be found in Istio and the recently announced Tetragon project.

Another is to build on INT. Whereas network devices historically were only minimally instrumented (e.g. with packet counters), INT builds on the rise in programmable networking hardware to enable fine-grained and programmable instrumentation of the data plane.

In both cases, the key insight is that it's difficult to know in advance (a) what questions you will want to ask, and (b) what specific workflows to zoom in on. Being able to programmatically re-instrument the code path (data plane) is sometimes the only option. Supporting that kind of flexibility is consistent with the ultimate goal of observability, but knowing where to embed "programmable instruments" is the $64,000 question. While we still have a lot of work to do, it's clear that Observability has achieved top billing with all the other desirable qualities of distributed systems, and the tools are rapidly evolving to keep up with the demand.

Larry Peterson, May 2022

What Happened to Network Automation?

Earlier posts have been discussing the limits of automation in the context of edge cloud operations. That got us thinking about the decade-plus worth of efforts to automate the configuration and operation of networks, of which intent-based networking may be the most well-known and ambitious example. Are we any closer to the automation of networking that we were a decade ago? In this post we look back at some early successes of network automation and limits on its adoption.

In thinking about these questions, I remember the moment when software-defined networking started to make sense for me. It was 2011 and I was in an auditorium at Stanford listening to Scott Shenker give a talk "The Future of Networking and the Past of Protocols". Up to that point, I had struggled to understand why the desire to make networks "software-defined" required a centralized controller that was separated from its data plane. The crux of Scott's argument was this: reasoning about the behavior of fully distributed algorithms is hard. And distributed algorithms are at the heart of networking. There is a reason why people who can configure BGP correctly in complex environments are highly sought after and widely viewed as wizards.

The solution proposed in Scott's talk, like so much of computer science, was to create a new layer of abstraction. The central SDN controller presents the abstraction of the network as one big switch, which is much easier to reason about than the distributed algorithms—notably, routing algorithms—that underpin traditional networking. Of course, abstracting away the complexity of the distributed algorithms inside a centralized controller is easier said than done, and there lies the challenge of building a working SDN system. But I, like many others, was sold on this new vision of how to build networks. At the same time, many of my colleagues remained unconvinced, having learned that (a) central control didn't scale (b) you could never sell a central controller into a real network because it was a single point of failure. Getting past those issues is indeed one of the key challenges of SDN.

Coincidentally, I ended up getting a chance to meet with Martin Casado a few days after Scott's talk. Martin, Scott, and Nick McKeown had founded Nicira a number of years earlier, and all that I really knew about the company was that they were active in OpenFlow standardization and implementation. Over the next few weeks I learned a lot more about Nicira as my interest in the company grew from curiosity to "maybe I should try to work there".

Network Automation Launches Nicira

By January 2012 I was indeed working for Nicira, just in time for the company to come out of stealth mode and launch the Network Virtualization Platform (NVP). While "network virtualization" was the use case of SDN that launched Nicira and led to its later acquisition by VMware, it's easy to lose sight of the importance of network automation in this story. In fact, all the Nicira customers that I can recall from before the acquisition were using NVP for some sort of network automation project.

A typical use case for NVP in these early days was to support a developer cloud. A developer wanting to run some code in a distributed environment with multiple virtual machines interconnected by some network topology would request the VMs and network resources via a self-service portal. Provisioning the VMs was a fairly well-solved problem by 2012, but the network provisioning was painfully manual.

The key insight at Nicira was that a central SDN controller could expose an API to be called (by the self-service portal) as part of the provisioning process. So while the motivation for central control in Shenker's talk was to make networks programmable, it also served to make them automatically configurable. The self-service portal calls the API to make requests such as "create a layer 2 network", "connect the following VMs to that network", "insert a router with NAT between the L2 network and the Internet". The SDN controller provides a single place to receive all those API requests, so that the self-service portal need not have any understanding of which network devices serve particular VMs. And importantly, even if VMs move around (as they are liable to do in modern virtualized data centers) the SDN controller ensures that the requested network capabilities followed the VMs around the data center.

In the time-honored tradition of software startups, we had our own "dog-food" environment that was used by our own developers. Anyone working on the NVP product could log into our local self-service portal (provided via OpenStack) and instantiate a set of VMs with appropriate networking services to run their code in a proper distributed environment. Our portal could provision a standard developer environment with one button push. We used to refer to this as "Inception" because of the layers of virtualization going on: many instances of NVP could be running in our developer cloud, each serving up virtual networks, with the networking that each instance required being provided by an underlying instance of NVP.

In a sense you could view this as the beginning of "intent-based net-working". Rather than provisioning VLANs and NAT rules on switches and routers, a developer only had to specify their intent: I want a network topology to interconnect this set of VMs I'm spinning up. The term "intent-based networking" would come later, and the vision was more expansive, but the basic idea was there.

Scaling Out Automation

But a funny thing happened as we tried to scale out the business of network virtualization. It turned out that automation was out of reach for most of our customers. When we joined VMware in late 2012 and started to talk to customers about NVP, one of the first questions we would ask is "what's your automation strategy". And in most cases we would get a blank look because there was no such strategy. The early customers of Nicira were, it turned out, unusually sophisticated. They had automated the provisioning of VMs to a level that was largely unheard-of among typical enterprise customers. And because they had lowered the friction needed for end-users to obtain virtual computing resources, the pain point of network provisioning had become extremely obvious. Thus, the need for NVP was clear, but only after automation had been put in place for computing. And it didn't help that automation platforms were seriously immature at this point, with the main options being OpenStack and the VMware platform later known as *vRealize Automation (VRA)*. Neither of these platforms were for the faint of heart.

Fortunately for VMware and the network virtualization team, the introduction of distributed firewalling in 2013 opened up a whole other use-case: microsegmentation. That turned out to be a huge success as we've discussed previously (see the chapter on Security). But that left network automation languishing on the sidelines again.

A good example of how a suitably sophisticated organization can automate their networking was reported by Jeff Mogul and his colleagues at Google in NSDI 2020. It's well worth reading the paper or watching the presentation. It illustrates both the complexity that needs to be managed before you can automate anything, and why smaller organizations might not go to such lengths to automate their networks: the pain is somewhat lower for a smaller network, and the resources needed to solve the problem cannot be found or justified.

I have the impression that the situation improved somewhat with the rise of microservices and Kubernetes in particular. For all its shortcomings, Kubernetes has brought the automatic provisioning of distributed computing and networking resources to a much larger audience. But the success stories that I can find for network automation are largely limited to situations where the network is virtual—whether it is to interconnect VMs as we did in 2012 or the more common case of container networking today. I am admittedly less plugged in (no pun intended) to the world of physical networks than I once was, but my conversations with colleagues make me doubt that we are closing in on full automation for physical networks. I'll be happy to be proven wrong here but I'm not sure the industry structure and incentives are set up to make this happen—a topic that I probably need another blog post to cover. And just as self-driving cars have been "just a few years away" for more than a few years, I suspect that automating the management of physical networks is going to remain out of reach (for most of us) for a while longer.

Bruce Davie, May 2024

Closing Remarks

It is something of a cliché in the networking community to speak of network management as an afterthought. However, we believe that a significant shift is underway to prioritize management and operations in networking, and this chapter presents some of the evidence for that claim. Much of the shift in thinking is the result of the rise of cloud computing. No-one would imagine that a modern cloud could rely on manual configuration to meet the requirements to acquire computing resources and deploy applications at scale. Many of the examples we have used to illustrate this chapter come from our experiences in building and deploying cloud services and all the automated processes that are involved in such services.

It is telling that the first big commercial success of SDN came from applying SDN techniques to the problem of automating network configuration in private clouds. That wasn't really what most of the research community thought SDN was aiming for, but it was the pain point that enabled SDN to escape from the lab into commercial usage. Networks have to be as easy to configure and manage in an automated manner as any other resource in a cloud.

Just as SDN was enabled by the adoption of ideas from the distributed systems community, network management is benefiting from ideas adopted from cloud computing. Managing both configuration state and runtime state at scale is essentially the same problem whether you are dealing with computational resources or networks. And because SDN has helped us to manage networks through programmatic APIs (rather than the old command line of traditional routers and switches) we can now rely on a large set of common tools and procedures to manage networks as part of an overall cloud system. This is not to say that cloud management is a solved problem—it remains challenging—but at least we now get to treat networks as just another system resource to be managed by the tools at our disposal.

Explore Further

Clifford Stoll. The Cuckoo's Egg. Doubleday, 1989.

Vivek Pai and Larry Peterson. Experience-driven Experimental Systems Research. Communications of the ACM, November 2007.

Amin Vahdat. Keynote: ONF Connect 2018. ONF, December 2018.

Aether Project. Linux Foundation.

OpenTelemetry. Cloud Native Computing Foundation.

Benjamin Sigelman, et al. Dapper, a Large-Scale Distributed Systems Tracing Infrastructure. April 2010.

Paramvir Bahl, et al. Towards Highly Reliable Enterprise Network Services via Inference of Multi-Level Dependencies. ACM SIGCOMM, August 2007.

Jeff Mogul, et al. Experiences with Modeling Network Topologies at Multiple Levels of Abstraction. USENIX NSDI, February 2020.

Looking Over The Fence

The title of this chapter was inspired by a National Research Council report, *Looking Over the Fence at Networks*, which takes a look at the field of networking from the perspective of neighboring fields in computer science and adjacent research fields. We at Systems Approach take a broad view of computer science, so we find ourselves looking over the fence at *our* neighbors. Two areas in particular have drawn our attention in recent years: quantum computing and large language models (along with AI more generally). One thing these areas have in common is an exceptional level of hype, which we hope to cut through by getting a deep enough understanding of what is going on under the covers to know what is real versus aspiration. We've made a few stabs at explaining these topics to a general computing audience, and this chapter collects the results.

Quantum Reality

I read a blog post recently from Scott Aaronson on his experiences at the Solvay conference on physics, which ultimately led me back down the rabbit hole of trying to understand what quantum computing is good for. At first glance this is a bit of a detour from normal Systems Approach material, but there is a networking and security angle to all of this (and it's interesting in its own right), so I hope you will read on.

Back when I was APJ field CTO for VMware, many of my colleagues expected me to know something about everything in tech, and it was sometimes hard to bring myself to say "I don't know". And so in 2018 when someone asked me to explain quantum computing I gave it a shot and made a complete mess of the explanation. In fact, I made the most typical mistake of a dabbling generalist (often made in the popular science press) which was to say something about trying lots of solutions in parallel, leveraging the quantum property of being in a superposition of multiple states. If you know only one thing about quantum mechanics, it's likely to be the thought experiment of Schrödinger's cat, in which the cat is supposedly in two states (alive and dead) at the same time. Well, that turns out to be just enough to produce a pretty bad explanation of quantum computing.

Much of what I do understand about quantum computing comes from Scott Aaronson via his blog and lecture notes. Right at the top of his blog is the line burned into my memory since I first read it: "quantum computers won't solve hard problems instantly by just trying all solutions in parallel." There is a Zach Weinersmith comic does a good job of debunking this line of thought as well.

Anyway, after botching my first attempt to explain it, I decided to go a bit deeper on quantum computing, which ended up being quite timely. The first claim of "quantum supremacy" came out the next year and I immediately wanted to understand whether this was the big deal it seemed to be. (Like so much in this space, it either may or may not be a big deal.) One thing led to another and I've become just knowledgeable enough (or foolish enough) to attempt a couple of lectures on quantum computing and its practical impact. While it's truly hard to get an intuitive feel for quantum computing, this talk (linked below) represents my best effort at giving that intuition.

Last week I came across Aaronson's post about his experience at the Solvay Conference on Physics, the topic this year being "The Physics of Quantum Information". Perhaps the most famous Solvay conference was the fifth, held in 1927, at which quantum theory was hashed out by an astonishing list of attendees including Einstein, Marie Curie, Bohr, Schrödinger and a dozen other Nobel prize winners.

Looking for Super-Polynomial Speedup

The Solvay conference could be the greatest poster child for the importance of interdisciplinary research—in this year's case, computer scientists exchanging ideas with particle physicists. There is still a huge amount of work to be done both in building practical quantum computers and in figuring out what they are actually good for, and broad expertise is needed to make progress. But I was inspired to write this post by Aaronson's suggestion that there is a "Law of Conservation of Weirdness". It's more of a hypothesis than a law, but it is at the heart of what many researchers are trying to understand about quantum computing: when does quantum computing provide significant (i.e., super-polynomial) speedup over classical algorithms? Scott's conjecture is: there has to be something "weird" about the problem for a quantum algorithm to be effective. What remains unsolved to date is the precise nature of that weirdness. But typically there is some sort of structure to the problem that makes it suitable for quantum speedup.

For us non-physicists, the most famous (and potentially most practically important) problem that displays an appropriate level of "weirdness" to benefit from quantum algorithms is factorization. Finding the prime factors of an integer is not just a matter of randomly trying different answers until you stumble on one that works; there is plenty of structure to the problem that allows an efficient quantum algorithm to be found. This is what Shor's algorithm does, and there is one part of Shor's algorithm that happens to be really efficient for quantum computers while not being efficient on classical computers. (It's called the quantum Fourier transform, and if you'd like a bit of intuition about how it works, Aaronson has you covered once again.)

Why does this problem, and Shor's algorithm, matter? Well, much of cryptography depends on the supposed difficulty of finding the prime factors of a large number, and a variety of similar computationally hard tasks. RSA and related public key algorithms are believed to be at risk within a decade or two of becoming ineffective. This is because the supposedly hard task of determining a private key given a public key depends on the hardness of factoring a large number (or some similarly expensive computation). If quantum computers continue to improve in terms of their number of quantum bits (qubits) and reliability as they have done in recent years, it seems only a matter of time before these algorithms will no longer be secure.

I would argue that there is no reason to panic since we have a while to wait before quantum computers are big enough and reliable enough to crack these algorithms, but the consensus is that we will need new algorithms eventually, and that by the time we know that the old algorithms have been broken, it will be too late. Hence, the wise choice is to plan ahead for "cryptographic agility", i.e., the ability to swap out algorithms in favor of new ones that are not susceptible to quantum solutions. NIST has been running a process for several years to identify suitable candidates for post-quantum cryptography (PQC).

What I find especially interesting about this situation is that the experts in this field are still figuring out which classes of problem are amenable to quantum solutions. This is the point of the "Law of Conservation of Weirdness." Only a narrow subset of problems that are hard to solve classically are easy to solve with quantum algorithms. What we need for PQC is algorithms that don't have efficient quantum (or classical) solutions. And while we can say "we haven't found an efficient quantum solution" to a problem, it is harder to say that no such solution exists. If nothing else, this underscores the need to be agile in our choices of cryptographic algorithms going forward.

Finally, there seems to be a bit of "irrational exuberance" about the ability of quantum computers to solve all sorts of problems, in areas such as machine learning and financial markets. While it's true that there is weirdness in both of those areas, I don't think that's what Aaronson means. My takeaway from his Solvay presentation is that the set of problems with efficient quantum solutions remains small, even as the latest research seeks to determine just what makes a problem a good fit for quantum computing.

Bruce Davie, July 2022.

––––––––––––––––––––

Putting Large Language Models in Context

In recent weeks it's been hard to avoid the buzz around the rise of Large Language Models (LLMs) and particularly the recent launch of ChatGPT. There have also been some notable failures ranging from the hilarious to the alarming. In fact we had to keep updating this post as new stories came out. So, we're shifting focus this week to go a bit outside our lane to look at some of the underlying issues with AI systems.

As someone whose primary field is networking, I'm not going to claim that I have deep expertise in Artificial Intelligence (AI). But in my role as regional CTO for VMware over the period from 2017 to 2020, I needed to be more of a generalist. So I sought to understand what was happening in AI and what it might mean for the technology industry as it moved into the mainstream. In this post I'm going to share some of what I learned, which is now proving helpful to process the daily onslaught of new developments in AI. I will note that there is some resistance to calling the latest round of LLM systems "AI" but that usage seems well established now.

When I was in the final year of my undergraduate electrical engineering degree, I happened to write my thesis on "Expert Systems for VLSI design". It was a bit of a random choice from a list of topics proposed by my favorite professor, but expert systems were "hot" in 1984, representing one promising line of research in AI at the time. There was a fairly direct line from that thesis to my applying to the PhD program at Edinburgh University. Edinburgh had one of the best Computer Science departments in the U.K. and one of the only AI departments in the world. What I didn't know until I arrived in Edinburgh from Australia was that the two departments had a dim view of each other, with the CS folks viewing AI as not serious, while the AI view of CS was no better. I sat in on a couple of AI courses but pretty soon I picked my side (CS) just in time to avoid the second of several "AI Winters".

That was about the extent of my AI knowledge until 2017, when I noticed a sort of anxiety among technical people I met about the rise of AI, including uncertainty about what it meant for the tech industry (and VMware in particular). So I started to read up on the state of the art and gather information from my co-workers who were closer to the field than I. One especially helpful article I read was "Machine Learning Explained" by noted roboticist Rodney Brooks (of iRobot fame). You should read it—it's fun, but long, so here is a quick summary: Donald Michie, who created the AI department in Edinburgh in the 1960s, built a mechanical computer called MENACE using matchboxes, which learned how to play tic-tac-toe (or noughts and crosses as it's called in the U.K.). It was a clever piece of design by an AI pioneer who couldn't get access to an electronic computer in those early days. The machine really did "learn": after every game of tic-tac-toe, it was given either positive or negative reinforcement in the form of the addition or subtraction of some colored beads into the relevant matchboxes, in much the same way that today we use training data to adjust the weights in a neural network. Eventually, with enough training, it was able to play decent but not optimal games against human players, even though no-one ever explained the rules of the game to it.

A Reconstruction of Michie's MENACE System by Matthew Scroggs

Brooks makes some good points about the similarity of this mechanical system to modern reinforcement learning systems. What strikes me is that no-one would be tempted to use the term "intelligent" or "sentient" to describe this machine. It learns to get better at a task through training, and there is something about "learning" that we associate with intelligence, but since this is just a few hundred matchboxes filled with colored beads, it's pretty easy to conclude that there is no intelligence. There is not even a concept of "three crosses in a row"—the machine just plays moves that have been rewarded because they led to wins in the past.

Not long before Brooks wrote his article, Alpha Go (a game-playing machine using deep learning) had managed to beat the world's best players at the game of Go, marking something of a milestone in the history of human-vs-computer competition. But Brooks suspected that the go-playing machine didn't understand the game in the way a human does, just as MENACE didn't understand what a row of crosses was. He asked the Deep Mind team if their machine would cope with a subtle change to the rules of Go (changing the board size) and they were quick to agree that it would not, because it had not encountered that situation in its training. That observation was effectively born out by the recent defeat of a system similar to Alpha Go. Quoting the report of the game:

The tactics used... involved slowly stringing together a large "loop" of stones to encircle one of his opponent's own groups, while distracting the AI with moves in other corners of the board. The Go-playing bot did not notice its vulnerability, even when the encirclement was nearly complete...

"As a human it would be quite easy to spot," he added.

In other words, the AI system, having been trained against typical Go strategies, didn't recognize a new strategy that would have been easy for a human to spot, because the AI system didn't recognize what a "loop" of stones looked like.

This lack of understanding is one of the key concerns about modern machine learning systems. And it has been on display in the various failures of ChatGPT and similar LLM systems. Douglas Hofstadter had some fun getting GPT-3 to give nonsensical answers when faced with questions that most humans would have quickly dismissed as unanswerable. Just as the game-playing systems lack an understanding of the game that would be obvious to a human, the chat systems lack an understanding of the meaning behind the words they are producing.

There are some other issues that are common to Michie's MENACE and modern machine learning systems. It is well known now that performance of these systems depends heavily on the training data that is fed in. Michie showed how MENACE learned different styles of play depending on the sort of human opponent it faced, and the Go-playing system was stumped by a style of play it had not been trained on.

It's also worth noting how much work it took to map a simple game like noughts and crosses onto a machine learning algorithm, and Brooks makes this point that ML is not just some sort of magic that we can sprinkle on hard problems and get results out the other side. "Every successful application of ML is hard won by researchers or engineers carefully analyzing the problem that is at hand." This makes me appreciate the hard work that has gone into making ML systems work at all and a bit less willing to believe that we are going to see all challenging human tasks taken over by machines soon.

The idea that LLMs have no understanding of the words they produce is conveyed by the term "stochastic parrots", coined by Emily Bender et al. in an influential paper. (This is also the paper that led to Timnit Gebru being forced out of Google.) The lack of understanding in large language models is easy to lose sight of because their conversational skills are so impressive (rather more so than the tic-tac-toe skills of MENACE) but I'm persuaded by the arguments made by Bender and team (and many others), especially as they come on top of the copious examples of wrong or bizarre answers coming out of LLMs. Bender has gone on to make the case that LLMs are a really bad choice for search engines—which is interesting as Microsoft and Google seem to be racing headlong in that direction. Maybe some of the recent speed bumps, such as the wrong answer about the James Webb telescope in Google's Bard launch announcement, will give the search giants pause. My approach, at least for now, is to treat these LLM-based systems as very large, efficient collections of matchboxes—and keep working in my chosen field of networking.

Bruce Davie, March 2023.

Looking Inside Large Language Models

While we're not quite ready to give the full Systems Approach book-length treatment to AI and machine learning, we like to think we can give our readers a bit of perspective on the field when there is no shortage of hyperbole and strong opinions. We're not claiming to be AI experts (although I very nearly ended up studying in the legendary AI department at Edinburgh in the 1980s, as discussed above). We've read many thousands of words on the topic and some of the central issues (in our view) are becoming clear.

A couple of questions put to me recently led me to think that perhaps it was time for another post on Large Language Models (LLMs) and the broader topic of AI. (As noted previously, I'm going to use "AI" in the way the term is most widely used now, an umbrella term that includes LLMs and other machine learning systems, in spite of some pushback. Rodney Brooks has a good piece that touches on the change in meaning of "AI" since the term was coined over 60 years ago.) First, in a recent podcast, I was asked about the biggest challenge at Systems Approach, and I immediately answered "figuring out what's important". This goes way beyond AI, but it's a challenge even to decide what aspects of AI warrant our attention.

And when a person in the investing community asked for my opinion on AI, my response (which might have verged on a rant) was this: my biggest concern with AI is that too many people, whether they are journalists, investors, business decision makers or whatever, are focused on the wrong problem. This issue is well captured in a recent Scientific American article by Emily Bender (of Stochastic Parrots fame) and Alex Hanna of DAIR. If you only read one article on AI, I'd suggest that one—even if that means skipping the rest of this post. To summarize, we should focus not on theoretical problems of some future superhuman intelligence, but on the harms that AI is already capable of causing, such as fostering discrimination in areas from housing to health care, or helping the spread of misinformation.

That said, I continue to find the inner workings of AI quite fascinating and it's worth understanding them well enough to know what AI is and is not capable of. In the last month I've read a number of more in-depth articles on LLMs, and these have given me a little more insight into why the question of what is really going on inside these systems remains, for most people, a matter of debate. I mostly agree with the position that LLMs have no idea what they are doing, but as with most topics, there is a bit more to this one than meets the eye.

Building a Model

If you want to go deep into the internals of LLMs such as ChatGPT, Stephen Wolfram has written an excellent (if long) article that is also available in book form. One of the aspects that he drills down on is what it means to have a "model" of something. For example, if we had a set of data showing how long it takes a cannonball to fall to earth from various heights, we could fit a straight line to the data, and extrapolate or interpolate to predict times to fall from other heights not in the data set. But by choosing a straight line, we've adopted a model that's not very accurate, and will be increasingly inaccurate as we go further outside the range of the original data. Knowing how gravity works, we'd be more inclined to fit a parabola, but that's only possible because we already have a model for gravity.

With LLMs, words are modelled in a vector space with hundreds of dimensions. The impressive feat is that an exceptionally complex model (with over a trillion parameters in GPT-4) can be trained (using vast amounts of input text) to do a pretty good job of mimicking human writing. In effect, GPT builds a model of language that captures a lot of the complexity of how humans string words together. With that model in place, an LLM is then able to generate strings of text not in the training data set—which is exactly what we observe when we interact with a system such as ChatGPT. As we know, the generated text often looks pretty authentic. As Timothy Lee and Sean Trott pointed out in another very helpful article at Ars Technica, LLMs deal with issues such as disambiguating the multiple meanings of words depending on context by passing the input text through multiple layers of neural networks. ("Fruit flies like a banana" is an example requiring some serious disambiguation.) Each layer is called a "transformer" (the T in GPT) and you can think of a line of text being passed through successive layers of transformers. Each layer adds metadata to the words: for example, having seen the sentence above, one transformer layer might add metadata to indicate that the word "flies" refers to insects rather than motion through the air.

There is a lot more in that article and I recommend you read it, but I had a disconcerting feeling as I was reading it that my confident assertion that LLMs have no understanding of the words they are producing was a bit overstated. At this stage, we all know of examples where LLMs have produced laughable results indicating a lack of understanding of the world, but the details of how they work show that they are very good at understanding language. I think the issue is the difference between understanding language (a set of symbols) and understanding the world. If a human understands language, we generally assume that they also understand the world, but making this extrapolation in the case of LLMs is a bridge too far. Here is a quote from the Ars Technica article that gave me pause:

> For example, as an LLM "reads through" a short story, it appears to keep track of a variety of information about the story's characters: sex and age, relationships with other characters, past and current location, personalities and goals, and so forth.

The description here comes awfully close to suggesting that the LLM "understands" what it is reading. Brooks calls out the issue here: we mistake performance (producing realistic text) for competence (understanding the world). Since he's a roboticist (he founded iRobot), I found his prediction that GPT won't be used for robots, because they have to understand the real world, very compelling. (Brooks is good at making predictions and he boosts his credibility by keeping his predictions online for the long haul and reporting back on them.) To quote:

> *... it will be bad if you try to connect a robot to GPT. GPTs have no understanding of the words they use, no way to connect those words, those symbols, to the real world. A robot needs to be connected to the real world and its commands need to be coherent with the real world. Classically it is known as the "symbol grounding problem". GPT+robot is only ungrounded symbols.*

This is the key takeaway for me: having a model for language is different from having a model of the world. For example, we know that LLMs have a tendency to make up citations. These citations look "correct" because they conform to the model of language (they have authors, realistic titles, journal names, etc.). But they fail a basic test: they are not drawn from real, legitimate publications. So the language model doesn't understand "what is a legitimate citation" - a fact about the world that is pretty basic for a human to grasp.

So I remain convinced that we need to be cautious about how LLMs and other AI techniques are put to work. Not because they are going to achieve superhuman intelligence, but because they have serious limitations, and because humans are already using them in ways that cause harm. This is certainly not limited to AI, but the difficulty of understanding what AI systems are actually doing and the human tendency to assume greater competence than they really have presents some unique challenges.

Bruce Davie, August 2023.

Making Computers Useful

In the 1990s and 2000s we were regular attendees at the End-to-end Research Group, part of the Internet Research Task Force. Surrounded by people whose history in networking went back quite a bit further than ours, it was a chance to appreciate the value of learning networking history. Computer scientists are perhaps not the greatest students of history, but just as the history of programming languages has something to teach us about elegance and simplicity, so too can we learn from the very long history of Artificial Intelligence, the topic of this article.

Regular readers of this newsletter will recall that I have a history with AI, having flirted with it in the 1980s (remember expert systems?) and then having safely avoided the AI winter of the late '80s by veering off into formal verification before finally landing on networking as my specialty in 1988. And just as Larry has classics like the Pascal manual on his bookshelf, I still have a couple of AI books from the 1980s on mine, notably P. H. Winston's Artificial Intelligence (1984). Leafing through that book is quite a blast, in the sense that much of it looks like it might have been written yesterday. For example, the Preface begins this way:

> *The field of Artificial Intelligence has changed enormously since the first edition of this book was published. Subjects in Artificial Intelligence are de rigueur for undergraduate computer-science majors, and stories on Artificial Intelligence are regularly featured in most of the reputable news magazines. Part of the reason for change is that solid results have accumulated.*

I was also intrigued to see some 1984 examples of "what computers can do". One example was solving seriously hard calculus problems—notable because basic arithmetic seems to be beyond the capabilities of today's LLM-based systems. If calculus was already solvable by computers in 1984, while arithmetic stumps the systems we view as today's state of the art, perhaps the amount of progress in AI in the last 40 years isn't quite as great as it first appears. (That said, there are even better calculus-tackling systems today, they just aren't based on LLMs, and it's unclear if anyone refers to them as "AI").

One reason I picked up my old copy of Winston was to see what he had to say about the definition of AI, because that too is a controversial topic. His first take on this isn't very encouraging:

> *Artificial Intelligence is the study of ideas that enable computers to be intelligent.*

Well, OK, that's pretty circular, since you need to define intelligence somehow, as Winston admits. But he then goes on to state two goals of AI:

- To make computers more useful.

- To understand the principles that make intelligence possible.

In other words, it's hard to define intelligence, but maybe the study of AI will help us get a better understanding of what it is. I would go so far as to say that we are still having the debate about what constitutes intelligence 40 years later. The first goal seems laudable but clearly applies to a lot of non-AI technology.

This debate over the meaning of "AI" continues to hang over the industry. I have come across plenty of rants that we wouldn't need the term "AGI" (Artificial General Intelligence) if only the term AI hadn't been so polluted by people marketing statistical models as AI. I don't really buy this. As far as I can tell AI has always covered a wide range of computing techniques, most of which wouldn't fool anyone into thinking the computer was displaying human levels of intelligence.

The Re-emergence of Neural Networks

When I started to re-engage with the field of AI about eight years ago, neural networks—which some of my colleagues were using in 1988 before they fell out of favor—had made a startling comeback, to the point where image recognition by deep neural networks had surpassed the speed and accuracy of humans (with some caveats). This rise of AI led to a certain level of anxiety among my engineering colleagues at VMware, who sensed that an important technological shift was underway that (a) most of us didn't understand (b) our employer was not positioned to take advantage of.

As I threw myself into the task of learning how neural networks operate (with a big assist from Rodney Brooks) I came to realize that the language we use to talk about AI systems has a significant impact on how we think about them. For example, by 2017 we were hearing a lot about "deep learning" and "deep neural networks", and the use of the word "deep" has an interesting double meaning. If I say that I am having "deep thoughts" you might imagine that I am thinking about the meaning of life or something equally weighty, and "deep learning" seems to imply something similar. But in fact the "deep" in "deep learning" is a reference to the depth, measured in number of layers, of the neural network that supports the learning. So it's not "deep" in the sense of meaningful, but just deep in the same way that a swimming pool has a deep end—the one with more water in it. This double meaning contributes to the illusion that neural networks are "think-ing". A similar confusion applies to "learning" (which is where Brooks was so helpful): a DNN gets better at a task the more training data it is exposed to, so in that sense it "learns" from experience, but the way that it learns is nothing like the way a human learns things.

As an example of how DNNs learn, consider AlphaGo, the game-playing system that used neural networks to defeat human grandmasters. Accord-ing to the system developers, whereas a human would easily handle a change of board size (normally a 19x19 grid), a small change would render AlphaGo impotent until it had time to train on new data from the resized board. To me this neatly illustrates how the "learning" of DNNs is funda-mentally unlike human learning, even if we use the same word. The neural network is unable to generalize from what it has "learned". And making this point, AlphaGo was recently defeated by a human opponent who re-peatedly used a style of play that had not been in the training data. This inability to handle new situations seems to be a hallmark of AI systems.

Language Matters

The language used to describe AI systems continues to influence how we think about them. Unfortunately, given the reasonable pushback on re-cent AI hype, and some notable failures with AI systems, there may now be as many people convinced that AI is completely worthless as there are members of the camp that says AI is about to achieve human-like intelli-gence. I am highly skeptical of the latter camp (as outlined above) but I also think it would be unfortunate to lose sight of the positive impact that AI systems—or, if you prefer, machine-learning systems—can have.

I am currently assisting a couple of colleagues writing a book on machine learning applications for networking, and it should not surprise anyone to hear that there are lots of networking problems that are amenable to ML-based solutions. In particular, traces of network traffic are fantastic sources of data, and training data is the food on which ML systems thrive. Appli-cations ranging from DoS-prevention to malware detection to geolocation can all make use of ML algorithms, and the goal of this book is to help net-working people understand that ML is not some magic powder that you sprinkle on your data to get answers, but a set of engineering tools that can be selectively applied to produce solutions to real problems. In other words, neither a panacea nor an over-hyped placebo. The aim of the book is to help readers understand which ML tools are suitable for different classes of networking problems.

One story that caught my eye some time back was the use of AI to help Network Rail (UK) to manage the vegetation that grows alongside British railway lines. The key "AI" technology here is image recognition (to identify plant species)—leveraging the sort of technology that DNNs delivered over the last decade. Not perhaps as exciting as the generative AI systems that captured the world's attention in 2023, but a good, practical application of a technique that sits under the AI umbrella.

My tendency these days is to try to use the term "machine learning" rather than AI when it's appropriate, hoping to avoid both the hype and allergic reactions that "AI" now produces. And with the words of Patrick Winston fresh in my mind, I might just take to talking about "making computers useful".

Bruce Davie, April 2024.

Closing Remarks

The systems approach reminds us to look at entire systems rather than just optimizing small components in isolation, so it is important to remember that networking sits in a large context alongside other engineering and computing disciplines. This chapter highlights some of the forays we have made "over the fence" to look at other technologies that bump up against networking.

It has been impossible to ignore the impact of machine learning, large language models, and the broader field of artificial intelligence in the last few years. The challenge for us as people trained in networking is to make sense of all the claims being made for AI, which sometimes seems likely to consume all the oxygen available for and field of computer science. Our approach has been to dig in deeply enough, guided by a few acknowledged experts, to gain a system-level view of LLMs and neural networks. While we continue to be impressed with some of the capabilities of modern AI systems, we're definitely not convinced by the more extreme hype. As with so much of our prior work, we're holding the middle ground: we don't think AI is useless but nor does it seem to be quite the game changer that its strongest proponents would have us believe.

Part of the problem with AI is one of language: much of "AI" is applications of less-exciting-sounding machine learning, a mature technology that is seeing plenty of networking applications. These include geolocation, DoS-prevention, and closed-loop control.

Quantum computing is fortunately a bit less over-hyped than AI, but it is also much harder to understand. If you can explain the double-slit experiment (which we still recall from high-school physics), you have a chance to understand quantum computing. The field is already having a direct impact on networking, with the standards for cryptography now moving away from algorithms that quantum computers will probably break withing a decade or two. Whether scalable quantum computers will arrive sooner than artificial general intelligence remains an open question, as both require advances that have not yet been proven possible.

Explore Further

Committee on Research Horizons in Networking. Looking Over the Fence at Networks. A Neighbor's View of Networking Research. National Academies Press, 2001.

Scott Aaronson. Computer Scientists Crash the Solvay Conference. Shtetl-Optimized Blog, 2022.

Scott Aaronson and Zach Weinersmith. The Talk. SMBC Comics, 2016.

Bruce Davie. Quantum Computing: How will it change the technology landscape?. Plamadiso seminar, November 2021.

Emily M. Bender, Timnit Gebru, Angelina McMillan-Major,and Shmargaret Shmitchell. On the Dangers of Stochastic Parrots: Can Language Models Be Too Big? Proceedings of the 2021 ACM Conference on Fairness, Accountability, and Transparency (FAccT '21).

Rodney Brooks. Machine Learning Explained. Rodney Brooks blog, 2017.

Rodney Brooks. What Will Transformers Transform? Rodney Brooks blog, 2023.

Alex Hanna and Emily Bender. AI Causes Real Harm. Let's Focus on That over the End-of-Humanity Hype. Scientific American, 2023.

Timothy B. Lee and Sean Trott. A jargon-free explanation of how AI large language models work. Ars Technica, 2023.

Stephen Wolfram. What Is ChatGPT Doing ... and Why Does It Work? Stephen Wolfram blog, 2023.

Image Credits

About The Authors

Larry Peterson and Bruce Davie have been collaborating on systems projects and writing networking textbooks since the 1990s. Their book *Computer Networks: A Systems Approach*, a staple of networking curricula for the last 30 years, is now in its sixth edition. That introductory textbook, along with several new books focused on emerging topics in network and cloud systems, are available as open source at `https://systemsapproach.org`.

Larry spent most of his career in academia, first at the Unviersity of Arizona and later at Princeton University, where he was the Robert E. Kahn Professor of Computer Science. While at Princeton he directed the PlanetLab Consortium, building a global testbed for research on Internet-scale services. A CDN startup he helped spin out of PlanetLab was acquired by Akamai in 2010. In 2013 Larry transitioned to Emeritus status at Princeton and joined the Open Networking Lab (now the Open Networking Foundation) where he served as CTO, leading the design of open source platforms for Software-Defined Networking (SDN) and edge cloud computing. He currently chairs the Technical Steering Team for Aether, a Private 5G Project of the Linux Foundation. He is a member of the National Academy of Engineering, a Fellow of the ACM and the IEEE, the 2010 recipient of the IEEE Kobayashi Computer and Communication Award, and the 2013 recipient of the ACM SIGCOMM Award. He currently lives in Tucson Arizona.

Bruce began his networking career at Bellcore where he worked on the Aurora Gigabit testbed, which led to his first collaboration with Larry on high-speed host-network interfaces. He then went to Cisco where he led a team of architects responsible for Multiprotocol Label Switching (MPLS). He worked extensively at the IETF on standardizing MPLS and various quality of service technologies. Bruce also spent five years as a visiting lecturer at the Massachusetts Institute of Technology. In 2012 he joined Software Defined Networking (SDN) startup Nicira as a lead architect and was then a principal engineer at VMware following the acquisition of Nicira. In 2017 he took on the role of VP and CTO for the Asia Pacific region at VMware, which gave him the opportunity to return to Australia. He is a Fellow of the ACM and chaired ACM SIGCOMM from 2009 to 2013.